Catholic Belief and Survival in Late Sixteenth-Century Vienna

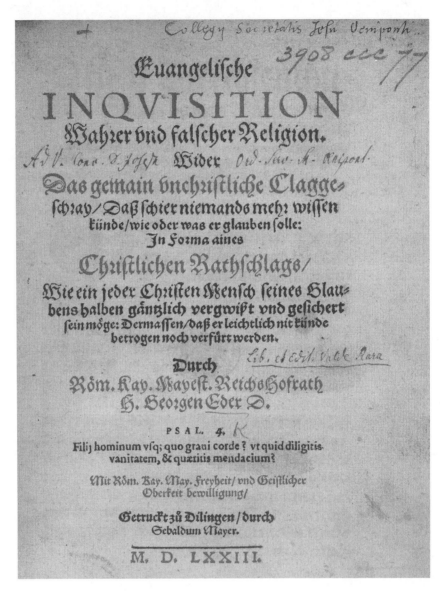

Euangelische

INQVISITION

Wahrer vnd falscher Religion.

Wider

Das gemain vnchristliche Claggeschray / Daß schier niemands mehr wissen künde / wie oder was er glauben solle:
In Forma aines

Christlichen Rathschlags /

Wie ein jeder Christen Mensch seines Glaubens halben gäntzlich vergwißt vnd gesichert sein möge: Dermassen / daß er leichtlich nit künde betrogen noch verfürt werden.

Durch

Röm. Kay. Mayest. ReichsHofrath
H. Georgen Eder D.

PSAL. 4.

Filij hominum vsq; quo graui corde ? vt quid diligitis
vanitatem, & quæritis mendacium?

Mit Röm. Kay. May. Freyheit / vnd Geistlicher
Oberkeit bewilligung /

Getruckt zů Dilingen / durch
Sebaldum Mayer.

M. D. LXXIII.

Title page from the 1573 edition of Eder's *Evangelische Inquisition*. By permission of the British Library (shelfmark 3908.ccc.77)

Catholic Belief and Survival in Late Sixteenth-Century Vienna

The Case of Georg Eder (1523–87)

ELAINE FULTON

ASHGATE

Published by
Ashgate Publishing Limited
Gower House
Croft Road
Aldershot
Hampshire GU11 3HR
England

Ashgate Publishing Company
Suite 420
101 Cherry Street
Burlington, VT 05401–4405
USA

Ashgate website: http://www.ashgate.com

British Library Cataloguing in Publication Data
Fulton, Elaine
    Catholic belief and survival in late sixteenth-century
    Vienna : the case of Georg Eder (1523–87). – (St Andrews studies in
    Reformation history)
    1. Eder, Georg, 1524–87 2. Catholic Church – Doctrines – History –
    Modern period, 1500– 3. Theologians – Austria – Biography 4. Lawyers –
    Austria – Biography 5. Counter-Reformation – Austria 6. Austria – Church
    history – 16th century
    I. Title
    230.2'092

    ISBN 978–0–7546–5652–4

Library of Congress Cataloging-in-Publication Data
Fulton, Elaine, 1975–
    Catholic belief and survival in late sixteenth-century Vienna : the case of
    Georg Eder (1523–87) / Elaine Fulton.
    p. cm. – (St. Andrews studies in Reformation history)
    Includes bibliographical references.
    ISBN 978–0–7546–5652–4 (alk. paper)
    1. Eder, Georg, 1524–87. 2. Catholic Church – Austria – Vienna.
    3. Catholic Church – History – 16th century. 4. Vienna (Austria) – Church
    history –16th century. I. Title. II. Series.

    BX4705.E34F85 2007
    282'.4361309031 – dc22
    2006016410

This book is printed on acid free paper

Printed in Great Britain by MPG Books, Bodmin, Cornwall

This book is dedicated to my parents, Ellen and Sidney Fulton, with love and deepest gratitude. It is also dedicated to the memory of my grandfather, Joseph Fulton (1911–2000).

Contents

Acknowledgements

The embarrassing length of this list of acknowledgements bears witness to the levels of generosity and support I have received from many quarters whilst researching and writing this book.

Based on a doctoral thesis examined in 2003, the main part of research for this study was carried out whilst a graduate student at the Reformation Studies Institute at the University of St Andrews, Scotland. This proved to be an invaluable base from which to work, and all those I met there, particularly Kenneth Austin, Fiona Campbell, Philip Conner, Max von Habsburg, Matthew Hall, Augustine Kelly, Alex Kess, Lauren Kim, Christine Linton, Steve Moulson, Paul Nelles, Michael Springer, Juliet Warren and Alexander Wilkinson, offered friendship and encouragement in equal measure. Professors Andrew Pettegree and Hamish Scott have been hugely generous patrons without whose support I could not have progressed in academia. Likewise, without the friendship and enthusiasm of Rona Johnston Gordon this book was unlikely to have been started and even less likely to have been finished. Most of all though, thanks are due to my supervisor, Bruce Gordon, for his wise guidance, not to mention infinite patience, over the past decade. I could not have wished for a better mentor, nor one to provide a better example of the integrity and commitment with which academic life should be conducted.

On research trips to Vienna I found another generous and supportive community of scholars. Beatrix Bastl, now of the city's Akademie der bildenden Künste, was an invaluable contact, introducing me to the archives and the cultural life of the city with her unique blend of efficiency and panache. Professors Friedrich Edelmayer and Gernot Heiss of the University of Vienna both offered very useful advice and a particular debt is owed to Professor Heiss who obtained for me, from Rome, copies of Eder's Jesuit correspondence. Dr Kurt Mühlberger of Vienna's Universität Archiv offered much guidance in the work's earlier stages. At the Haus-, Hof- und Staatsarchiv, I am especially grateful to Dr Michael Hochedlinger and the archive's director, Professor Leopold Auer, without whose time and help the workings of the HHStA might have forever remained a mystery.

The wider, international community of early modern scholars has also been an important source of advice and encouragement. Encounters at various stages with Maria Crăciun, Howard Louthan, John O'Malley, Ray Mentzer, Joseph Patrouch and Regina Pörtner have all been fruitful, while particular thanks must go to Professor Robert Evans of the University of Oxford for sharing with me the benefit of his extensive knowledge in this area. I have been delighted to find a further mine of expertise and enthusiasm in my current position in the department of modern history at the University of Birmingham. Here I have found a collegiality that makes it hard to single out individuals, but specific mention must be made of the members of the new Centre for Reformation and Early Modern Studies, in particular Richard Cust, Graeme Murdock, Catherine Richardson and Alec Ryrie, for all their support thus far.

In addition to those above, many friends have made this process far less painful than it could have been, and for that thanks go to Francesca Carnevali, Janet Deatherage, Barbara Ferguson, Ben Garstad, Heather Huntley, Alex Mold, Antje Pieper and Noelle Plack. I am particularly indebted to Emma and Spencer Adair whose friendship, generosity and good humour helped me survive three university degrees and their aftermath. Last but certainly not least, I wish to thank Deborah Jewison, for being all that she is.

On a practical level, this work could not have been undertaken without financial assistance from a number of sources. A three-year doctoral scholarship from the Caledonian Research Foundation provided the bulk of required funding, while a substantial grant from the Carnegie Trust enabled me to make further research trips to Vienna, Munich and London in the summer of 2000. Generous additional funding from the University of St Andrews modern history department contributed further to the cost of research trips, as did a sum of money from the Friends of the St Andrews Reformation Studies Institute. Help with the substantial range of translation work required to transform the thesis into a book came from Fiona Campbell, Francesca Carnevali, Ben Garstad, Tom Holland and Nicholas Da Costa. A grant from the School of Historical Studies Research Strategy Group at the University of Birmingham helped pay costs incurred in the reproduction of the images used in this book, while Tom Gray, Celia Hoare, Anne Keirby and Ann Newell of Ashgate Publishing Limited have shown great patience with a first-time author. Andrew Pettegree offered some wise words on the book's overall structure, while rigorous proofreading by Deborah Jewison and especially Michael Springer saved me from making a number of errors in the text. As always, however, any remaining blunders are entirely my own.

Elaine Fulton, Birmingham, December 2005

List of Figures

Abbreviations

AHY	*Austrian History Yearbook*
AÖG	*Archiv für Österreichische Geschichte*
ARG	*Archiv für Reformationsgeschichte*
ARSI	Archivum Romanum Societatis Iesu, Rome
BHStA	Bayerisches Hauptstaatsarchiv, Munich
CEH	*Central European History*
CH	*Church History*
CHR	*Catholic Historical Review*
DAW	Diözesanarchiv, Vienna
Fasz.	Faszikel
fol.	Folio
fols	Folios
HHStA	Haus-, Hof- und Staatsarchiv, Vienna
HKA	Hofkammerarchiv, Vienna
HZ	*Historische Zeitschrift*
Jb.f.Lk.v.NÖ	*Jahrbuch für Landeskunde von Niederösterreich*
JEH	*Journal of Ecclesiastical History*
JEMH	*Journal of Early Modern History*
JMH	*Journal of Modern History*
MIÖG	*Mitteilungen des Instituts für Österreichische Geschichtsforschung*
nö	Niederösterreich
Nr	Nummer (number)
ÖNB	Österreichisches Nationalbibliothek, Vienna
P&P	*Past and Present*
RQ	*Römische Quartalschrift*
SCJ	*Sixteenth Century Journal*
UAW	Archiv der Universität Wien

Glossary

The following terms are used more than once throughout the text. The definitions refer to their meaning in the context of Eder's life and work. Plurals, where relevant, are given in brackets. Other terms are explained where necessary as they occur in the text.

Auslaufen – Word used to describe the weekly exodus of thousands of Viennese from the city to the outlying properties of Protestant nobles, where Lutheran services were held.

Consistorium – Term used to describe the general assembly, concilium generale or senatus of a university. In the case of Vienna, it was usually composed of the rector, the Kanzler and Superintendent as well as the Dekans of the four faculties and Prokurators of the four nations.

Dekan – Term referring to the dean or head of each university faculty.

Diet – Term used to describe a meeting of the estates.

Geheimer Rat – Privy Council: a small group of senior Habsburg courtiers who usually met daily to advise on matters of state including foreign affairs and legal and financial matters.

Herrenstand – Upper nobility.

Herrschaft – Term for the collection of privileges, rights and responsibilities of the landowner over those living within the bounds of their particular property. Sometimes also used to refer to the act of exercising these powers.

Hofburg – Habsburg residence in the centre of Vienna.

Hofkammer – Literally, 'court chamber' comprised of approximately 15 councillors with responsibility for Habsburg financial affairs, in particular the administration of crown estates and the collection of indirect taxes such as those on wine or meat.

Hofkriegsrat – Title of the imperial war council.

Hofstaatsverzeichnis(se) – List(s) of court members.

Kammerprokurator – Title used by the councillors responsible for the Hofkammer.

Kanzler – In the context of Vienna University, this term refers to the chancellor who, as episcopal representative, was also dean or provost of Stephansdom.

Klosterrat – Name of the imperial body, founded in 1568, for the visitation of religious houses.

Landhaus – Meeting place of the estates in Vienna; also home to the Lower Austrian government.

Landtag(e) – Meeting(s) of the estates in a provincial Diet.

Obersthofmarschall – Title given to the marshal, one of the four major posts at the Habsburg court which included jurisdiction over all courtiers.

Obersthofmeister – Title of the high steward, the emperor's key adviser who headed the Geheimer Rat and represented the ruler in his absence.

Passau Offizial – Title of the representative of the bishop of Passau in Vienna.

Prokurator – In the university context, a term for the representative of the four academic 'nations'.

Protokolle – Term used to describe court or university records, minutes or transcripts.

Reichshofkanzlei – Imperial Chancellery, nominally under partial control of the archbishop of Mainz.

Reichshofrat(räte) – The Aulic Council, subject to the emperor alone and the ultimate source of justice throughout the empire. The word can refer to the institution or its member(s).

Reichskammergericht – The Imperial Chamber Court or Imperial Exchequer Court. This court was heavily subject to the influence of the estates.

Reichstag – Meeting or Diet of the representatives of the electors, knights, princes, prelates and free cities of the Holy Roman Empire.

Reichsvizekanzler – Imperial Vice-Chancellor, head of the Reichshofkanzlei and also a key member of the Reichshofrat and Geheimer Rat.

Ritterstand – Knights, or lower nobility.

Superintendent – Term used to describe the representative in the university of the local secular ruler. In the case of Vienna, this was the representative of the Habsburg ruler.

Editorial Conventions

In this book, any quotations from primary sources will reflect the exact spelling and punctuation of the original. To facilitate reading, however, early modern usage of 'f' for 's' and 'v' for 'u' has usually been modernised.

In the same spirit, throughout my own text all place names will be anglicised where there is an established and commonly used English form: for example, 'Vienna' will replace 'Wien' and 'Munich' will replace 'München'. Other place names will, where possible, be spelt according to their modern form, with any former variations added in the relevant footnotes. For example, the place Eder calls 'Intzerstorff' will be referred to in the text by its modern spelling of Inzersdorf.

The vagaries of early-modern spelling also mean that few personal names were spelt consistently, even within the same source. The most commonly used spelling will therefore be employed, with any important variations indicated in the relevant footnote.

Lastly, due to their length, the titles of Eder's published works will generally be cited by their short title only. Full versions of the titles may be found in the bibliography.

Introduction

Georg Eder was one of sixteenth-century Vienna's most prominent figures.[1] His rise was swift: by 1552, within a mere two years of his arrival in Vienna, the 29-year-old Bavarian jurist was elected to his first post at the city's university, as Prokurator of the German nation.[2] Entry to office at the Habsburg court came just two years later, with the position of Kammerprokurator, while nine years later, at the age of 40, Eder received promotion to one of the court's and indeed the Holy Roman Empire's highest positions: that of Reichshofrat.[3] Eder was to remain active in this prestigious legal post for 20 years, while his university career was one of equal longevity. By his death in 1587 he had been elected university rector a total of 11 times, a role that placed him right at the heart of one of the city's key institutions.[4]

Eder's contemporary fame, however, was based on much more than this considerable legal and administrative status: he was also the author of 12 books that sought to defend the Catholic faith against the onslaught of Protestant heresy.[5] That one of these, the *Evangelische Inquisition*, was inflammatory enough to anger no less than the Emperor Maximilian II, Eder's own employer and champion of confessional moderation, only added to Eder's profile.[6] The subsequent imperial condemnation of Eder's book saw his name reach the courts of Madrid and Rome itself, while closer to home, his cause was taken up by the Society of Jesus and the

---

1   Georg Eder almost always spelt his surname in this manner, and the vast majority of secondary works in which he has been mentioned follow suit. For this reason his name will be spelt 'Eder' throughout this book. There were, however, alternate spellings in his own day: the compiler of a volume of the Hofkammer records, for instance, spells his name as 'Eder' on one page having spelt it 'Öder' the page before: HKA, Expedit. Regist. nö 52, fols 248r–v. A letter dated 3 May 1559 is similarly addressed to 'Georgius Öder', HKA, Reichsakten, Fasz. 150/A fol. 351r.

2   For more on the evidence surrounding Eder's biographical details, see pp. 3–13.

3   On Eder's career at the Habsburg court, see Chapter 2.

4   For details of Eder's career at Vienna University, see Chapter 2.

5   These will be discussed below, pp. 10–13 and at some length in Chapters 3, 4 and 6.

6   Eder, Georg (1573), *Evangelische Inquisition Wahrer und falscher Religion Wider Das gemain unchristliche Claggeschray, Das schier niemand mehr wissen Künde, wie oder was er glauben solle: In forma aines Christlichen Rathschlags, wie ein jeder Christen mensch seines Glaubens halben ganzlich vergwißt und gesichert Sein moge: Dermassen, daß er leichtlich nit künde Betrogen noch verfurt werden*, Dillingen: Sebald Mayer.

Habsburgs' own rivals, the Wittelsbach Dukes of Bavaria. Eder and his career survived the crisis, but only due to the intervention of powerful patrons and some judicious reading on his part of the volatile confessional climate of late sixteenth-century Vienna.

There has been some examination of this remarkable career in the four centuries since his death, and recent literature suggests, rightly, that Eder's was indeed a significant career in the Vienna of the latter half of the sixteenth century. In Howard Louthan's 1997 work on the court of Emperor Maximilian II, Eder is characterised as 'the most vociferous and effective opponent of the irenic faction'.[7] Louthan highlights the content of Eder's most controversial work, the *Evangelische Inquisition*, while Robert Evans' seminal 1979 study, *The Making of the Habsburg Monarchy*, describes Georg Eder as 'our most candid witness for the 1580s'.[8] Pertinent as these treatments have been, however, such appearances in recent literature are few and fleeting.[9] In this they reflect a pattern set by much earlier studies, published mainly in the eighteenth and nineteenth centuries, in which Eder's role was discussed only for the warmth of his relationship with the hierarchy of the Catholic Church, for his literary career, or for his position at Vienna University.[10]

---

[7]   Louthan, Howard (1997), *The Quest For Compromise: Peacemakers in Counter-Reformation Vienna*, Cambridge: Cambridge University Press, p. 127.

[8]   Ibid., pp. 127–9. Evans, Robert J.W. (1979), *The Making of the Habsburg Monarchy, 1550–1700*, Oxford: Oxford University Press, p. 63. Evans hints at the significance of Eder's life but goes no further than to intriguingly describe him as 'helped by undoubted talent and good connections in Munich rather than by his cantankerous religiosity' and as a man who 'devoted his literary oeuvre, correspondence, and professional persuasiveness to disinterested advocacy of the Roman cause', p. 42.

[9]   The most recent works in which Eder makes a number of passing appearances are Sutter Fichtner, Paula (2001), *Emperor Maximilian II*, New Haven, CT: Yale University Press, and MacHardy, Karin J. (2003), *War, Religion and Court Patronage in Habsburg Austria. The Social and Cultural Dimensions of Political Interaction, 1521–1622*, Basingstoke: Palgrave Macmillan. The only work dedicated exclusively to Eder in recent years is a dissertation by Katharina Kronberger (1995), 'Der Reichshofrat Dr Georg Eder und sein Werk Evangelische Inquisition', unpublished Diplomarbeit, University of Vienna. This dissertation is of limited value in that it is highly reliant on the century-old works described below.

[10]   Works that bear at least brief witness to early recognition of Eder's ties with the Catholic hierarchy and the Society of Jesus are: Duhr, Bernhard (1907), *Geschichte der Jesuiten in den Ländern deutscher Zunge*, vol. 1, *Geschichte der Jesuiten in den Ländern deutscher Zunge im XVI. Jahrhundert*, Freiburg im Briesgau: Herder; Janssen, Johannes (1885), *Geschichte des deutschen Volkes seit dem Ausgang des Mittelalters*, vol. 4, Freiburg im Breisgau: Herder; Socher, Antonius, S.J. (1740), *Historia Provinciae Austriae Societatis Jesu Pars Prima*, Vienna: Kurtzböck; Wiedemann, Theodor (1880, 1884), *Geschichte der Reformation und Gegenreformation im Lande unter der Enns*, vols 2 and 4, Prague: Tempsky. Eder's writings were noted in Denis, Michael (1782 and 1793), *Wiens Buchdruckergeschicht bis M.D.L.X.*, 2 vols, Vienna: Wappler; Kobolt, Anton Maria (1795), *Baierisches Gelehrten Lexikon*, vols 1 and 2, Landshut: Hagen; Mayer, Anton (1883), *Wiens Buchdrucker-Geschichte*, vol. 1, *1482–1682*, Vienna: Verlag d. Comites z. Feier d. vierhundertj. Einführung

While identification of these themes is not incorrect, no single work has ever successfully examined in any depth how all of these aspects of Eder's career interacted with one another in the environment in which he lived. The year 1895 saw one attempt to synthesise the existing material, but this was restricted by its failure to utilise the full range of primary sources available.[11] One year earlier, the director of the Vienna University archive, Dr Karl Schrauf, also had scribbled the promising words 'für Biographie Geo. Eders' on the front cover of a folder. After ten years and 135 pages of painstaking work, however, these notes were terminated suddenly.[12] In 1904 Schrauf died, and the efforts of Georg Eder's most recent would-be biographer remain a series of incomplete notes now stored in a filing cabinet at the Vienna University archive.

So why return to Eder now? Aside from the simple fact that Eder's was an important career that deserves a much closer look, it is also the case that there survives a remarkable wealth and variety of relevant source material that has never been examined fully. Just before he died, Karl Schrauf did have some of his research on Eder published, in *Der Reichshofrath Dr Georg Eder. Eine Briefsammlung*, a useful collection of 109 letters written to, by and concerning Eder.[13] This was, however, restricted in scope in that it focused heavily on the flurry of

---

d. Buchdruckerkunst in Wien, and Raupach, Bernard (1736), *Evangelisches Osterreich, das ist, Historische Nachricht von den vornehmsten Schicksalen der Evangelisch Lutherischen Kirchen in dem Ertz-Hertzogthum Oesterreich*, Hamburg: Felginer. Earlier works with information on Eder's career at Vienna University include: Aschbach, Joseph Ritter von (1888), *Geschichte der Wiener Universität. Die Wiener Universität und Ihre Gelehrten, 1520 bis 1565*, Vienna: Adolph Holzhausen; Locher, D. Joanne Joseph (1773–75), *Speculum Academicum Viennense, sen magistratus antiquissimae et celeberrime Universitatis Viennensis, a primo eiusdem auspicio ad nostra tempora chronologice, historice, et lemmatice, exhibitus a D. Joanne Josepho Locher J.U.D.*, 3 vols, Vienna: Kaliwoda; Mitterdorffer, R.P. Sebastiano (1724, 1725), *Conspectus historiae universitatis Viennensis ex actis veteribus que documentis erutae atque a primis illius initiis ad annum usque 1701 deductae. (etc.)*, vols 2 and 3, Vienna: Schwendimann.

11   Paulus, N., 'Hofrath Dr Georg Eder. Ein katholischer Rechtsgelehrter des 16. Jahrhunderts', *Historisch-politische Blätter für das katholische Deutschland*, 115 (1895), 13–28, 81–94, 240.

12   Many thanks are due to the current holder of Karl Schrauf's post, Dr Kurt Mühlberger, for allowing me to examine this folder of notes. It is presently housed at the Archiv der Universität Wien under the signature 'Schrauf, Karl, Konvolut, Altes Biographisches Material-Eder'.

13   Schrauf, Karl, ed. (1904), *Der Reichshofrath Dr Georg Eder. Eine Briefsammlung. Als Beitrag zur Geschichte der Gegenreformation in Niederösterreich*, Vienna: Adolf Holzhausen. In this, Schrauf adds a wry but telling comment on the difficulties involved in deciphering Eder's script: 'as soon as he [Eder] writes of an at all interesting theme, he loses all control of the pen, leaves out letters, syllables, indeed whole words, writes instead others twice, and glides so fleetingly over the paper that his script becomes illegible in places', p. vii.

communication immediately following the emperor's furious reaction to Eder's *Evangelische Inquisition*.[14] The work of two other editors from the same period also failed to complete the task of utilising the full extent of Eder's correspondence. An 1885 contribution of Felix Stieve was always going to be limited, consisting as it did of a mere sample of five letters from the much wider total collection.[15] The publication of a third and final edition of Eder's Bavarian correspondence in 1909, however, was a much more ambitious effort. Victor Bibl's 'Die Berichte des Reichshofrates Dr Georg Eder an die Herzoge Albrecht und Wilhelm von Bayern über die Religionskrise in Niederösterreich (1579–1587)' consisted of 68 of the reports, written by Eder either to Duke Albrecht or his successor Duke Wilhelm of Bavaria, between 1579 and 1587.[16]

There is no doubt that Bibl's collection of Eder's letters, like that of Schrauf, is a piece of careful scholarship that provides valuable insights into Eder's perspective on the situation in which he lived. The very selective editing on Bibl's part must, however, be taken into equal account. Unlike Schrauf, whose foreword indicated his concern to allow the sources to speak in full, Bibl excised substantial passages from almost three-quarters of the letters in his collection.[17] The resultant compilation

---

[14]   Schrauf's 'Vorwort' to his edition of Eder's letters betrays this wish to focus on the crisis that resulted from the publication of Eder's *Evangelische Inquisition*. His coverage of material begins with the imperial decree against Eder, published 2 October 1573, and ends with a letter from Eder to Duke Albrecht dated 30 December 1578.

[15]   Stieve, Felix, ed., 'Briefe des Reichshofrathes Dr G. Eder zur Geschichte Rudolfs II und der Gegenreformation in Österreich unter der Enns', *MIÖG*, 6 (1885), 440–49.

[16]   Bibl, Victor, ed., 'Die Berichte des Reichshofrates Dr Georg Eder an die Herzoge Albrecht und Wilhelm von Bayern über die Religionskrise in Niederösterreich (1579–1587)', *Jb.f.Lk.v.NÖ*, Neue Folge 8 (1909), 67–154. The first letter in Bibl's edition is dated 17 February 1579, while the last is dated 14 March 1587.

[17]   Approximately 50 of the 68 letters in Bibl's edition had substantial amounts of original material missing. Examples can range from the loss of the seven-line postscript (BHStA, Kurbayern Äußeres Archiv, Status Ecclesiasticus-Religionsacta des Erzhauses Österreich, signature 4241, Tom. XI, fol. 92v) excluded from Bibl's edition of a letter from Eder to Duke Albrecht dated 25 March 1579, 'Die Berichte', pp. 73–5, to much more serious losses. For example, a total of 16 folio pages from a letter from Eder to Duke Wilhelm dated 1 December 1579 are present in the original (BHStA, Kurbayern Äußeres Archiv, Status Ecclesiasticus-Religionsacta des Erzhauses Österreich, signature 4241, Tom. XI, fols 180r–187r), but not in Bibl's version of the same, 'Die Berichte', pp. 99–100. For Schrauf, this was bad practice. He wrote that he had the impression 'that the available documents are too detailed and too valuable to be simply placed in a bibliography or to be picked out and broken up for a database, to be half published and half thrown away, which recently has been the fashion', *Der Reichshofrath Dr Georg Eder. Eine Briefsammlung*, p. vi. Bibl's focus was deliberately narrower, indicating that he had limited himself to the 'reports over the religious nature of Austria'. His view was that the 'remaining contents of the correspondence were almost exclusively personal affairs of little interest', Bibl, 'Die Berichte', p. 69, note 1.

of source material, like the other century-old works on the same topic, thus fails to capture the full complexity of Eder's position.

The research on which this book is based, however, reveals the full extent and value of Georg Eder's documentary legacy. Not only has the aforementioned Bavarian correspondence now been enumerated and evaluated in full, but further source materials relating to Eder's career in Vienna and to his relationship with the hierarchy of the Catholic Church have also been uncovered and employed for the first time. The resulting, greatly enlarged body of evidence allows for a fresh reconstruction of the career of Georg Eder, and points to a life of significance not only within the sphere of late sixteenth-century Vienna, but also at the Bavarian court and indeed throughout the wider European Catholic network.

The research entailed in this project has, firstly, greatly enhanced the existing picture of Eder's relationship with the Dukes of Bavaria, the near neighbours and close rivals of his Habsburg employers in Vienna. It is now clear that Eder wrote more and fuller letters to the Wittelsbach Dukes than had previously been utilised by the likes of Schrauf and Bibl. My research in the Bayerisches Hauptstaatsarchiv has identified and re-examined the substantial passages excluded by Bibl from his published collection of Eder's letters. A further 23 of Eder's letters to the Wittelsbachs wholly unused by any of his previous editors were also uncovered, bringing the known number of letters sent from Eder to the Wittelsbachs between 1577 and 1587 to a total of 123.[18] Revealingly, the same research also suggests that there may well have been even more letters sent by Eder to the Wittelsbachs in the same period which have not survived: short summaries of two of Eder's letters that had apparently been dated 31 October 1581 and 19 April 1582, were also found, but are no longer extant in their original form.[19] Still preserved, however, is another previously unused manuscript containing a judgment given by Eder in his legal capacity to Duke Wilhelm in Munich and dated 26 October 1580.[20]

Additional sources from the same archive throw still further light on Eder's connection with the Dukes of Bavaria. Eder, it seems, was not their only Vienna-based correspondent: he was one of a number who sent reports to the Bavarian court throughout this period of religious and political tension. At least six others were compiling reports from

---

[18] These letters were extracted from analysis of the BHStA, Kurbayern Äußeres Archiv, Status Ecclesiasticus-Religionsacta des Erzhauses Österreich, signature 4240, Tom. X; signature 4241, Tom. XI and signature 4242, Tom. XII, and date from 8 January 1579 to 18 April 1587. They will be discussed fully in Chapters 5 and 6.

[19] BHStA, Staatsverwaltung, Auswärtige Staaten und bayerische Beziehungen zu denselben, signature 1931 fols 20r–v.

[20] BHStA, Jesuitica, signature 960. For more on the significance of this manuscript, see pp. 124–5.

Vienna for the Bavarian Dukes during the same period in which Eder acted as correspondent. These included Reichshofräte Johann Hegenmüller and Timotheus Jung; Reichshofrat and Reichsvizekanzler Siegmund Viehauser; Passau Offizial and eventual Bishop of Vienna, Melchior Khlesl, and two further office-holders in the Habsburg court's administration, Georg Ehrenpreis and Andreas Erstenberger. The wider holdings of the Kurbayern Äußeres Archiv further suggest a significant level of Wittelsbach interest in the affairs of all courts, but in particular that of the emperor. There survive more than 21 000 pages of reports sent to the Wittelsbachs between 1552 and 1595, approximately half of which concern news from the various Habsburg courts.[21] That Eder's letters form part of this information network flowing from Vienna to Munich suggests an even more intriguing role on his part.

The identification of previously unused material relating to Eder's relationship with the Catholic hierarchy in Rome as well as with leading members of the Society of Jesus suggests a second important realm in which Eder was active. Unlike the evidence relating to Eder's Bavarian connection, barely any substantial material had been uncovered in this area. Some sources required little excavation: that Eder's religious writings had gained him at least the notional attention of two popes, Pius V in 1568 and Gregory XIII in 1580, is plainly evident from the letters printed at the start of the books Eder had published in these years.[22] Of greater political import, however, are the nuncio reports in which Eder is also mentioned. That these total 99 separate reports, written between 19 June 1567 and 20 August 1585, offers telling evidence of the extent of interest Eder's fluctuating fortunes drew from Rome.[23]

---

[21]   BHStA, Kurbayern Äußers Archiv, Korrespondenzakten-Auswärtige Residenten, signatures 4292–347.

[22]   The publication in 1568 of the first edition of Eder's 714 page *Oeconomia Bibliorum*, Cologne: Gervinus Calenius and Johanne Quentel, was apparently noted by Pope Pius V, as all three subsequent editions of the work open with his letter of praise to Eder dated 2 January 1569. Both the 1580 and 1581 editions of another pedagogical work from the latter part of Eder's career, *Malleus Haereticorum*, Ingolstadt: David Sartorius, were also prefaced by a letter, this time dated February 1580 from Eder to Pope Gregory XIII, fols 2*r–**7v. A further, manuscript copy of this letter is held in the ÖNB, Bibl. Pal. Vind. Cod. 11648, fols 92v–96r.

[23]   These reports were found in Bues, Almut, ed. (1990), *Nuntiaturberichte aus Deutschland 1572–1585*, part 3, vol. 7, Tübingen: Niemayer; Dengel, Ignaz Philipp, ed. (1939), *Nuntiaturberichte aus Deutschland 1560–1572*, part 2, vol. 6, Vienna: Adolf Holzhausen; Hansen, Joseph, ed. (1892), *Nuntiaturberichte aus Deutschland 1572–1585*, part 3, vol. 1, Berlin: A. Bath; Hansen, Joseph, ed. (1894), *Nuntiaturberichte aus Deutschland 1572–1585*, part 3, vol. 2, Berlin: A. Bath; Keussen, Hermann, ed. (1979), *Die Matrikel der Universität Köln*, vol. 2, Düsseldorf: Droste; Kramer, Hans, ed. (1952), *Nuntiaturberichte aus Deutschland 1560–1572* part 2, vol. 7, Vienna; Rainer, Johann, ed. (1967), *Nuntiaturberichte aus Deutschland 1560–1572*, part 2, vol. 8 Graz, Cologne: Niemayer; Reichenberger, Robert, ed. (1905), *Nuntiaturberichte aus Deutschland 1585 (1584)–1590*, Part 2, *Die Nuntiatur*

Numerically less striking but none the less highly significant is the existence of further material, again unused and unmentioned by any of Eder's previous historians, pointing to his career-long association with key members of the Society of Jesus. Otto Braunsberger's magnificent eight-volume collection of sources relating to Peter Canisius reveals a total of 17 letters in which Eder is mentioned, the first in a letter by Canisius himself, dated as early as 1544.[24] Materials housed at the Jesuit archive in Rome bear further witness to Eder's connections with the society. There survive three letters from 1573, two of which are from Eder to the society's General, Mercurian, and another of which is a discussion of Eder's situation in Vienna sent to Mercurian from the Jesuit Provincial Magius.[25]

It is however evidence relating to Eder's life in the city from which all of these Bavarian, Roman and Jesuit relations were conducted – Vienna – that represents the most varied source base. Eder's career in Vienna was not only long, beginning in 1550 and continuing right up to his death 37 years later, but extremely active. Eder held a number of positions at Vienna University over a large part of this time, and spent substantial periods at the Habsburg court as both a member of the Hofkammer and Reichshofrat as well as Kammerprokurator to the Lower Austrian government.[26] As a result his name appears in a wide and complex variety of materials, which reveal much of the status of Eder's career there throughout the period under examination.

---

am Kaiserhofe. Erste Hälfte, Paderborn; Schellhass, Karl, ed. (1896), Nuntiaturberichte aus Deutschland 1572–1585, part 3, vol. 3, Berlin: A. Bath; Schellhass, Karl, ed. (1903), Nuntiaturberichte aus Deutschland 1572–1585, part 3, vol. 4, Berlin: A. Bath; Schellhass, Karl, ed. (1909), Nuntiaturberichte aus Deutschland 1572–1585, part 3, vol. 5, Berlin: A. Bath; Schwarz, W.E., ed. (1898), Die Nuntiatur-Korrespondenz Kaspar Groppers (1573–1576), Paderborn: Ferdinand Schöningh; Steinherz, S., ed. (1914), Nuntiaturberichte aus Deutschland 1560–1572, part 2, vol. 4, Vienna: Alfred Hölder. It is worth noting that Eder's career also drew interest from Madrid: his predicament in Vienna is named in letters from the Count of Monteagudo to Philip II dated 18 October and 25 December 1573, in Fernandez de Navarrete, Martin, ed. (1842), Por el Marquís de la Fuensanta del Valle (Colección de documentos inéditos para la historia de Espanya), vol. 111, Madrid: Impenta de la Viuda de Calero, pp. 332–9 and pp. 346–50 respectively.

[24] Braunsberger, Otto, ed. (1896–1923), Beati Petri Canisii, Societatis Iesu, Epistulae et Acta, 8 vols, Freiburg im Briesgau: Herder. The first specific reference to Eder is in a letter sent from Cologne by Canisius to Peter Faber dated 30 December 1544, vol. 1, p. 126. The last is from a letter from Canisius to General Mercurian dated 19 July 1574, vol. VII, p. 226.

[25] Many thanks are due to Professor Gernot Heiss of the University of Vienna for obtaining copies of these letters for me, and indeed for alerting me to their existence. ARSI, Epistolae Germaniae 153, fols 56r–58v, Eder to Mercurian, 5 May 1573; fols 235r–v, Provincial Magius to Mercurian, 4 October 1573; fols 293r–294r, Eder to Mercurian, 28 October 1573.

[26] Eder's career in Vienna will be examined in detail in Chapter 2.

The sources indicate such details as which posts Eder held in Vienna, when he held them, what his responsibilities were and the names of those with whom he had dealings. Some of this material from the Vienna University archives has already been edited and published, including the matriculation registers and transcripts from the records of the faculty of medicine for the period when Eder was rector.[27] Similar material from the theology and philosophy faculties has not, and remains in manuscript form.[28] The Hofkammerarchiv and Haus-, Hof- und Staatsarchiv, however, contains the bulk of the relevant material.[29] Regarding Eder's role at the Habsburg court, the holdings of the Haus-, Hof- und Staatsarchiv reveal a number of as yet unpublished Hofstaatsverzeichnisse in which Eder's name appears.[30] Similar work was done at the Hofkammerarchiv, where material from Expedit. Regist. nö indicates how long Eder had served within the Hofkammer, and in what capacity.[31]

The finer details of Eder's court career could be traced still further, however. Samples of material from the Reichshofrat Protokolle offer a precise record of which Reichshofrat sessions Eder attended and with whom, while Eder himself left a report of his own work as

---

[27]   Gall, Franz and Szaivert, Willy, eds (1971), *Quellen zur Geschichte der Universität Wien. I Abteilung. Die Matrikel der Universität Wien*, vol. 3, 1518/II–1579/I and vol. 4 1579/II–1658/59, Vienna, Cologne, Graz: Publikationen des Instituts für Österreichische Geschichtsforschung; Schrauf, Karl, ed. (1904), *Acta Facultatis Medicae Universitatis Vindobonensis III 1490–1558*, Vienna: Verlag des Medicinischen Doctorcollegiums; Senfelder, Leopold, ed. (1908), *Acta Facultatis Medicae Universitatis Vindobonensis IV 1558–1604*, Vienna: Verlag des Medicinischen Doctorcollegiums. In addition, Albert Starzer's 'Fortsetzung' in his own, 1906 edition of *Quellen zur Geschichte der Stadt Wien*, part 1, vol. 5, Vienna: Verein für Geschichte der Stadt Wien, pp. 11–397, contains a transcript from the minutes of the Consistorium of 7 December 1569 detailing aspects of Eder's administration, no. 5480, p. 128.

[28]   UAW, Theol. Akten Th3 (1508–49) and Th4 (1567-1644), microfilm 075; Th15 (1395–1549) and Th16 (1569–1666), microfilm 076. UAW, Phil. Akten Ph9 (1497–1559) and Ph10 (1559–1616), microfilm 066.

[29]   I am grateful to Dr Michael Hochedlinger for his friendly guidance through the intricacies of the Haus-, Hof- und Staatsarchiv.

[30]   HHStA, Hofarchiv, Hofstaatsverzeichnis O Me A /SR 183 (1563–1600), Nr 50 fol. 6r; Nr 56 fol. 1v, December 1574 and December 1576 respectively. Eder's name also appears in three Hofstaaten edited by Thomas Fellner and Heinrich Kretschmayr in a 1907 volume, *Die Österreichische Zentralverwaltung I Abteilung Von Maximilian I. bis zur vereinigung der Österreichischen und Böhmischen Hofkanzlei (1749)*, vol. 2, *Aktenstücke 1491–1681*, Vienna: Veröffentlichungen der Kommission für neuere Geschichte Österreichs. These date from 1563 (p. 183), 1567 (p. 188), and 1576 (p. 193). The Hofstaatsverzeichnis for 1567 only exists in manuscript form in the ÖNB, Bibl. Pal. Vind. Cod. 14458, fol. 5v.

[31]   HKA, Expedit. Regist. nö 26 (1552), 30 (1554), 37 (1557), 41 (1558), 42 (1558), 45 (1559), 48 (1560), 50 (1561), 51 (1561), 52 (1561), 54 (1562), 56 (1562), 64 (1564), 68 (1565), 71 (1566), 72 (1567), 76 (1567), 80 (1568), 84 (1569), 85 (1570), 90 (1570), 95 (1571), 98 (1572), 100 (1573), 103 (1574), 107 (1575), 108 (1575), 132 (1582), 136 (1583), 145 (1586).

Kammerprokurator to the Lower Austrian government in the form of 'Die Relationen des nö Kammerprokurators Dr Georg Eder 1561'.[32] Research in the Hofkammerarchiv also reveals something of the status of Eder's work: there exist three previously unexamined letters sent from the Emperor Ferdinand I to Eder in 1559, while the Haus-, Hof- und Staatsarchiv reveals another such missive from the same year.[33] In addition, the Österreichische Nationalbibliothek holds the only manuscript copy of a document mentioned by just one of Eder's past historians. Entitled 'Consilia doctorum Viennensium Philippi Gundelii, Georgii Eder et Georgii Gienger in negotio imperii adversus objecta papae et quidem pro Ferdinando I imperatore contra Paulus IV papam', the document was partly composed by Eder in his capacity as a jurist for the Emperor Ferdinand I in 1558.[34]

The sources resulting from Eder's life in Vienna do not, however, reveal only the significance of his court or university career. Research in Vienna's Diözesanarchiv revealed the existence of seven previously unused letters exchanged between Eder and the local Catholic bishop, Johann Neuböck, between 29 May 1581 and 12 April 1586.[35] The same archive also reveals Eder's involvement in the selection of Melchior Khlesl as Passau Offizial in 1579.[36] In addition, Albert Starzer edited documents in which Eder's concern for the religious life of the city can further be seen.[37] All of these

---

[32] HHStA, Reichshofrat, *RHR Protocollum rerum resolutarum* XVI 26a (January 1565–April 1569), 36a (January 1572–December 1574), 37 (January–December 1573), 38 (January–December 1574), 39 (August 1574–December 1575), 41 (January 1575–December 1577), 42 (January–November 1577), 44 (August 1577–March 1578), 45 (December 1577–October 1579), 47 (January 1578–December 1580), 48A (October 1579– December 1582), 50 (January 1581–December 1584), 51 (June 1582– January 1583). 'Die Relationen des nö Kammerprokurators Dr Georg Eder' (2 vols) comes from K und K Reichsfinanzarchiv Cod. Mscr. Nro 22 D but was transcribed in the nineteenth century into two volumes now housed in the HHStA as part of the Graf Chorinsky Quellensammlung.

[33] HKA, *Reichsakten*, Fasz. 150/A, fols 351r–v (3 May 1559), fols 353r–v (5 June 1559), fol. 355r (8 July 1559). HHStA, *Staatenabteilung Italien*, Rom Varia 1551–59, Fasz. 2 (alt 1, 2) fol. 9r: 3 March 1559. For more on these, see p. 46.

[34] Although apparently unused by any historian thus far, there is a reference to this work in Aschbach, *Geschichte der Wiener Universität*, p. 175. The only surviving copy exists in manuscript at the Österreichische Nationalbibliothek, Bibl. Pal. Vind. Cod. 8727. For more on this, see pp. 45–6.

[35] Johann Weißensteiner of Vienna's Diözesanarchiv is due thanks for helping me locate the material relevant to Eder: Bischofsakten Johann Kaspar Neuböck (1574–94), Kop. Reg. Nr 101–200 (1582–93), letters 133 and 138; Epistolare des Bischofs Neuböck (1578–82), Wiener Protokolle 9, Standort I B 1, numbers 55 (69), 57 (71), 77 (93), 92 (113), 97 (119).

[36] DAW, Bischofsakten Melchior Khlesl (1598–1630), Kop. Reg. Nr. 1–100 (1555-84), letters 33 and 34. These letters were dated 20 June and 17 July 1579 respectively.

[37] In Albert Starzer's 1895 'Regesten aus dem k.k. Archive für Niederösterreich (Statthalterei-Archiv)', in Mayer, Anton, ed., *Quellen zur Geschichte der Stadt Wien*, part 1, vol. 1, Vienna: Verlag und Eigenthum des Alterthums-Vereines zu Wien, pp. 210–78, Eder's name appears in documents dated 24 May 1573 (no. 1138, pp. 242–3) and 29 August 1579 (no. 1199, p. 265).

materials, however, must be regarded synoptically with a final major range of sources that also stem from Eder's career in Vienna and which also, until now, have been inadequately examined. These are Eder's own published works, the extent and nature of which are here accurately listed for the first time, and which add another crucial layer of understanding to Eder's career in Vienna and his association with Bavaria, Rome and the Society of Jesus.

Eder's earlier historians were all aware that he was the author of a number of works, but scant attention had been paid to this important aspect of Eder's career. Paulus came closest to providing a full inventory of Eder's writings, but even he failed to mention three titles.[38] Other existing bibliographies of Eder's publications were often riddled with inaccuracies.[39] Examination of the library catalogues of all major European libraries indicated that between them, the Österreichische Nationalbibliothek in Vienna, the Bayerisches Staatsbibliothek in Munich, and the British Library in London together held at least one copy of all editions of Eder's surviving published works. Approximately ninety copies of Eder's publications were consulted in these three locations, the result of which survey makes Eder a writer more prolific than any of his previous historians had recognised. Georg Eder was the author of 22 titles published in four separate decades and composed for various purposes: as a university rector, as a Catholic educator, and as a Catholic polemicist.

Ten of the speeches Eder made in his capacity as Vienna University rector survive. Some of these were made solely for the occasion of doctoral promotions, but others marked moments of greater note: the funeral of a military hero, the funeral of an emperor, the accession of another emperor and the proclamation of a new king of Hungary.[40] Four

---

[38]   N. Paulus, 'Hofrath Dr Georg Eder'. Paulus omits 1559's *Orationes sex In Celeberrimo Archigymnasio Viennen*, Vienna: Raphael Hofhalter; 1573's, *Orationes II. Gratulatoriae, Ad Rudolphum Sereniss*, Vienna: Stephan Creutzer, and 1585's, *Symbolum der Evangelischen Predicanten*, Prague: printer unknown.

[39]   For example, Bauer, Johann Jacob (1774), *Bibliothecae Librorum Rariorum Universalis Supplementorum oder des vollständigen Verzeichnißes rarer Büccher*, vol. 1, Nuremberg: Martin Jacob Bauer, p. 40, asserts that there was a further edition of Eder's *Orationes sex* from 1569. There may have been a copy in Bauer's day that is no longer extant, but that no library catalogue at all records this work casts doubt that it ever existed. Both Paulus ('Hofrath Dr Georg Eder', p. 26) and Anton Maria Kobolt (*Baierisches Gelehrten Lexikon*, vol. 1, 1795, p. 183) also assert the existence of a Venetian edition of Eder's *Oeconomia Bibliorum* from 1577. Similarly, there is no remaining evidence that any such work existed.

[40]   Speeches made by Eder for doctoral promotions include: Eder, Georg (1557), *Ius Non Opinione Inductum*, Vienna: Raphael Hofhalter; Eder, Georg (1570), *Ad Rubricam Codicis De Summa Trinitate*, Bautzen: Johannis Vuolrab, and Eder, Georg (1581), *Quaerela Iustitiae*, Vienna: Stephan Creuzer. The two funeral orations made by Eder are: Eder, Georg (1551), *Georgii Eder De Illustriss. Principis et D.D. Nicolai Comitis a Salm & Neuburg ad Oenum*, Vienna: Egidius Aquila, and Eder, Georg (1559), *Luctus Archigymnasii Viennen: Pro Funere*

of these speeches were even collected and reprinted in an abbreviated form in 1559 as *Orationes sex In Celeberrimo Archigymnasio Viennen* ....[41] Another collection of speeches, *Laurea Poetica*, points to Eder's ability amongst even the talented rhetoricians of late sixteenth-century Vienna, as does his authorship of the *Catalogus Rectorum*, an attempt to chart aspects of the history of the city's university.[42]

Such displays of learning and status were with one exception published in Vienna and with only three exceptions all come from the 1550s, at the outset of Eder's career.[43] Most striking about the bibliography of Eder's writings however is the extent to which it is dominated for the last two decades of his life by purely religious works. There survive a total of 12 of Eder's Catholic instructional and polemical writings, published in two quite distinct phases.[44] The first phase, from 1568 until 1573, saw the publication of five religious titles by Eder, almost all in Latin and almost all of which were first published in Cologne.[45] The one exception to this,

---

D. *Caroli Quinti*, Vienna: Raphael Hofhalter. His speech on the accession of Ferdinand I as Holy Roman Emperor is (1558), *Triumphus D. Ferdinando I. Ro. Imperator*, Vienna: Raphael Hofhalter, while that on Rudolf's accession as King of Hungary is Eder, Georg (1573), *Orationes II. Gratulatoriae, Ad Rudolphum Sereniss*, Vienna: Stephan Creutzer.

[41]   *Orationes sex In Celeberrimo Archigymnasio Viennen*, contains the speech made on the promotion of a Rotis as well as those from the funerals of Charles V and Salm and that made on the accession of Ferdinand I as Holy Roman Emperor. It also contains two further speeches which do not appear to have been published separately elsewhere: 'Politicum ordine etiam in ecclesia retinendum esse, & quid ad rem conferat Iurisprudentia: habita Vien: in aedibus D. Stephani dum clariß: viro D. Marco Faschang Doctoream dignitatem in V.I. conferret. I Octobris Anno M. D. LV.', and 'De Maiestate legum & ordinum sive gradu dignitate & vsu, Qua Excellent iss: viro D. Laurentio Leemanno Grecarum literarum professori Doctorea dignitas in VI. ab Authore in tertio Rectoratu suo collata fuit. XIX. Ianuarii Anno M.D.LIX'.

[42]   Eder, Georg (1558), *Laurea poetica, ex caesareo privilegio in celeberrimo archigymnasio Viennensi tribus nuper viris eruditiss: Eliae Corvino, Ioanni Lauterbachio, & Vito Iacobaeo*, Vienna: Raphael Hofhalter.

[43]   *Ad Rubricam Codicis De Summa Trinitate*; *Orationes II. Gratulatoriae, Ad Rudolphum Sereniss*; *Quaerela Iustitiae*.

[44]   Examination of the collation and pagination of one of these works, *Oeconomia Bibliorum*, indicated that it could be counted as two separate books. This was confirmed by the existence in Munich of a copy of the 1571 version (signature: Exeg 189) in which another book had been bound between the two parts of Eder's work. It should also be noted that these books tend to be much more substantial and more strongly bound than the flimsier speeches, suggesting that 12 is the true number of Eder's religious works while some published versions of his speeches may not have survived.

[45]   Eder, Georg (1568), *Oeconomia Bibliorum*, Cologne: Gervinus Calenius and Johanne Quentel; Eder, Georg (1568), *Partitiones, Catechismi, Catholici*, Cologne: Gervinus Calenius and Johanne Quentel; Eder, Georg (1569), *Catechismus Catholicus*, Cologne: Gervinus Calenius and Johanne Quentel; Eder, Georg (1570), *Compendium Catechismi Catholici*, Cologne: Gervinus Calenius and Johanne Quentel.

1573's *Evangelische Inquisition*, was the work that brought a temporary halt to Eder's writing, such was the level of condemnation it received from the Emperor Maximilian II.[46] Equally striking is the speed with which and the extent to which Eder's career as a religious writer appears to have recovered. Between 1579 and 1585 seven further religious works bearing Eder's name were published, this time predominantly in Ingolstadt and revealing a greater mix between Latin and German.[47] Eder's position as a writer can also be traced through more than the mere number of titles he produced. His works were not only published in Vienna, Cologne, and Ingolstadt but also as widely as Dillingen, Prague, Lyon and Venice. Moreover, Eder's works were influential: a number of them made it into

---

[46]   Eder, Georg (1573), *Evangelische Inquisition Wahrer und falscher Religion*, Dillingen: Sebald Mayer; Eder, Georg (1574), *Evangelische Inquisition Wahrer und falscher Religion*, new edition, place of printing and name of printer unknown; Eder, Georg (1580), *Evangelische Inquisition Wahrer und falscher Religion*, new edition, Ingolstadt, David Sartorius. There has been considerable debate over the printing history of this work. Vogt, Johannes (1747), *Catalogus historico-criticus librorum rariorum, iam curis tertiis recognitas et copiosa accessione ex symbolis et collatione bibliophilorum per germaniam doctissimorum adauctus*, Hamburg: Heroldus, p. 253; Bauer, *Bibliothecae Librorum Rariorum Universalis Supplementorum*, p. 40 and then Kobolt, *Baierisches Gelehrten Lexikon*, p. 184, all maintained that the first edition was printed in 1572 as opposed to 1573. My own research has brought no such work to light, and a much more recent analyst of the Dillingen presses concurs that the first printing of the *Evangelische Inquisition* was not until 1573: Bucher, Otto (1960), *Bibliographie der Deutschen Drucke des XVI Jahrhunderts*, vol. 1, Dillingen, Bad Bocklet: Krieg, p. 159. There exists further debate over the number of editions from 1574 and their place of origin. Bauer, p. 40 and Paulus 'Hofrath Dr Georg Eder', p. 81, assert that there was an edition from Cologne in 1574, printed at the press of Dietrich Baum. Another camp insist that there was an edition printed in Dillingen in 1574 but without a place name or printer's name appearing in the text: Bucher, p. 172. While such works may have existed, my own research can only confirm that existing copies from 1574 bear no indication at all of their place of origin. That their pages are however printed and bound in a completely different fashion from the earlier and later editions of the same work would suggest that the Mayer press at Dillingen and the Sartorius press at Ingolstadt are unlikely to have been the source.

[47]   Eder, Georg (1579; 1580 reprint), *Das guldene Flüß Christlicher Gemain Und Gesellschaft*, Ingolstadt: David Sartorius; Eder, Georg (1579), *Methodus Catechisimi Catholici*, Lyon: Joannes Parant; Eder, Georg (1580), *Malleus Haereticorum*, Ingolstadt: David Sartorius; Eder, Georg (1581), *Confessio Catholica S.S. Concilii Tridentini*, Lyon: Joannes Parant; Eder, Georg (1580), *Ein Christliche Gutherzige und Notwendige Warnungschrifft*, Ingolstadt: David Sartorius; Eder, Georg (1581), *Mataeologia Haereticorum* (Ingolstadt: David Sartorius); Georg Eder (1585), *Symbolum der Evangelischen Predicanten*, Prague: printer unknown.

more than one edition or went through more than one printing, while others acted as a foundation for the work of later authors.[48]

This wide range and high quality of source material is of such inherent value that it offers in itself grounds for an examination of the man at its centre. A study of Georg Eder is, however, much more than a reconstructive exercise. The second major reason why he is at the heart of this book is for what the changing contours of his career can contribute to existing historiography, in particular that of early modern Catholic reform.[49] The case of Georg Eder not only builds on and adds to existing work, but simultaneously extends the parameters of debate yet further.

The study of Catholic reform has already seen much highly constructive recent work.[50] As John O'Malley has noted, 'For serious historians of the Protestant and secular tradition, Catholicism until quite recently lacked interest as a subject of research ... For them, Catholicism was the backward and lacklustre stepsister to the Reformation.'[51] The past few decades have however seen a valuable historiographical exploration of Catholic reform that has tended to emphasise three main themes: the importance of the support of the secular authorities to the progress of Catholic ecclesiastical and spiritual revival, the significance of local factors in determining the nature and speed of reform, and the sheer slowness of the entire process.[52]

---

[48]   See bibliography for full details. The *Oeconomia Bibliorum, Partitiones, Catechismi Catholici, Das guldene Flüß Christlicher Gemain Und Gesellschaft*, and *Confessio Catholica S.S. Concilii Tridentini* were all reprinted once. The first two titles also went through two new editions as did the *Evangelische Inquisition*, while the *Malleus Haereticorum* went through one. Eder's *Catalogus Rectorum* acted as the foundation for two updated versions from the seventeenth century: Litters, Jonas (1645), *Catalogus Rectorum et illustrium virorum archigymnasii Viennensis ... 1237–1644*, Vienna: Rictius; Sorbait, Paul de (1669), *Catalogus Rectorum et illustrium virorum archigymnasii Viennensis 1237–1669*, Vienna: Matthaeus Cosmerov; Sorbait, Paul de (1670), *Catalogus Rectorum et illustrium virorum Archigymnasii Viennensis 1237–1670*, Vienna: Matthaeus Cosmerov. In addition, Eder's religious writings influenced that of Heinrich Fabricius and the Jesuit Antonio Possevino: see p. 80 and pp. 80–81.

[49]   Such is the extent and variety of writing on Vienna and Catholic reform in this period that this discussion can be little more than an overview of the general historiographical tendencies. It is not, however, the intention to offer an exhaustive survey of past work, but rather to demonstrate how this book can add to paths of examination already in existence.

[50]   For a helpful and up-to-date overview of the historiography of the Catholic Reformation, see Johnson, Trevor (2006), 'The Catholic Reformation', in Ryrie, Alec (ed.), *The European Reformations*, Basingstoke: Palgrave Macmillan, pp. 190–211.

[51]   O'Malley, John W. (2000), *Trent And All That. Renaming Catholicism in the Early Modern Era*, Cambridge, MA: Harvard University Press, p. 10.

[52]   The other main area of debate of less relevance to this particular discussion concerns terminology: Counter-Reformation, Catholic Reformation or, as John O'Malley proposes, 'Early Modern Catholicism'. See his book named above, or O'Malley, John W. (1993), 'Was Ignatius Loyola a Church Reformer? How to look at Early Modern Catholicism', in O'Malley, J.W. (ed.), *Religious Culture in the Sixteenth Century*, Aldershot: Variorum XII,

These themes have been coherently and convincingly examined by a wide range of historians. German historiography of the past two decades has tended to emphasise the 'confessionalization' thesis. Not to be confused with 'confessionalism', which refers to the formation of the different confessions themselves, confessionalization draws parallels between the confessions, to examine how the close co-operation of church and state resulted in identifiably 'modern' states.[53] Wolfgang Reinhard, following Zeeden and accompanied in methodology by Schilling, focuses in particular on the interpenetration of secular and religious authority to create a Catholic state.[54] In this, such work bears comparison with that of John Bossy and Jean Delumeau whose 'acculturation' thesis regards Tridentine Catholicism as an attempt by central authorities to 'Christianise' and control the body of the Church.[55]

The main growth area in recent years has however been that historiography which points rather to the significance of factors peculiar to each locality. These factors result in what scholars such as Marc Forster regard as a negotiated Catholicism, a mere version of that desired by the ecclesiastical authorities and as much a product of the enduring vitality of pre-Tridentine Catholicism as post-Tridentine attempts to enforce conformity.[56] Despite the majestic scholarship of Jedin, the

---

pp. 177–93. The nature of Eder's Catholicism and the extent to which it could be described as 'anti-evangelical' or 'Tridentine' will however be a theme that runs throughout this book as a whole.

[53]   For an accessible discussion of the complexities of this theory, see Bireley, Robert (1999), *The Refashioning of Catholicism, 1450–1700. A Reassessment of the Counter Reformation*, Basingstoke: Macmillan, pp. 6–7, and Po-Chia Hsia, R. (1989), *Social Discipline in the Reformation: Central Europe 1550–1750*, London: Routledge.

[54]   For example, Reinhard, Wolfgang (1985), 'Reformation, Counter-Reformation and the Early Modern State: A Reassessment', *CHR*, 75, 383–404. See too Ernst Walter Zeeden (1967), *Das Zeitalter der Gegenreformation von 1555 bis 1648*, Freiburg im Briesgau: Herder, and Schilling, Heinz (1992), *Religion, Popular Culture and the Emergence of Early Modern Society*, Leiden: Brill.

[55]   Bossy, John (1985), *Christianity in the West 1400–1700*, Oxford: Oxford University Press; Delumeau, Jean (1977), *Catholicism between Luther and Voltaire: A New View of the Counter-Reformation*, London: Burns and Oates.

[56]   Forster, Marc R. (1997), 'With and Without Confessionalization. Varieties of Early Modern German Catholicism', *JEMH*, 1, 315–343, p. 315. Here, Forster notes that while the confessionalization thesis 'asserts that confessionalism originated in the policies of church officials and state bureaucrats intent on imposing order, discipline, and religious uniformity on the population from above', it cannot explain the development of Catholic culture in areas where states were weak. See too Forster's 1992 *The Counter-Reformation in the Villages. Religion and Reform in the Bishopric of Speyer, 1560–1720*, Ithaca, NY: Cornell University Press and his 2001 *Catholic Revival in the Age of the Baroque. Religious Identity in Southwest Germany, 1550–1750*, Cambridge: Cambridge University Press. In this approach, Châtellier, Louis (1989), *The Europe of the Devout: The Catholic Reformation and the Formation of a New Society*, Cambridge: Cambridge University Press, has been influential. Châtellier's preface notes his wish to produce 'a study of modern Catholicism as a social phenomenon', p. ix.

decrees of the Council of Trent are thus no longer regarded as the sole key to understanding the true nature of Catholic reform.[57] Forster's own exemplary study, for example, draws on the evidence of visitation reports, cathedral chapter minutes, and court records to demonstrate that the 'beliefs, practices, and modes of behaviour of the Catholic population of Speyer changed and developed through a dynamic relationship between Catholic reform and popular reaction'.[58] Numerous other studies of different localities in the empire and beyond bolster this view while stressing the need to regard the entire process of the implementation of Catholic reform through a much longer chronological lens.[59] In David Gentilcore's 1992 work on Terra D'Otranto for example, a timescale of 1563 to 1818 is suggested for a true sense of the processes involved in early modern Catholic reform.[60]

In its approaches and subsequent conclusions, the newest historiography of Catholicism in the early modern Austrian lands follows such trends. In the context of the historiography of Austrian Catholicism, attention has now moved from the emphasis of the likes of Bibl and Duhr on the achievements of late sixteenth-century Catholic reform, to a much more conservative estimate of its speed and success.[61]

Acting in tandem with the work of Mecenseffy and Reingrabner on the extent of evangelical belief in the late sixteenth-century Austrian lands, the studies by Gernot Heiss, Joseph Patrouch, Rona Johnston Gordon

[57]   *Geschichte des Konzils von Trient* (4 vols, 1949–75, Friburg: Herder) was Jedin's massive work outlining the progress of Trent. He also addressed the question of the extent of anti-Protestantism within Catholic reform in his 1946 essay, *Katholische Reformation oder Gegenreformation? Ein Versuch zur Klärung der Begriffe nebst einer Jubiläumsbetrachtung über das Trienter Konzil*, Lucerne: Josef Stocker.

[58]   Forster, *The Counter-Reformation in the Villages*, p. 5.

[59]   In addition to Forster's own work, key examples include: Po-Chia Hsia, R. (1984), *Society and Religion in Münster, 1535–1618*, New Haven, CT: Yale University Press, and Wolfgang Zimmermann (1994), *Rekatholisierung, Konfessionalisierung und Ratsregiment: Der Prozeß des politischen und religiösen Wandels in der österreichischen Stadt Konstanz, 1548–1637*, Sigmaringen: Thorbecke. For an example from the Italian context, see Simon Ditchfield (1995), *Liturgy, Sanctity and History in Tridentine Italy*, Cambridge: Cambridge University Press.

[60]   Gentilcore, David (1992), *From Bishop to Witch. The System of the Sacred in Early Modern Terra d'Otranto*, Manchester: Manchester University Press, p. 2.

[61]   Bibl, Victor (1900), *Die Einführung der katholischen Gegenreformation in Niederösterreich durch Kaiser Rudolf II*, Innsbruck: Wagner; Bibl, Victor (1901), 'Erzherzog Ernst und die Gegenreformation in Niederösterreich (1576–1590)', *MIÖG*, 6, 575–96; Duhr, Bernhard (1907), *Geschichte der Jesuiten in den Ländern deutscher Zunge*, vol. 1, *Geschichte der Jesuiten in den Ländern deutscher Zunge im XVI. Jahrhundert*, Freiburg im Briesgau: Herder. Bibl in particular tends to present a very positive view of the achievements of Ernst's administration as regards Catholic reform. It should also be remembered that older Catholic historiography frequently has strong confessional undertones.

and Regina Pörtner, to name the most recent, have helped challenge the image of 'Catholic Austria'.[62] While Heiss has taken the more traditional approach of analysis of the role of the first Jesuits to mission within such an environment, Patrouch and Johnston Gordon both have conducted studies of the nature and timing of Catholic reform at parish level.[63] Basing her work on the perspective of the episcopal authorities in Lower Austria, Rona Johnston Gordon notes that it was not until the late seventeenth century that the region became 'a bastion of reformed Catholicism', and that even in 1628 there was still the need to order all Lower Austrian subjects to attend Catholic worship.[64] Patrouch's work, although on

---

[62]   On the influence of evangelicals in Lower Austria and Vienna, see in particular the numerous works of Grete Mecenseffy and Gustav Reingrabner. The most helpful include: Mecenseffy, Grete (1974), 'Wien im Zeitalter der Reformation des 16. Jahrhunderts', *Wiener Geschichtsblätter*, 29 (1), 228–39; Mecenseffy, Grete and Rassl, Hermann (1980), *Die Evangelischen Kirchen Wiens*, Vienna: Zsolnay; Reingrabner, Gustav (1976), *Adel und Reformation. Beiträge zur Geschichte des Protestantischen Adels im Lande Unter Der Enns Während des 16. und 17. Jahrhunderts*, Vienna: Verein für Landeskunde von Niederösterreich und Wien; Reingrabner, Gustav (1981), 'Religiöse Lebensformen des Protestantischen Adels in Niederösterreich', in Klingenstein, Grete and Lutz, Heinrich (eds), *Spezialforschung und 'Gesamtgeschichte'*, Wiener Beiträge zur Geschichte der Neuzeit, vol. 8, Vienna: Verlag für Geschichte und Politik, pp. 126–38. There is, furthermore, a long-running tradition of historiography dealing with the diocese of Vienna, including work by Josef Kopallik (1890–94), *Regesten zur Geschichte der Erzdiözese Wien*, Vienna; Tomek, Ernst (1935–59), *Kirchengeschichte Österreichs*, vol. 2, *Humanismus, Reformation und Gegenreformation*, Innsbruck, Munich, Vienna: Tyrolia, and most recently Loidl, Franz (1983), *Geschichte des Erzbistums Wien*, Vienna: Herold. All such works remain indebted to the sources collected by Theodor Wiedemann earlier in the nineteenth century. Note that there have been numerous studies of aspects of Austrian Catholicism but these are frequently overviews based on secondary literature. For example: Krexner, Martin and Loidl, Franz (1983), *Wiens Bischöfe und Erzbischöfe*, Vienna; Lechner, Karl (1969), '500 Jahre Diözese Wien. Vorgeschichte und geschichte des Wiener Bistums', *Unsere Heimat*, 40, 53–70; Loidl, Franz (1983), *Geschichte des Erzbistums Wien*, Vienna: Herold.

[63]   Heiss, Gernot (1986), 'Die Jesuiten und die Anfänge der Katholisierung in den Ländern Ferdinands I. Glaube, Mentalität, Politik', 2 vols, unpublished Habilitation, University of Vienna; Heiss, Gernot (1991), 'Princes, Jesuits and the Origins of Counter-Reform in the Habsburg Lands', in Evans, R.J.W. and Thomas, T.V. (eds), *Crown, Church and Estates. Central European Politics in the Sixteenth and Seventeenth Centuries*, London: Macmillan in association with the School of Slavonic and Eastern European Studies, University of London, pp. 92–109.

[64]   Johnston, Rona Gordon (1996), 'The Bishopric of Passau and the Counter-Reformation in Lower Austria, 1580–1636', unpublished D. Phil. dissertation, University of Oxford, p. 8; Johnston, Rona (1997), 'Patronage and parish: the nobility and the recatholicization of Lower Austria', in Maag, Karin (ed.), *The Reformation in Eastern and Central Europe*, Aldershot: Ashgate, pp. 211–27, p. 211. On this theme also see Regina Pörtner (2001), *The Counter-Reformation in Central Europe: Styria 1580–1630*, Oxford: Oxford University Press. Her examination of the Counter-Reformation in Styria is intended 'as a case study of the Counter-Reformation in one of the provinces of the Habsburg Monarchy from the beginnings of forcible recatholization in the late sixteenth century to the definite termination of religious persecution by the end of the eighteenth', p. 1.

Upper Austria, reaches a similar conclusion. Reliant on the gaining of influential local allies in each parish, the implementation of Catholic reform was a slow and piecemeal process heavily at the mercy of secular sanction and generational change.[65]

The contribution of this book to the historiography of Catholic reform in the Austrian lands, and indeed to the genre in general, simultaneously builds on and goes beyond such foundations. Firstly, that a man such as Eder could be so heavily involved in the processes of Catholic reform contributes a new element to the equation: the role of the laity in bringing religious change. Studies such as those named above have tended to focus rather on the position of the secular and ecclesiastical authorities, in large part due to the relative availability of primary sources.[66] As demonstrated above, however, the case of Eder and the wealth of attendant sources offer generous access to the viewpoint of this often fairly anonymous group. That the career of Eder also points to the considerable potential for action of certain members of the laity, particularly in co-operation with the Jesuits, suggests that the instigation and survival of Catholic reform is a matter over which exclusive study of rulers and churchmen is insufficient.

Secondly, the fact that Georg Eder was most active in the decades immediately following the conclusion of the Council of Trent places him at the coalface of the implementation of Catholic reform at precisely its most important moment. The studies described above have indeed demonstrated the slowness of bringing religious change to the local level, but it is inevitable that this was a long process. It is hardly a surprise that the results of Trent-inspired reform, such as the proper training of new priests, would take several generations to bear fruit. What these studies reflect rather is the importance of the foundations laid in the later sixteenth century, by the likes of Eder, which contributed to such future change but were hotly disputed in their own day.

---

[65]   Patrouch, Joseph F. (1991), 'Methods of Cultural Manipulation: The Counter-Reformation in the Habsburg Province of Upper Austria, 1570–1650', unpublished PhD dissertation, University of California; Patrouch, Joseph F. (1994), 'The Investiture Controversy Revisited: Religious Reform, Emperor Maximilian II, and the Klosterrat', *AHY*, 25, 59–77. For a helpful recent summary of the literature on the eventual return to Catholic orthodoxy at the highest levels of the Habsburg court, see Murdock, Graeme (2006), 'Central and Eastern Europe', in Ryrie, Alec (ed.), *The European Reformations*, Basingstoke: Palgrave Macmillan, pp. 36–56, in particular pp. 48–50. As Murdock concludes, 'Above all, it was the drift of nobles back to the Catholic fold which ensured the decline of Central European Protestantism', p. 49. See too MacHardy, Karin J. (2003), *War, Religion and Court Patronage in Habsburg Austria. The Social and Cultural Dimensions of Political Interaction, 1521–1622*, Basingstoke: Palgrave Macmillan.

[66]   An exception is Rößner, Maria Barbara (1991), *Konrad Braun (ca. 1495–1563) – ein katholischer Jurist, Politiker, Kontroverstheologe und Kirchenreformer im konfessionellen Zeitalter*, Münster: Aschendorff.

Thirdly, that Eder's formative years were pre-Tridentine and his most active years post-Tridentine, makes him a telling case study of the physical and intellectual survival of lay Catholicism throughout the most troubled decades of the sixteenth century. The available sources offer compelling evidence that lay Catholicism did not disintegrate between the rise of Lutheranism and the end of Trent; nor was it something that ever lay prone: it remained a creative and vibrant force in its own right. It was furthermore a Catholicism that had to react to two notions of itself: one that could see the potential for middle ground and one that made its claims solely for Rome. It was a Catholicism that had to respond to the two contrasting models of Christian rule: that of Eder's employers, the Austrian Habsburgs, who would tolerate a middle way in exchange for unity, and that of the neighbouring Bavarian Wittelsbachs, willing to abandon the ideal of a universal Christendom in exchange for confessional purity in their own territory. It was, in addition, a Catholic body with a disputed head, facing Rome's demands for allegiance on the one side and those of the local secular ruler on the other. Catholic identity was in real flux in the middle decades of the sixteenth century, and the three major groupings with whom Eder had to deal: the Austrian Habsburgs, the Bavarian Wittelsbachs, and the Rome-directed Jesuits all had their own view on what it meant to be a Catholic.

There remains, then, the question of how best to employ Eder's life and attendant range of surviving sources to explore such themes. Adhering loosely to the path of Eder's working life provides a particularly helpful method of approach.[67] Such an organisation of the material rightly highlights a central achievement of this project: the recovery of little-known details of the life of a man so clearly significant in the Vienna of the later sixteenth century. It should be noted at the outset, however, that this book is not a biography. The concern is less with Eder's life per se as with the implications of his career for the confessional context in which he worked. Eder's personal life, for example the role of his family, is of interest only in so far as it casts light on his political or

---

[67]   In this approach the precedent set by Thomas Brady in his 1995 work, *Protestant Politics: Jacob Sturm (1489–1553) and the German Reformation*, Atlantic Highlands [NJ]: Humanities Press, has been helpful. Brady states in his introduction: 'What held the entire project together was the strand of biography, Jacob Sturm's biography, around which could be braided the stories of the conjuncture of Imperial structure and Reformation movement', p. xiv. Similarly, Craig Harline and Eddy Put introduce their study of the career of Mathias Hovius, Archbishop of Mechelen, with the argument that 'in seeking to understand a world long past, we found it highly illuminating to begin with a single human being rather than a large abstraction such as "society"', Harline and Put (2000), *A Bishop's Tale. Mathias Hovius Among His Flock in Seventeenth-Century Flanders*, New Haven, CT:Yale University Press, 2000), p. vii.

confessional position.[68] Nor would Georg Eder's life be of such inherent interest without the career and religious allegiance that put him in such an interesting situation in the first place.

The book is, none the less, loosely chronological in that it gradually tells the tale of the rise, fall and recovery of Eder's career in the confessionally piranha-infested waters of Vienna in the latter half of the sixteenth century. Each chapter has, however, a particular focus that casts light on much broader themes. Chapter 1, 'Eder's Vienna', looks at the political and religious topography of early modern Vienna. Chapter 2, 'Promotion and prominence, 1550–73' focuses on the nature of political survival at Vienna's university and court in this deeply divided period, while Chapter 3, 'Service to the Church, 1550–73', deals with the role of the educated laity in the survival of embattled Catholicism. Chapter 4, '1573: imperial condemnation', focuses on the nature of an imperial authority that was so affronted by criticism such as that of Eder, while Chapter 5 looks at the Dukes of Bavaria as rival patrons of Catholic reform in the absence of clear Habsburg leadership. Chapter 6 ends the study by focusing on the one group that never deserted Eder, even after his death: the Jesuits. As such, this book is simultaneously a study of one man's life and the political, religious, cultural and social context in which he lived.

---

[68]   It is worth noting, however, that the surviving records almost all derive from Eder's working life. As a result, any rare glimpses of his family life are so valuable for putting his working life in its wider context that virtually all have been included in the discussion.

CHAPTER 1

Eder's Vienna

The Vienna in which Georg Eder lived and worked was a far cry from the city that would later be known for the physical splendour and Catholic vigour of its Baroque period.[1] By the time of his arrival at the mid-point of the sixteenth century, the city was still suffering from the after-effects of a Turkish siege, a series of epidemics and a major fire which had destroyed one-third of the 1250 buildings estimated to have stood within the city walls.[2] Together, these disasters led to a drop in the city's population, a decline in trade and a subsequent rise in the cost of living for those who remained.[3] At the university, these circumstances resulted in a drastic downturn in student matriculation rates which, despite the gradual return of notable

---

[1]   On all aspects of social, political, economic, and religious life in early-modern Vienna, see the 2003 volume edited by Karl Vocelka and Anita Traninger, *Wien. Geschichte einer Stadt*, vol. 2, *Die frühneuzeitliche Residenz (16. bis 18. Jahrhundert)*, Vienna, Cologne, Weimar: Böhlau. There are other useful works such as that by Csendes, Peter (1981), *Geschichte Wiens*, Munich: Oldenbourg, but these cover a much broader period, consequently in less depth.

[2]   The first major Ottoman siege of Vienna took place over two weeks in 1529. It had been preceeded four years earlier by a major fire: on this see Weigl, Andreas (2003), 'Frühneuzeitliches Bevölkerungswachstum', in Vocelka and Traninger (eds), *Wien. Geschichte einer Stadt*, vol. 2, pp. 109–32, especially p. 109. Kurt Mühlberger notes that plague broke out in Vienna approximately every eight to ten years in the sixteenth century, with major outbreaks occurring in 1541–42, 1552, 1560–62, 1570 and 1575–76. Mühlberger, Kurt (1991), 'Zu den Krisen der Universität Wien im Zeitalter der konfessionellen Auseinandersetzungen', *Bericht über den achtzehnten österreichischen Historikertag in Linz veranstaltet vom Verband Österreichischer Geschichtsvereine in der Zeit vom 24. bis 29. September 1990*, Veröffentlichungen des Verbandes Österreichischer Geschichtsvereine 27, pp. 269–77.

[3]   Andreas Weigl suggests that the city's population fell dramatically in the 1520s, from around 30 000 in 1520 to only 12 000 in 1530. Though rates recovered slowly in the next three decades, by 1563 Vienna's population was still only around 25 000, less than in the pre-siege years. Weigl, 'Frühneuzeitliches Bevölkerungswachstum', pp. 109–10. John Spielmann suggests that the total population of Vienna had even been as high as 80 000 in the fourteenth century. He distinguishes between figures for the 'inner' part of the city, within the walls, and the 'outer' part, beyond the walls. Weigl's statistics appear to refer to those living in the 'inner' part of the city. Spielman, John P. (1993), *The City and the Crown. Vienna and the Imperial Court 1600–1740*, West Lafayette, IN: Purdue University Press, pp. 12, 30. On the rising cost of living, Mühlberger has estimated that in Vienna in 1514, a loaf of bread would have cost the equivalent of one Pfennig: by 1566, the same item would have cost four times as much. Mühlberger, 'Zu den Krisen der Universität Wien', p. 273.

and attractive humanist figures, were by the mid-point of the century, still nowhere near pre-siege numbers.[4]

One of the few draws left was the Habsburg court, which had, since the Archduke Ferdinand's arrival in 1522, acted not only as something of a military high command but as a growing administrative centre for the dynasty's hereditary lands.[5] Ferdinand's eventual accession as Holy Roman Emperor in 1556 gave Vienna an important share in his reflected glory, and the city remained the primary base for the emperor during the reign of Ferdinand's eldest son, Maximilian II, 1564–76.[6] Though Rudolf II, Maximilian's son and successor as Holy Roman Emperor, chose to spend much of his reign in Prague, Rudolf's younger brother Archduke Ernst, who administered Lower Austria between 1576 and his death in 1596, remained in Vienna and maintained the Habsburg presence.[7] The Habsburg court became, as John Spielmann has put it, 'the most important resident of the city', and played a central role in defining the

---

[4]   Mühlberger, 'Zu den Krisen der Universität Wien', p. 271. According to Mühlberger's graph, by 1520, Vienna University enjoyed approximately 3200 annual matriculations compared to only 1200 for Ingolstadt and 1700 for Wittenberg. By 1530, Vienna's number had all but collapsed to a mere 300 matriculations. By 1555, while Wittenberg received 3200 matriculations and Ingolstadt 1000, Vienna's total still only reached 800, a quarter of its 1520 rate.

[5]   Holy Roman Emperor Charles V had granted his younger brother Ferdinand control of the dynasty's so-called 'Erblande' through the Treaty of Brussels in 1522. This included the archduchies of Upper and Lower Austria; the duchies of Styria, Carinthia and Carniola and principalities of Istria, Gorizia and Trieste that comprised Inner Austria; and the Tyrol, also known as Outer Austria. Ferdinand was also elected King of Bohemia in 1526, and in 1531 was elected King of the Romans, making him Charles' successor-designate to the imperial title. Though he was a peripatetic ruler, Vienna became central to Ferdinand's administration of the whole region. For a detailed study of the career of Ferdinand I, see Sutter Fichtner, Paula (1982), *Ferdinand of Austria: The Politics of Dynasticism in the Age of the Reformation*, New York: Columbia University Press.

[6]   Maximilian's control over Vienna came in the first instance from his inherited status as archduke of Lower Austria. Ferdinand I's death in 1564 saw the division of the hereditary lands: his eldest son Maximilian retained control of Upper and Lower Austria, while younger sons Charles and Ferdinand ruled Inner Austria and Outer Austria from Graz and Innsbruck respectively. Volker Press has noted, however, that even in the diets of the hereditary lands such as those of Lower Austria, Maximilian II would have been dealt with in his capacity as emperor, as in the imperial diet. Press, Volker (1991), 'The System of Estates in the Austrian Hereditary Lands and in the Holy Roman Empire: A Comparison', in Evans, R.J.W. and Thomas, T.V. (eds), *Crown, Church and Estates. Central European Politics in the Sixteenth and Seventeenth Centuries*, London: Macmillan in association with the School of Slavonic and Eastern European Studies, University of London, pp. 1–22, p. 1. On the career of Maximilian II, see Sutter Fichtner, Paula (2001), *Emperor Maximilian II*, New Haven, CT: Yale University Press.

[7]   The only exclusive study of Ernst is now more than a century old: Victor Bibl, 'Erzherzog Ernst und die Gegenreformation in Niederösterreich (1576–1590)' (1901), *Mitteilungen des Instituts für Österreichische Geschichtsforschung*, VI Ergänzungsband, pp. 575–96.

political and religious culture of Vienna in the second half of the sixteenth century.[8]

This was not, however, always to the taste of all the city's inhabitants. For those as devoutly Catholic as Georg Eder, Habsburg policy often seemed to be at best ambivalent toward the Catholic cause, and at worst actively hostile.[9] This impression came in large part from the religious concessions wrung from the Habsburgs during a period of severe political and military vulnerability. The extent of the Ottoman threat to Europe in the sixteenth century has been reasonably well-documented, at least from the perspective of the Christian powers.[10] Its impact on Habsburg policy at imperial level is also well-known: it had been Ferdinand I who, desperate for military aid against the Turks from the Protestant princes of the empire, had first accepted the temporary principle of the 'cuius regio, eius religio' formula at the Diet of Speyer in 1526. Less than thirty years later it was the same ruler who was forced to accept the formula as permanent in the Peace of Augsburg, thereby permitting Lutheran freedom of worship within the empire.[11] What has received much less attention, though, is how the even greater geographical proximity of the Ottoman threat impacted on Habsburg policy in their own archduchy of Lower Austria and its most vulnerable city of Vienna.

Lutheranism had infiltrated Vienna in the early 1520s, and despite frequent efforts by Ferdinand I, was never fully suppressed.[12] Whether this form of Protestantism was accepted by the Lower Austrian nobility for doctrinal reasons or political ones is hard and perhaps unnecessary to fathom, but whatever their reasons, by 1568, the Lower Austrian Herrenstand or upper nobility was overwhelmingly dominated by nobles describing themselves as Lutheran.[13] By then too, Maximilian II

---

[8]   Spielman, *The City and the Crown*, p. 4. Spielmann's is one of the few studies to look directly at the relationship between court and city in early-modern Vienna. Though Vienna had its own municipal structures, these were usually subordinate to the will of the crown, particularly since one of Ferdinand's first acts in Lower Austria had been to execute the leaders of an urban rebellion led by the then mayor of Vienna, Dr Martin Siebenbürger, in 1522.

[9]   Eder's views on the situation in Vienna will be explored fully in Chapter 5.

[10]   See in particular Daniel Goffman (2002), *The Ottoman Empire and Early Modern Europe*, Cambridge: Cambridge University Press.

[11]   For an account of these negotiations, see Stephan A. Fischer-Galati (1959), *Ottoman Imperialism and German Protestantism 1521–1555*, Cambridge, MA: Harvard University Press.

[12]   As early as 1523 Ferdinand had issued a mandate against the spread and possession of Lutheran books. Similar decrees followed, such as that of 1551 against Lutheran schoolmasters and the publication of Lutheran works, and that of 1554 which forbade the partaking of communion in both kinds.

[13]   As Robert Evans has remarked of this complex situation, 'By the middle of the sixteenth century the ethos of the Austrian Habsburg lands was Protestant. That cannot be a precise statement; rather it indicates what religion was not', Evans, Robert J.W. (1979), *The*

was struggling to contain the Turkish threat that seemed continually on the verge of enveloping Vienna. The year 1566 had seen humiliation for the Habsburg forces in Hungary, which only increased fears of a further Ottoman attack on the city. This was to be avoided at all costs. Maximilian's father Ferdinand had stated in a letter of 1546 that 'our city of Vienna is almost a frontier town against them [the Turks] ... Vienna is important and precious not only for the hereditary dominions, but for all Christendom and the German nation ... ', and his son clearly appreciated the same.[14] Attempts were duly made to negotiate terms between ruler and estates, but with a state debt standing at 2.5 million gulden, the result was inevitable.[15] In return for the financial and military aid of the Lower Austrian estates, Maximilian II was not only forced to grant the Lower Austrian 'Religions-Konzession' in 1568, but to confirm the same three years later with the so-called 'Religions-Assekuration' of 1571. Maximilian had permitted the seemingly unthinkable on his own doorstep. Although Lutheran worship was not formally permitted in Vienna, both Konzession and Assekuration granted members of the noble estates the right to worship according to the confession of Augsburg 'in all their castles, houses and possessions'. In the countryside, this also included the provision of churches for their Lutheran subjects.[16]

Maximilian II's provision, however, contained a rapidly exploited legal loophole that made regular worship according to Lutheran rites

---

Making of the Habsburg Monarchy 1550–1700, Oxford: Clarendon Press, p. 3. According to Gustav Reingrabner, by the 1580s approximately 90 per cent of the Lower Austrian nobles claimed allegiance to Lutheranism. *Adel und Reformation. Beiträge zur Geschichte des Protestantischen Adels im Lande Unter Der Enns Während des 16. und 17. Jahrhunderts* (Vienna, Verein für Landeskunde von Niederösterreich und Wien, 1976), p. 79.

[14]   Letter from June 1546, regarding Ferdinand I's wish to raise funds to pay for the additional fortification of Vienna. Barea, Ilsa (1966), *Vienna. Legend and Reality*, London: Secker & Warburg, p. 38, citing material in Starzer, Albert (1906) 'Fortsetzung' in Starzer, Albert (ed.), *Quellen zur Geschichte der Stadt Wien*, part I, vol. 5, Vienna: Verein für Geschichte der Stadt Wien, pp. 11–397, p. 104.

[15]   Sutter Fichtner, *Emperor Maximilian II*, p. 148. Each diet – held for Lower Austria in the Landhaus on Vienna's Herrengasse – was a forum for the discussion of the public affairs of the territory, with members of each estate as participants. The monasteries comprised the first estate while the second was composed of the higher nobility or Herrenstand. Knights or the lower nobility (Ritterstand) made up the third estate, while the fourth estate was that of the cities. It was also, however, the place where these same estates could wield their most important power: that of the right of the grant of taxes. That these taxes funded the Habsburg ruler's own court, administration and, above all, military defence, made them a vital bargaining chip for the estates. For more on such negotiations, see MacHardy, Karin J. (2003), *War, Religion and Court Patronage in Habsburg Austria. The Social and Cultural Dimensions of Political Interaction, 1521–1622*, Palgrave Macmillan: Basingstoke, pp. 30–33.

[16]   Quotation from the Religions-Assekuration of 11 January 1571, cited in Johnston, 'Patronage and Parish', p. 214.

just as possible for those living within Vienna's walls as for those living without. Lower Austrian nobles installed Lutheran Schloßprediger, or 'castle preachers', at their own properties, as permitted under the terms of the Konzession. Indeed, a Lutheran visitation of Lower Austria in 1580 uncovered a total of 138 such preachers in what is a relatively small area.[17] What Maximilian had perhaps not anticipated, was that such was the Viennese hunger for Lutheranism, every Sunday several thousand people would flock from the city, technically excluded from the terms of the Konzession, to hear the Protestant preachers on the nobles' own land. Eder himself observed bitterly in 1585, almost two decades after the issue of the Konzession, that as many as 3000 people were still participating in the so-called 'Auslaufen' to hear a Lutheran preacher at just one such location, Inzersdorf.[18] In a fruitless bid to stop such embarrassing infringements of Habsburg authority, Maximilian bowed even further to Protestant demands and granted a room for worship in the Viennese Landhaus, right in the heart of the city, and close to the Hofburg itself. With their own preachers, and soon a school and even a bookshop all under noble protection, Habsburg religious policy had done nothing less than permit the exercise of Protestantism in Vienna as well as Lower Austria.[19]

No less damaging to the reputation of the Austrian Habsburgs as defenders of Catholicism was the enthusiasm of Ferdinand I and particularly Maximilian II to turn the Viennese court into a centre of humanist scholarship.[20] There was, of course, nothing inherently damaging to Catholicism in this. The men they invited to Vienna were famed primarily for their scholarship, and between them they turned what was an unglamorous Habsburg court into a base of patronage and production for humanist intellectuals working in a wide range of fields.[21]

---

[17]   Reingrabner, *Adel und Reformation*, p. 85, citing Bernleithner, *Konfession in Österreich um 1580*, sheet 21.

[18]   Eder to Duke Wilhelm of Bavaria, 19 March 1585, in Bibl, Victor (ed.) (1909), 'Die Berichte des Reichshofrates Dr Georg Eder an die Herzoge Albrecht und Wilhelm von Bayern über die Religionskrise in Niederösterreich (1579–1587)', *Jb.f.Lk.v.NÖ*, Neue Folge 8, 67–154', 144–6.

[19]   Between 1576 and 1578 the Lutheran school flourished, with five members of teaching staff. Mecenseffy, Grete (1974), 'Wien im Zeitalter der Reformation des 16. Jahrhunderts', *Wiener Geschichtsblätter*, 29 (1), 228–39, 236.

[20]   Robert Evans has described the reign of Maximilian II in particular as 'the climax of orthodox Humanism in Austria', *The Making of the Habsburg Monarchy*, p. 20.

[21]   Aspects of this court culture would only reach their apogee in Prague after Rudolf II moved the imperial court there. For an examination of Prague-based humanist culture under the Emperor Rudolf II, see Evans, Robert J.W. (1973), *Rudolf II and his World: A Study in Intellectual History 1576–1612*, Oxford: Oxford University Press. Another useful collection is Fučíková, E., et al. (eds) (1997), *Rudolf II and Prague: the Court and the City*, London: Thames & Hudson.

As a result, by the middle decades of the sixteenth century the court of Vienna could boast the presence of many of the leading scholars of the day, including Wolfgang Lazius, physician, court historian and author of the first history of Vienna; Jacopo Strada, court antiquary and artist; Hugo Blotius, keeper of the imperial library; Augerius Busbequius, Ottoman ambassador, botanist and collector; Johannes Sambucus, historian and philologist, and Johannes Crato and Carolus Clusius, botanists.[22]

This wish to act as patrons of humanism was in large part due to the two emperors' own deep personal interest in scholarship and learning. Maximilian II in particular was well known for his interest in natural science and antiquities. Humanist writer Andreas Camutius recorded how the emperor liked to participate in debates on literature and inscriptions, while the correspondence of his ambassadors in Spain contains many references to the supply of Maximilian's requests for rarities from the new world, especially exotic plants and animals.[23] These interests may, it seems, have been passed down by his father: Ferdinand too had once been described by a Venetian ambassador as 'a most curious investigator of nature, of foreign countries, plants and animals'.[24]

There was, however, another reason why the Emperors Ferdinand and Maximilian were so keen to espouse this late, central European manifestation of humanism, and that was for its emphasis on religious moderation and compromise in the interests of political peace, social harmony and the salvaging of Christian unity.[25] As politicians, both

---

[22]   See in particular Mühlberger, Kurt (1992), 'Bildung und Wissenschaft. Kaiser Maximilian II. und die Universität Wien', in Edelmayer, Friedrich and Kohler, Alfred (eds), *Kaiser Maximilian II. Kultur und Politik im 16. Jahrhundert*, Wiener Beiträge zur Geschichte der Neuzeit, vol. 17, Vienna: Verlag für Geschichte und Politik, pp. 203–31. On Blotius (1533–1608), Crato (1519–85), Lazius (1514–92) and Strada (1515–88), see Louthan, Howard (1997), *The Quest For Compromise: Peacemakers in Counter–Reformation Vienna*, Cambridge: Cambridge University Press, passim. For more on Lazius, see Aschbach, Joseph Ritter von (1888), *Geschichte der Wiener Universität. Die Wiener Universität und Ihre Gelehrten, 1520 bis 1565*, Vienna: Adolph Holzhausen, pp. 204–33; on Strada, see too Jansen, Dirk Jacob (1992), 'The Instruments of Patronage. Jacopo Strada at the Court of Maximilian II: A Case-Study', in Edelmayer and Kohler (eds), *Kaiser Maximilian II*, pp. 82–202. On the career of Busbequius (1520–92), see Martels, Zweder von (1992), 'On His Majesty's Service. Augerius Busbequius, Courtier and Diplomat of Maximilian II', in Edelmayer and Kohler (eds), *Kaiser Maximilian II*, pp. 169–81. For details on Sambucus (1531–84), see Aschbach, *Geschichte der Wiener Universität. Die Wiener Universität und Ihre Gelehrten*, pp. 260–66; on Clusius (1526–1609) see Mühlberger, 'Bildung und Wissenschaft', p. 213.

[23]   See Evans, *The Making of the Habsburg Monarchy*, p. 21 and Herrnleben, Susanne (1992), 'Zur Korrespondenz Kaiser Maximilians II. mit seinen Gesandten in Spanien (1564–1576)', in Edelmayer and Kohler (eds), *Kaiser Maximilian II*, pp. 95–108, p. 105.

[24]   Mühlberger, 'Bildung und Wissenschaft', p. 217.

[25]   See Evans, *The Making of the Habsburg Monarchy* and *Rudolf II*, and Louthan, *Quest for Compromise*, passim, on the many manifestations of this spirit. Though Louthan refers to an 'Erasmian dynamic operative within Vienna', p. 2, he prefers use of the term

rulers already had had to compromise in the name of the higher goals of peace and unity: the Peace of Ausgburg which Ferdinand I had accepted and Maximilian II sought to maintain was one case in point. Robert Evans has also seen Ferdinand I's efforts to press Rome for the authorisation of clerical marriage and the use of the lay chalice as 'not simply a gesture from weakness, but a real movement towards conciliation within the area of adiaphora', while the correspondence of the future Maximilian II with none other than Philip Melanchthon points to a similar desire.[26] Maximilian first approached Melanchthon in 1555 for his views on the key areas of doctrinal debate between Lutherans and Catholics, in itself a bold move towards inter-confessional understanding. Melanchthon's replies challenged the then 28-year-old Maximilian to work as 'God's tool for his universal church', and offered advice on the rebuilding of Christian unity.[27]

Humanism therefore provided an ideology and an impetus to the tricky politics of compromise being exercised on a daily basis at the Habsburg court of sixteenth-century Vienna. For those less open to the paths of moderation, however, such humanist impulses not only looked like a sign of weakness, but seemed to provide yet another dangerous 'back-door' through which Protestant heresies could continue to creep. Indeed, to a hostile observer, the composition of the Habsburg court itself provided a perfect example of the dangers of overlooking Catholic purity in the interests of confessional unity and temporal gain. Of the humanist scholars named above, for example, every one except Lazius and Strada would have described themselves as Protestant, while Hugo Blotius even came from a Reformed background.

In part through a need to appear even-handed, and in part through the urgent need for competent functionaries to carry out policy, the administrative branches of the Viennese court of the late sixteenth century also housed a significant number of Protestants or at least non-Catholics in high places.[28] A key figure in this regard was Johann Baptist Weber,

---

'irenicism' to describe the mood of the Viennese court in this period. Sutter Fichtner also refers to the 'general Erasmianism' of Ferdinand I, while Evans makes mentions of the 'Erasmian sympathies' of some of Ferdinand's advisors. Sutter Fichtner, *Emperor Maximilian II*, p. 38; Evans, *The Making of the Habsburg Monarchy*, p. 19.

[26] Ibid., p. 19. Evans adds that on his death, Ferdinand I even won praise from the Anglican, Edmund Grindal.

[27] Louthan, *Quest for Compromise*, p. 102.

[28] Evans has noted that 'We find in the professional ranks of Habsburg government the beginnings of a court étatism which originated perhaps among the bourgeois advisers to Ferdinand I', *Rudolf II*, pp. 61–2. On the significance of court positions and its overall structure, see Evans, Robert J.W. (1977), 'The Austrian Habsburgs: the dynasty as a political institution', in Dickens, A.G. (ed.), *The Courts of Europe: Politics, Patronage and Royalty, 1400–1800*, London: Thames and Hudson, pp. 121–45; Evans, Robert J.W. (1991), 'The Court: A Protean Institution and an Elusive Subject', in Asch, R.G. and Birke, A.M.

Reichsvizekanzler between November 1563 and April 1577. In spite of the Emperor Maximilian II's personal dislike for Weber, he did espouse the political virtues of religious tolerance and confessional moderation that were the Habsburgs' political watchwords in these years.[29] Another significant court office-holder who claimed no particular confessional allegiance was doctor of law, Andreas Gail.[30] Gail not only served in the Reichshofrat from 1569 until 1582, but was sent on numerous missions to Italy, France and Belgium.[31] Two other members of the Reichshofrat were, however, openly Protestant and powerful in their own right. Gabriel Strein, Herr zu Schwarzenau, was member of a long-established, well-connected Lower Austrian noble family. Strein's uncle Richard served as a member of Maximilian II's Hofkammer, while Gabriel Strein, himself Reichshofrat from December 1564 until the end of September 1578, later served in the court of Rudolf II.[32] Similarly, Joachim von Sinzendorf, Reichshofrat in 1576 and 1577, was the son of a Lower Austrian knight and served the imperial dynasty in various functions in Vienna and Constantinople throughout the 1570s and 1580s.[33]

Nor was heresy in high places confined to the Habsburg court. Vienna University had long had a reputation for the harbouring of Protestants and Protestant ideas. As early as 1520 the rector of the university had refused to publish the papal bull against Luther: nearly four decades later,

---

(eds), *Princes, Patronage and the Nobility*, Oxford: Oxford University Press, pp. 481–92; Press, Volker (1986), 'The Habsburg Court as Centre of the Imperial Government', *JMH* Supplement, 58, 23–45, and Ehalt, Hubert C.H. (1980), *Ausdrucksformen Absolutischer Herrschaft. Der Wiener Hof im 17. und 18. Jahrhundert*, Munich: Oldenbourg. Also useful is a 1999 volume edited by John Adamson, *The Princely Courts of Europe: Ritual, Politics and Culture under the Ancien Régime 1500–1750*, London: Weidenfeld & Nicolson.

29   Weber's readiness to avoid religious extremes may have been due to something of a carnal appetite on his part. Weber's drinking bouts were well known in court circles: not for nothing did Duke Albrecht V of Bavaria refer to him as a 'fat rogue'. From Vienna, Maximilian had also revealed similar views to his brother-in-law Albrecht, indicating that he feared Weber was not sufficiently qualified for the post of Reichsvizekanzler. See Gross, Lothar (1933), *Inventare des Wiener Haus-, Hof- und Staatsarchivs*, vol. 1, *Der Geschichte der deutschen Reichshofkanzlei von 1559 bis 1806*, Vienna: Haus-, Hof- und Staatsarchiv, pp. 312ff.

30   Floridus Röhrig, however, does note in his 1961 article: 'Protestantismus und Gegenreformation im Stift Klosterneuburg und seinen Pfarren', *Jahrbuch des Stiftes Klosterneuburg*, Neue Folge 1, 105–70, 145, that Gail was in the same circle of friends as the Catholic courtier Wolfgang Unversagt and the Jesuit Georg Scherer. For more on Gail, see pp. 52 and 126; for more on Unversagt, see pp. 36 and 88; and on Scherer, see pp. 131 and 136–7.

31   Gschließer, Oswald von (1942), *Der Reichshofrat. Bedeutung und Verfassung, Schicksal und Besetzung einer obersten Reichsbehörde von 1559 bis 1806*, Vienna: Veröffentlichungen der Kommission für neuere Geschichte des ehemaligen Österreich. pp. 125–6. Also spelt 'Gayl'.

32   Sometimes spelt Streyn, Streun, or Strain. For more, ibid., pp. 111–12.

33   Ibid., p. 133.

in 1559, the university was still being criticised by Rome for possessing Lutheran works and employing Lutheran professors. [34] By the 1560s, even the emperor himself seemed to be involved in the protection of such heresy within the city's university. Shortly after his coronation as emperor, Maximilian II permitted a change in the university oath to aid the promotion of Lutheran doctors and professors. [35] Instead of swearing to 'romanae fidei', they merely had to express belief in 'christianae fidei'. In April 1569 Vienna University had its first Protestant rector in the shape of Kornelius Grünwald, and the same period saw the promotion of numerous other Protestants to high university ranks. [36] Paulus Fabricius, for example, sat as a member of the university's consistorium for a total of 17 semesters between 1555 and 1580, 12 times as Prokurator of the Hungarian nation and five as the dean of the faculty of medicine. [37] Fabricius' talents ranged from medicine and mathematics to botany and astronomy, with skill in rhetoric and poetry as well. Another Protestant, Georg Tanner, a renowned professor of Greek language and literature, sat on the consistorium a total of four times, while the anatomist and botanist Johann Aicholtz was also openly Protestant. [38] Nor was a teaching post a pre-requisite to membership of Vienna University's intellectual circle of Protestants: as Kurt Mühlberger has suggested, the aforementioned Carolus Clusius, 'the most famous botanist of his time'

---

[34]   For more on this see Mecenseffy, 'Wien im Zeitalter der Reformation' and Mühlberger, 'Bildung und Wissenschaft'. Mecenseffy in particular notes a connection between Vienna University and the initial progress of the Swiss Reformation, presumably due to the university's early reputation for humanism. Huldrich Zwingli and Konrad Grebel both studied at Vienna at the end of the fifteenth century, while Joachim Watt or Vadian had been university rector in the winter semester of 1516–17.

[35]   This was a change from the policy of Ferdinand I, whose Reformatio Nova of 1554 had insisted that all university members 'belong to the orthodox religion, and are in communion with and adherents of the Holy Roman Church'. Cited in Heiss, Gernot (1991), 'Princes, Jesuits and the Origins of Counter-Reform in the Habsburg Lands', in Evans, R.J.W. and Thomas, T.V. (eds), Crown, Church and Estates, pp. 92–109, p. 94.

[36]   Grünwald was not to be the only one: a rector of 1576, Doctor of Law Sigismund Eisler, was also known to be a Protestant. Locher, D. Joanne Joseph (1773), Speculum Academicum Viennense, sen magistratus antiquissimae et celeberrime Universitatis Viennensis, a primo eiusdem auspicio ad nostra tempora chronologice, historice, et lemmatice, exhibitus a D. Joanne Josepho Locher J.U.D., Vienna: Kaliwoda, vol. 1, pp. 27–8.

[37]   On Fabricius see Mühlberger 'Bilding und Wissenschaft', p. 213 and Aschbach, Geschichte der Wiener Universität. Die Wiener Universität und Ihre Gelehrten, pp. 187–9. On his university posts see Locher, Speculum, vol. 1, pp. 126–9 and pp. 254–7.

[38]   On Tanner (1520–80) see Mühlberger, 'Bildung und Wissenschaft', p. 214, Aschbach, Geschichte der Wiener Universität. Die Wiener Universität und Ihre Gelehrten, pp. 279–90 and Locher, Speculum, vol. 1, pp. 102–104 and pp. 175–6. On Aicholtz (1520–88), see Aschbach, Geschichte der Wiener Universität. Die Wiener Universität und Ihre Gelehrten, pp. 119–124. His conversion to Lutheranism had come about after a period of study at the University of Wittenberg.

was connected to many holders of Viennese professorships simply by the bonds of friendship.[39]

Vienna in the sixteenth century was, therefore, far from the bastion of Catholicism that might have been expected from a city so dominated by members of the Habsburg dynasty. Maximilian II's cousin Philip II of Spain, regularly expressed deep concern about the extent to which the Austrian branch of the family had permitted heresy to thrive in the territories for which they were responsible.[40] For the court of Madrid, defence of Catholicism meant an uncompromising, speedy and emphatic overthrow of heresy in all its guises. This was, furthermore, to be a Roman Catholicism, with its content and direction emanating from Rome and sanction coming from all true Christian rulers.

The Austrian Habsburgs, particularly Ferdinand and Maximilian had, however, developed quite a different conception of Catholicism.[41] In part this was forced on them by the circumstances under which they had to operate, circumstances quite different from those faced by the Spanish branch of the family. Ferdinand and Maximilian had both had to compromise with Protestant nobles for the sake of military security, at an imperial and local level. Both had seen value in the principles of humanism which advocated a more conciliatory approach to confessional difference. Both also realised, however, another need: the bolstering of the dynasty's vulnerable authority in the German-speaking lands by showing their independence in policy-making from Rome and Spain alike. The estates of the empire with whom Maximilian and his father Ferdinand had to deal were extremely sensitive to even the appearance of what they saw as 'foreign' interference from Spain or Rome.[42] In order to enhance their image as 'German' emperors and 'Austrian' archdukes, and to emphasise their own authority, Ferdinand I and Maximilian II were anxious to avoid any sign of susceptibility to outside influence, or lack of control in their own realms.[43] Thus it was that in the Austrian lands neither Inquisition nor Index saw any imperial sanction, while the decrees of the Council of Trent were not promulgated in the Austrian territories

---

[39]   Mühlberger, 'Bildung und Wissenschaft', p. 213.

[40]   Sutter Fichtner, *Emperor Maximilian II*, pp. 113–16.

[41]   On the rivalry between Madrid, Vienna and Rome, Robert Evans notes: 'With the accession of Philip II in the Spanish lands and Ferdinand in the Empire, together with the new Papal militancy following the Tridentine decrees of 1563, it becomes clear that there are now three contenders for one ideology. Reviving Papal claims to temporal dominion are matched by two Habsburg monarchies, both deriving their authority from an apostolic succession to a traditional "Imperium"', Evans, *The Making of the Habsburg Monarchy*, p. 13.

[42]   Sutter Fichtner, *Emperor Maximilian II*, pp. 32–3.

[43]   Ibid., p. 1. Sutter Fichtner comments that Leopold von Ranke saw virtue in the stance of Maximilian II, as his politics in the empire furthered Lutheranism, the German 'national' religion.

until 1637, and even then only in part. Their Catholicism was, therefore, what Robert Evans has described as an 'aulic Catholicism', a distinctively Austrian Habsburg religious policy that was Catholic in essence, but to be carried out in the dynasty's time, on the dynasty's terms, and above all intended to demonstrate the dynasty's own political and ecclesiastical authority.[44]

The results were a telling hybrid of Catholic reform and Austrian Habsburg politics. To take the case of the implementation of the Gregorian calendar reform as one particularly potent example, the papal bull 'inter gravissimas' of 24 February 1581 announced that in order to realign the calendar, ten days were to be 'lost' between 4 October and 15 October 1582. While areas such as Spain and Bavaria did exactly as Rome asked on the dates that Rome asked, in Lower Austria the calendar reform was not introduced until 1583, in part due to local resistance but also due to a symbolic Habsburg insistence on autonomy over affairs in the Austrian lands.[45]

Similarly, Maximilian II's establishment of the Klosterrat or monastery commission in 1568, for the monitoring of the quality of preaching, appointment of abbots and administration of sacraments in every monastery within Lower and Upper Austria, can on one level be seen as nothing more than an attempt to reform the Catholic Church in these territories.[46] As Joseph Patrouch has noted, however, the Klosterrat also represented 'the first step towards an imperial ecclesiastical policy operated with secular sanctions'.[47] The subsequent diplomatic posturing that accompanied the establishment of the Klosterrat suggests that Maximilian's statement of ecclesiastical independence had hit its target. As a direct response to the commission's establishment, in the very

---

[44]   Evans, *The Making of the Habsburg Monarchy*, pp. 59–61. Evans refers to this as 'the dynastic ideology of the Habsburgs ... an aulic Catholicism revivified by the example of Counter-Reformation, especially after 1600, yet never identical with it.' He later expands on this as a distinction between '... Papal and dynastic Catholicism', p. 62. This is a particularly helpful concept with which to explain the often apparently contradictory religious policies emanating from the Vienna court in this period. I use it again in an essay from 2005 entitled, '"Wolves and Weathervanes": Confessional Moderation at the Habsburg Court of Vienna', in Racaut, Luc and Ryrie, Alec (eds), *Moderate Voices in the European Reformation*, Aldershot: Ashgate, pp. 145–61. Thanks are due to the editors of that volume for allowing me to draw again on parts of that material for this chapter, and to reproduce some brief sections.

[45]   This point is based on an as-yet unpublished paper by Rona Johnston Gordon delivered at the 2001 meeting of the Sixteenth Century Studies Conference in Denver, Colorado. Given in a session on 'Confessional Identity in the Austrian Habsburg Lands: Court, Cloister and Calendar', the paper was entitled 'Confessional Tensions in Lower Austria: The Gregorian Calendar Reform' and is cited here with the author's permission.

[46]   Patrouch, Joseph F. (1994), 'The Investiture Controversy Revisited: Religious Reform, Emperor Maximilian II, and the Klosterrat', *AHY*, 25, 59–77.

[47]   Ibid., 61

same year Pope Pius V ordered one of his cardinals, Commendone, to undertake a visitation of Austria as, it has been observed, 'more a staking out of claims and territory than a well-thought-out attempt to reform the monasteries visited'.[48] In 1572 the Klosterrat officially warned the local representative of the Bishop of Passau, Thomas Ruf, not to interfere in the secular affairs of the clergy in Austria. It was 1592 before an uneasy peace was reached between the secular and ecclesiastical authorities over the source, direction and supervision of Catholic reform in the Austrian Habsburg lands.[49]

What is also telling about the Klosterrat episode, however, is that it underlines what can easily be overlooked: despite the clear political agenda of the Austrian Habsburg rulers in this period, they remained fundamentally devoted to the reform and revival of Catholicism.[50] Although their attempts to defend the faith and foster its reform had to be tailored to fit the political exigencies of the time, the court of Vienna in the second half of the sixteenth century remained one in which Catholic belief still thrived.

Ferdinand I's personal credentials as a Catholic have rarely been doubted, despite his role in the creation and maintenance of the Peace of Augsburg of 1555.[51] Thanks in part to the policies of Ferdinand, Lower Austria became the territory of one of the first executions of a Lutheran, with the beheading of one Kaspar Tauber on 17 September 1524 before Vienna's Stubentor. The year before, Ferdinand had issued a mandate against the spread and possession of Lutheran books; that similar decrees were passed throughout his reign indicates not only the persistence of the problem but also Ferdinand's determination to eradicate the same,

---

[48]   Patrouch, Joseph F. (1991), 'Methods of Cultural Manipulation: The Counter-Reformation in the Habsburg Province of Upper Austria, 1570–1650', unpublished PhD dissertation, University of California, p. 117.

[49]   This was via the Passau Treaty of 6 November 1592, signed in Prague by Rudolf II and Bishop Urban of Passau.

[50]   For the classic treatment of this subject, see Anna Coreth's 1959 work, recently translated and published in 2004 as *Pietas Austriaca. Austrian Religious Practices in the Baroque Era*, trans. W. Bowman, and A.-M. Leitgeb, West Lafayette [IN]: Purdue University Press. 'Pietas Austriaca' is Coreth's term for the Austrian Habsburgs' religious ideology in the early modern period, one that was inextricably linked to what they saw as their 'holy, binding heritage' as defenders of Catholic purity, p. xxii. Recent scholarship on the sixteenth-century Vienna court has, however, tended to dwell more on the extent of its religious moderation.

[51]   See Sutter Fichtner, Paula (1980), 'The Disobedience of the Obedient: Ferdinand I and the Papacy, 1555–1564', *SCJ*, 11 (2), 25–34; also Sutter Fichtner, Paula (1982), *Ferdinand of Austria: The Politics of Dynasticism in the Age of the Reformation*, New York: Columbia University Press. In her monograph, Fichtner's restatement of the Emperor Ferdinand's ultimate if pragmatic orthodoxy echoes the position of earlier scholars including Joseph von Aschbach, *Geschichte der Wiener Universität. Die Wiener Universität und Ihre Gelehrten*, pp. 310–11 and pp. 335–46.

whatever the cost to his popularity with the Protestant nobility.[52] It was also Ferdinand who first called the Jesuits to Vienna in 1551.[53] Soon after their arrival the society opened a school which, by 1554, had accrued no less than 300 students.[54] Such was Ferdinand's approval of this work, he later requested that Peter Canisius compose what would become his highly influential Catholic catechism.[55]

Maximilian II, by contrast, has received a worse press as a 'Catholic' ruler. Like some of Maximilian's own contemporaries, it seems historians have sometimes found it difficult to reconcile the emperor's rank and dynastic obligations with his personal determination to receive communion in both kinds and his association with and patronage of Protestants.[56] Despite being dubbed 'der rätselhafte Kaiser' or 'the mysterious emperor' in a 1929 biography by Victor Bibl, Maximilian's policies in Vienna also point, none the less, towards a concern to strengthen Catholicism and arrest the progress of Protestantism as far as his straitened circumstances would allow.[57] The negotiations over the Konzession, for example, took a full two years in a period when the Emperor Maximilian's need for

---

[52]   For example, in 1551 Ferdinand passed a decree against Lutheran schoolmasters and the publication of Lutheran works. 1554 saw another decree forbidding the partaking of communion in both kinds.

[53]   According to 'Historia Collegii SJ Viennensis ab anno 1550 usque ad annum 1567, auctore (secundum sententiam traditam) Laurentio Maggio SJ', Ferdinand called the Jesuits to Vienna because of the orthodoxy of their teaching and also 'because of the endless number of heretics, which multiplied daily like the ancient warriors from the Trojan horse ...'. On 11 December 1550 he wrote to Loyola from Vienna stating that he wanted a Jesuit college in Vienna with which to protect the 'ancient orthodox and Catholic faith, our Chistian religion, for the sake of the salvation of the people'. Translations by Gernot Heiss, 'Princes, Jesuits and the Origins of Counter-Reform in the Habsburg Lands', in Evans, R.J.W. and Thomas, T.V. (eds), *Crown, Church and Estates*, pp. 92–109, citing Magius, pp. 7–8. Friedrich Staphylus wrote on 16 February 1555 to Stanislaus Hosius, then Bishop of Ermland, that Ferdinand loved the Viennese Jesuits Bobadilla, Le Jay and Canisius like brothers. Duhr, Bernhard (1901), 'Die Jesuiten an den deutschen Fürstenhöfen des 16. Jahrhunderts' in Pastor, Ludwig (ed.), *Erläuterungen und Ergänzungen zu Janssens Geschichte des deutschen Volkes*, vol. 2, Freiburg im Breisgau: Herder, p. 7, citing Hosius *Epistulae* vol. 2, pp. 337, 363.

[54]   Denk, Ulrike (2003), 'Schulwesen und Universität', in Vocelka, K. and Traninger, A. (eds), *Wien. Geschichte einer Stadt*, vol. 2, *Die frühneuzeitliche Residenz (16. bis 18. Jahrhundert)*, Vienna, Cologne, Weimar: Böhlau, pp. 365–422, p. 374.

[55]   O'Malley, John W. (1993), *The First Jesuits*, Cambridge, MA: Harvard University Press, pp. 207, 123. Canisius' first version of the catechism, the *Summa doctrinae christianae* was first published in 1554 and was the largest he would produce. The *Catechismus minimus* of 1556–57 was aimed at very young children, while it was his *Catechismus parvus*, an intermediate text first published in 1558, that would go through so many editions.

[56]   For more on the question of Maximilian II's seemingly ambiguous personal confession, see pp. 89–91.

[57]   Victor Bibl (1929), *Maximilian II. Der rätselhafte Kaiser. Ein Zeitbild*, Hellerau. He had already investigated this earlier, in Bibl, Victor (1917), 'Zur Frage der religiösen Haltung K. Maximilians II', *Sonderabdruck aus dem Archiv für österreichische Geschichte*.

finance was urgent, and demands for a Lutheran church in Vienna were met with provision of a single room. And in a decree of 18 February 1572, Maximilian commanded prelates to evict heretical clergy from their parishes and make sure that vacancies were replenished with Catholic candidates only.[58]

Allegiance to Catholicism was also evident elsewhere in the upper echelons of the court. Maximilian II's Spanish wife María, the sister of Philip II and therefore also her husband's first cousin, was so known for her devout Catholicism that she was publicly praised by Pope Pius V, no doubt partly as a snub to her seemingly equivocal husband.[59] The empress personally ensured that her children were raised according to the Roman rites, going against her husband's wishes so to do, and María also acted both as patron of the Jesuits in Vienna as well as representative of the pro-Catholic Spanish interest.[60]

Catholic allegiance continued, furthermore, to the following generation in the shape of Maximilian's second son Ernst and his daughter Elisabeth. Governing Lower Austria in his elder brother Rudolf's stead, it was Ernst who announced the closure of the Lutheran church in Vienna on 6 May 1578, along with the Lutheran book shop and school. Under Ernst the Auslaufen to Lutheran services outside Vienna was also forbidden, the Lutheran preacher Joshua Opitz expelled from the city, and the so-called Sturmpetition of the people was resisted, albeit somewhat nervously. In this incident of 19 July 1579, a protest at the anti-Lutheran laws of the previous year saw the Lower Austrian evangelical burghers, nobles and knights appeal for the restoration of their worship before the Hofburg, but to no avail.[61] Recent research has also brought to light Ernst's sister Elisabeth's equally significant if less dramatic efforts to bolster Catholicism. As the 27-year-old widow of King Charles IX of France, Elisabeth returned to Vienna in 1581 where she spent the remaining eleven years of her life working for the establishment of a house of Poor Clares in the city, known as the 'Queen's Cloister, Our Lady Queen of Angels'.[62]

---

[58]   Pörtner, Regina (2001), *The Counter-Reformation in Central Europe: Styria 1580–1630*, Oxford: Oxford University Press, p. 23.

[59]   Sutter Fichtner, *Emperor Maximilian II*, p. 19.

[60]   Laferl, Christopher F. (1997), *Die Kultur der Spanier in Österreich unter Ferdinand I. 1522–1564*, Vienna: Böhlau.

[61]   For Eder's dramatic description of this, see p. 118.

[62]   On Elisabeth, see the most recent work of Joseph F. Patrouch (1999), 'Ysabell/Elisabth/Alzbeta: Erzherzogin. Königin. Ein Forschungsgegenwurff,' *Frühneuzeit-Info 10*, 257–65; and Patrouch, Joseph F. (2000), 'The Archduchess Elizabeth: Where Spain and Austria Met,' in Kent, Conrad, Wolber, Thomas and Hewitt, Cameron M.K., (eds), *The Lion and the Eagle: Interdisciplinary Essays on German-Spanish Relations over the Centuries*, New York: Berghahn Books, pp. 77–90. According to a paper entitled 'The Queen's Cloister: Female(s) Religious in 1580s Vienna' delivered at the 2001 meeting of the Sixteenth Century Studies Conference and here cited with the author's permission, the original 12 members

The court administration also had its share of openly Catholic personnel. Within the Reichshofrat were the likes of Johann Andreas von Schwanbach, a member from May 1570 until September 1573, and from a noble Catholic family from Überlingen am Bodensee, and Bologna-trained Doctor of Law Johann Hegenmüller, Reichshofrat from 1566 until 1583.[63] Hegenmüller also taught law to Ferdinand I's younger sons and later became Hofkanzler under Rudolf II, rewarded as early as 1568 with promotion into noble ranks. Yet it seems Hegenmüller was also well-known for his devotion to the Catholic faith: the Bavarian Chancellor Simon Eck had described him as one of several 'warm-hearted, Catholic ... advisors' in service at the Viennese court. Another Reichshofrat had a similar reputation: after his death, Christoph Pirckhaimer was described by the Jesuits as a man who had done good deeds.[64] Siegmund Viehauser was another Catholic in Habsburg employ. Having emerged from Wittelsbach service in Bavaria, Viehauser rose rapidly, from Reichshofrat in 1573 to membership of the Geheimer Rat in 1576 and finally to the rank of Reichsvizekanzler in 1577.[65] Lastly, Dr Timotheus Jung, a regular member of the Reichshofrat between 1568 and 1579, was a convert from Lutheranism. His insistence on attending Catholic services even at the Reichstag in Augsburg in 1559, much to the disgust of the powerful Protestants all around him, did not hinder his promotion at the Viennese court, and he continued to attend almost every Reichstag as a valued member of the Austrian delegation.[66]

Nor was such a Catholic presence at the Vienna court of the second half of the sixteenth century limited to members of the Reichshofrat. Leonhard von Harrach, a representative of a leading Lower Austrian noble family, acted as Obersthofmarschall until 1567.[67] Such was this man's reputation as a devout Catholic that the dying Emperor Ferdinand I reputedly charged him with the defence of the faith in the Austrian lands.[68] Adam von Dietrichstein evidently had a similar reputation. It was he whom the Emperor Maximilian II sent as his representative to Madrid

---

of the revamped Viennese Poor Clares had come from Munich where Duke Albrecht V's Habsburg wife Anna had acted as their patron.

[63]   Gschließer, *Der Reichshofrat*, p. 128 and pp. 119–21.

[64]   Ibid., pp. 120, 142. Pirckhaimer served as Reichshofrat between 1581 and 1591.

[65]   On Viehauser, ibid., pp. 131–2. He replaced Weber in the final post, and held it until his death in April 1587.

[66]   Ibid., pp. 112–13.

[67]   Fellner, Thomas and Kretschmayr, Heinrich (eds) (1907), *Die Österreichische Zentralverwaltung I Abteilung Von Maximilian I. bis zur vereinigung der Österreichischen und Böhmischen Hofkanzlei (1749)*, vol. 2, *Aktenstücke 1491–1681*, Vienna: Veröffentlichungen der Kommission für neuere Geschichte Österreichs, p. 188.

[68]   Louthan, *Quest for Compromise*, p. 132, citing Mencik, F. (1899), 'Das religiöse Testament Kaiser Ferdinands I', *MIÖG* 20, pp. 105ff.

while his sons Rudolf and Ernst spent eight years there at the court of their uncle, Philip II.[69] So impressed was the King of Spain with Dietrichstein that he made him and his sons knights of Calatrava, while also paying him additional wages to urge a greater degree of adherence to Rome on his imperial master in Vienna, Maximilian II.[70] Andreas Khevenhüller of Frankenburg and Hochosterwitz was another Austrian noble known for his Catholicism: such was his reputation as a Catholic, he spent 32 years in a post similar to that held by Dietrichstein, as ambassador in Madrid between 1574 and 1606. Wolfgang Unversagt, another known Catholic from Vienna itself, is listed in the Hofstaatsverzeichnis of December 1576 as having served as 'Reichs- und Hofsecretarien' since 28 May 1567: that he also served in the Geheimer Rat and briefly in the Reichshofrat places him at the heart of the Habsburg administration in Vienna.[71]

There was, furthermore, a significant Catholic core at Vienna University. Wolfgang Lazius and Paulus Weidner in the faculty of medicine, Andreas Dadius in the faculty of philosophy and Petrus a Rotis in the law faculty were all open in their allegiance to Rome. Of these, Andreas Dadius, professor of dialectic and Aristotelian philosophy, served on the consistorium four times.[72] It is Wolfgang Lazius, however, who was the highest-profile Catholic active at Vienna University during the period under scrutiny. Not only did he hold the prestigious court positions mentioned earlier in the chapter, but he acted as dean of the medical faculty four times between 1552 and 1561 as well as superintendent from 1563 until his death two years later.[73] Even university legislation of the 1570s attempted to limit the impact of Lutheranism on the student body, in spite of the concessions on the promotion of Lutheran staff made by Maximilian II in 1564. In 1577, for example, all members of Vienna

---

[69]   The boys were in Spain between 1563 and 1571; Dietrichstein was with them between 1564 and 1571, and was also in the country 1572 to 1573. On the Viennese ambassadors in Spain, see Susanne Herrnleben 'Zur Korrespondenz Kaiser Maximilians II. Mit Seinen Gesandten In Spanien', and Friedrich Edelmayer, 'Ehre, Geld, Karriere. Adam von Dietrichstein im Dienst Kaiser Maximilians II.', both in Edelmayer and Kohler (eds) (1992), *Kaiser Maximilian II.*, pp. 95–108 and pp. 109–42.

[70]   Sutter Fichtner, *Emperor Maximilian II*, p. 213. Dietrichstein's reputation is all the more impressive in view of the fact that he had been born a Lutheran but had converted.

[71]   Fellner and Kretschmayr, *Die Österreichische Zentralverwaltung*, p. 194. According to Lothar Gross, *Inventare des Wiener Haus-, Hof- und Staatsarchivs*, vol. 1, pp. 372ff, Unversagt became Sekretär to the Geheimer Rat in 1568, just a year after his initial appointment, and also participated in some Reichshofrat business.

[72]   On Dadius see Mühlberger, 'Bildung und Wissenschaft', p. 213 and Aschbach, *Geschichte der Wiener Universität. Die Wiener Universität und Ihre Gelehrten*, pp. 162–6. On his positions in the Consistorium see Locher, *Speculum*, vol. 1, pp. 126–9 and pp. 215–22.

[73]   On Blotius' position, see Locher *Speculum* vol. 1, p. 220. For Lazius' offices, ibid. pp. 54–5 and pp. 126–9.

University were forbidden to participate in the Auslaufen to Lutheran services outside the city, and in 1578 the election of the Protestant jurist Johann Baptist Schwarzenthaler as rector was declared invalid by Rudolf II and a new election held. The year after, a young Jesuit-educated priest, Melchior Khlesl was made chancellor.[74] Later to become Bishop of Vienna, it was Khlesl who would become one of the city's champions of Catholic reform well into the seventeenth century.

This, then was the environment through which Georg Eder had to negotiate a path, one in which his Habsburg employers sought to maintain peace and revive Catholicism whilst challenging Roman ecclesiastical control and compromising with Lutheranism. The keystone that held this fragile construct together was the authority of the dynasty itself, and it was this that Eder defended in key areas of Viennese court, university and civic life at particularly sensitive points in the history of all three.

---

[74]   For more on this, see Denk, 'Schulwesen und Universität', p. 380. For more on Khlesl, see pp. 135–6 and p. 142.

CHAPTER 2

Promotion and prominence, 1550–73

For Georg Eder, the years 1550–73 were ones in which it seemed he could do no wrong. His star rose steadily at the court and the university, and he and his young family appear to have settled well into the city.[1] For example, we know from the court quartering records that by 1566 at the latest, Eder had attained the status of burgher and was living right in the heart of Vienna in a two-storey house at number 956 Weihburgasse, not far from Stephansdom.[2] We know too that Eder's confessional stance as a staunch Catholic was well known from his first arrival in Vienna, but far from being an obstacle to his promotion to high office, it gave his Habsburg employers another way in which the Catholic presence could be strengthened at the court and in the city. But this had to be an aulic Catholicism, one that was first and foremost about the preservation and proclamation of the authority of the ruling dynasty. For the first part of his career in Vienna, up to 1573, Georg Eder followed the complex rules of the game to the letter, and his early success in court and university life stemmed directly from his very public support of the dynasty's interests.

The path of Eder's career at the Habsburg court in Vienna was summarised succinctly by Eder himself in 1574, noting that he had served the Emperor Ferdinand from 1552, 'firstly as Kammerprocurator, thereafter as a member of the government of Lower Austria, and finally as Hofrat'.[3] Although

---

[1]   Eder married twice in his lifetime, and fathered at least eight children. For more on Eder's family and their significance for his relationship to the Church, see pp. 64–8 and pp. 126–7.

[2]   Camesina Ritter v. San Vittore, Albert (ed.) (1881), *Urkundliche Beiträge zur Geschichte Wien's im XVI. Jahrhundert*, Vienna: Alfred Hölder, p. 38. The court-quartering system was one in which the court could essentially commandeer space in 'private' dwellings within the city for the compulsory quartering of court officials, workers or even troops as Vienna's precarious defensive situation demanded. That Eder's house was not listed as a 'Freihaus' indicates that he was not exempt from paying taxes, and that rooms in his home were liable for temporary seizure. For more on the court-quartering system, see Spielman, John P. (1993), *The City and the Crown. Vienna and the Imperial Court 1600–1740*, West Lafayette, IN: Purdue University Press, Chapter 4. On the position of the burgher in Viennese civic life, see Pils, Susanne C., and Weigl, Andreas (2003), 'Die frühneuzeitliche Sozialstruktur', in Vocelka, K. and Traninger, A. (eds), *Wien. Geschichte einer Stadt*, vol. 2, *Die frühneuzeitliche Residenz (16. bis 18. Jahrhundert)*, Vienna, Cologne, Weimar: Böhlau, pp. 241–81. Pils and Weigl suggest that in the sixteenth and seventeenth centuries, only 2000 of the city's total population held this status, p. 255.

[3]   Eder made this recollection in two separate letters to Duke Albrecht of Bavaria, the first dated 21 January 1574, and the other dated 11 February 1574: Schrauf, Karl (ed.) (1904), *Der Reichshofrath Dr Georg Eder. Eine Briefsammlung. Als Beitrag zur Geschichte*

Eder's editor Schrauf attempted to correct his subject's recollection of the date, court sources support Eder.[4] He is first mentioned in Hofkammer records on 1 April 1552, though not described as 'Kammerprocurator' until an entry of 12 June 1554.[5] Eder appears to have held this post until September 1586 and during this time also operated as Kammerprokurator to the Lower Austrian government.[6] According to his own account of his work in this office, he was called to this post by Ferdinand I and served in it from 16 July 1556 until 1564.[7] These dates are further supported by Eder's self-description in his own history of Vienna University, the *Catalogus Rectorum* published in 1559. The entry for 1557 lists him as 'Georgius Eder I.U.D., Regis Ferdinandi Consiliarius & Fisci provinciarum inferioris Austriae Advocatus', and he bears a similar title in the university registers of 1557.[8] Eder's highest promotion, held alongside these offices, was however to the rank of Reichshofrat. The Hofstaatsverzeichnis of December 1563 is the first to list Eder as a member after his installation in the post, again by the Emperor Ferdinand, on 22 November 1563.[9] Eder remained Reichshofrat just two months short of 20 years: his final mention in the Reichshofrat Protokolle is dated 24 September 1583.[10]

   The Reichshofrat or Aulic Council has been described as 'the highest court of appeal for the whole empire'.[11] As the fount of temporal justice,

---

der Gegenreformation in Niederösterreich, Vienna: Adolf Holzhausen, p. 78 and p. 81, respectively.

   [4]   Ibid., p. 78.

   [5]   HKA, Expedit. Regist. nö 26, fol.168r, and Expedit. Regist. nö 30, fol. 416v respectively.

   [6]   Eder is last mentioned in HKA, Expedit. Regist. nö 145, fol. 357r, on 27 September 1586.

   [7]   'Die Relationen des nö Kammerprokurators Dr Georg Eder 1561' (2 vols) comes from K und K Reichsfinanzarchiv Cod. Mscr. Nro 22. D but was consulted for this thesis in its transcribed form as part of the Graf Chorinsky Quellensammlung held in the HHStA. This reference, p. 14.

   [8]   Eder, Georg (1559), *Catalogus Rectorum*, Vienna: Raphael Hofhalter, p. 88. In the university's register for the entry dated 13 October 1557, the new rector Eder is described as 'caesarae maiestatis consiliarius et fisci provinciarum inferioris Austriae advocatus', Gall, Franz and Szaivert, Willy (eds) (1971), *Quellen zur Geschichte der Universität Wien. I Abteilung. Die Matrikel der Universität Wien*, vol. 3, 1518/II–1579/I and vol. 4 1579/II–1658/59, Vienna, Cologne, Graz: Publikationen des Instituts für Österreichische Geschichtsforschung, p. 116.

   [9]   HHStA, Hofarchiv, Hofstaatsverzeichniss O Me A /SR 183 (1563–1600), Nr 45a, fol.1v line 13. On Eder's promotion to Reichshofrat, see Gschließer, Oswald von (1942), *Der Reichshofrat. Bedeutung und Verfassung, Schicksal und Besetzung einer obersten Reichsbehörde von 1559 bis 1806*, Vienna: Veröffentlichungen der Kommission für neuere Geschichte des ehemaligen Österreich, pp. 108–109.

   [10]   HHStA, RHR Protocolla rerum resolutarium XVI 24, fol. 217v.

   [11]   Evans, Robert J.W. (1973), *Rudolf II and his World: A Study in Intellectual History 1576–1612*, Oxford: Oxford University Press, p. 10. Robert Evans notes that large territorial princes such as those of Saxony and the Palatinate held the 'privilegium de non appellando'

none other than the emperor himself was the notional head of the Reichshofrat. It was he who personally appointed each member: Eder, for example, was the penultimate appointment of Ferdinand I. By the time of Eder's official entry to this institution in 1563, it had evolved from its original incarnation by Maximilian I as a 'Hofratkolleg', intended as a means of retaining the emperor's personal influence in the administration of justice and to act as a counterweight to the Reichskammergericht.[12] Ferdinand I's Reichshofratsordnung of 3 April 1559 not only reflected the institution's new imperial title but confirmed and updated an older Hofratsordnung of 1541 which had defined its remit as covering all matters of justice.[13] This stood, but the decree of 1559 also emphasised a wider role for the Reichshofrat. As Gschließer has noted, the Reichshofrat rapidly became involved in a series of matters concerning the Reich and beyond, from the negotiations between Denmark and Sweden at Rostock, the position of three ecclesiastical princes on confessional issues over the lay chalice and clerical marriage, to preparations for future Reichstage.[14] The details of administering imperial justice usually fell on the shoulders of the Reichshofräte themselves. For this, as one historian has noted, 'members of the Aulic Council in general enjoyed precedence in rank over all other councillors of the emperor except members of the imperial Privy Council'.[15]

The Reichshofrat was not only an office that was prestigious in itself, however: it was also a post to which the already highly-ranked could be elected. The Reichshofratsordnung of 1559 distinguished between two types of Reichshofrat member. The Gelehrten or 'learned' members were to have specialist legal knowledge and to be 'graduate or other learned, well experienced, stately, pious and intelligent persons'.[16] 'Lay' members

---

which protected them from Reichshofrat judgments. Evans, Robert J.W. (1979), *The Making of the Habsburg Monarchy 1550–1700*, Oxford: Clarendon Press, p. 151. For more on the Reichshofrat, see Wilson, Peter H. (1999), *The Holy Roman Empire 1495–1806*, Basingstoke: Macmillan Press Limited, pp. 45–48.

[12]   Gschließer, *Der Reichshofrat*, p. 1. Although the focus of this book is on the centuries after the sixteenth, it is none the less the most recent and most comprehensive monograph on this important institution. Gschließer also notes that 1498 and 1501 have both been suggested as the date of Maximilian I's foundation. According to Henry Schwarz, 'the aim in creating a judiciary in immediate contact with the emperor and subject to him alone was primarily to strengthen the emperor's power against the ... Kammergericht, a court subject largely to the influence of the imperial estates.' Schwarz, Henry Frederick (1943), *The Imperial Privy Council in the Seventeenth Century*, Cambridge, MA: Harvard University Press, p. 16.

[13]   Gschließer, *Der Reichshofrat*, p. 90.

[14]   Ibid., pp. 5–6.

[15]   Schwarz, *The Imperial Privy Council*, p. 18.

[16]   Gschließer, *Der Reichshofrat*, p. 68.

were members of the upper or lower nobility, and always supplied the Reichshofrat with its president. As a result, when Eder entered as one of ten serving Gelehrten he found himself mingling with those who were influential by birth as well as those who had sought their own rank.[17] The three Reichshofrat presidents under whom Eder served – Philipp Freiherr zu Winnenberg, Otto Heinrich Graf zu Schwarzenberg and Paul Sixt Graf von Trautson – all came from noble backgrounds and had a history of service to the Habsburg dynasty.[18] The family of Winnenberg, president from 1563 until 1576, held the Herrschaft of Winnenberg and Philipp himself went on to serve Rudolf II as part of the Reichskammergericht in Speyer. Von Trautson, who took over as president the year before Eder's career as Reichshofrat terminated, was the son of the Hans Trautson, Freiherr zu Matrei, Sprechenstein, Schrofenstein and Falkenstein who had served in the Geheimer Rat as Obersthofmeister and Obersthofmarschall under both Ferdinand I and Maximilian II. Schwarzenberg, Reichshofrat president between 1576 and 1582, came from a family of Catholic Bavarian nobles, and would later became Rudolf II's Obersthofmarschall.

So how did Georg Eder not only join such company, but actually thrive in it? Firstly, it seems that Eder's Catholic allegiance may well have helped him enter high court circles. When he first arrived in Vienna in 1550, he was from an indisputably orthodox Catholic background.[19] Born in Bavaria, Eder had studied in the faculties of philosophy, arts and law at the University of Cologne between 1543 and 1549.[20] Apparently from a

---

[17]   Numbers of Reichshofräte fluctuated: Gschließer notes that by the mid-seventeenth century there could have been as many as 18 serving members. Ibid., p. 69.

[18]   On these three see Gschließer, *Der Reichshofrat*, pp. 104–105, pp. 136–8, and pp. 138–9 respectively.

[19]   In his *Ein Christliche Gutherzige und Notwendige Warnungschrifft* of 1580, Eder wrote that he had already spent 30 years in Vienna: 'I am now in the thirtieth year of being in this country, and have seen how the false prophets have toyed with religion', fol. H iii v. Eder's precise birthdate has been the subject of some debate. N. Paulus took Eder's statement that he was 'almost' in his forty-fifth year from the dedication to his *Oeconomia Bibliorum* of 1568 and reasonably calculated that Eder must have been born in 1523: Paulus, N., 'Hofrath Dr Georg Eder. Ein katholischer Rechtsgelehrter des 16. Jahrhunderts', *Historisch-politische Blätter für das katholische Deutschland*, 115 (1895), pp. 13–28, 81–94, 240, p. 13; *Oeconomia Bibliorum*, fol. *br. Paulus went on to speculate, however, that Eder may have been born or baptised on the feast of St George, on 23 April, while Karl Schrauf concluded more reliably, based rather on the evidence of one of Eder's letters, that he must have been born on 2 February 1523. In a letter dated 21 January 1574, Eder indicated that he had turned 50 on the Feast of the Purification of the Virgin Mary, also known as Candlemass: Schrauf (ed.), *Der Reichshofrath Dr Georg Eder. Eine Briefsammlung*, p. 78.

[20]   Uncertainty exists over Eder's exact place of origin. Eder himself occasionally uses the title 'Frisingensis', for example, on the front pages of his *Catechismus Catholicus* of 1569 and *Compendium Catechismi Catholici* of 1570. However, this seems to contradict his other claim of having been born a subject of the Dukes of Bavaria, whose territories in the sixteenth century excluded Freising: Eder describes himself as a 'subject' of the Wittelsbachs

family of restricted means, Eder had received there the financial support of members of the Society of Jesus.[21] He had benefited, furthermore, from the patronage of a powerful Catholic family. Between his time in Cologne and his arrival in Vienna, Eder worked briefly as rector of a school in Passau. The year after his arrival in Vienna Eder offered public thanks to the von Salm family for their support during this period. The printed version of the speech was dedicated to none other than Wolfgang von Salm, Bishop of Passau.[22]

Such credentials seem likely to have marked the young doctor of law as a safe representative of the Catholic cause, and therefore one ripe for promotion.[23] When Eder later gave credit for his rapid rise and success in Vienna to five influential men, one of these was himself known to be a Catholic and an uncompromising one at that. In his *Catalogus Rectorum* Eder named Ferdinand I's advisers Stephan Schwarz and Bartholomäus

in the preface to *Das guldene Flüß Christlicher Gemain Und Gesellschaft* of 1579, p.)(iiii r. It has been suggested by way of resolution that Eder may well have merely been born in a village near Freising which did fall under Wittelsbach jurisdiction: see N. Paulus, 'Hofrath Dr Georg Eder', p. 14; it may also be that by 1579, Eder wanted to associate himself with the Wittelsbachs in whatever way he could, regardless of where he was born: see Chapter 5.

[21]   Wiedemann, Theodor (1880), *Geschichte der Reformation und Gegenreformation im Lande unter der Enns*, vol. 2, Prague: Tempsky, p. 143. This connection between Eder and the fledgling Jesuit order will be discussed at greater length in Chapter 3. Otherwise, nothing is known about Eder's familial background.

[22]   Eder, Georg (1551), *Georgii Eder De Illustriss. Principis et D.D. Nicolai Comitis a Salm & Neuburg ad Oenum*, Vienna: Egidius Aquila, fol. Aii verso. This was also reprinted in part in Eder's *Orationes sex* of 1559. The speech was delivered on 8 January 1551 at the funeral of Feldherr Nikolaus von Salm, brother of the Bishop of Passau and the man who had led the defence of Vienna in the Ottoman siege of 1529. The implications of this speech for Eder's position in the Vienna of his day will be discussed later in this chapter, p. 56.

[23]   Another more practical reason for the Habsburgs' willingness to employ and promote representatives of a spectrum of religious positions lay in the desperate need for competent functionaries. Owing to the dramatic expansion of central European territories under his command from the 1520s, Ferdinand I had greatly expanded the number of Habsburg administrative bodies based at his court in Vienna. A decree of 1 January 1527 reorganised the central government of his states: it was now to consist of an Aulic Council, a Privy Council, a court chancellery and a chamber of accounts. As the holder of a doctorate in canon and civil law, Georg Eder was therefore a prime candidate to hold such office. Eder graduated with this degree from Vienna in 1551. He had, however, commenced these studies at Cologne. On Eder's qualifications see Locher, D. Joanne Joseph (1773), *Speculum Academicum Viennense, sen magistratus antiquissimae et celeberrime Universitatis Viennensis, a primo eiusdem auspicio ad nostra tempora chronologice, historice, et lemmatice, exhibitus a D. Joanne Josepho Locher J.U.D.*, 3 vols, Vienna: Kaliwoda, vol. 1, p. 8 and p. 38.

a Cataneis as having been instrumental in his initial appointments.[24] The other three he mentioned much later in a letter to Duke Albrecht of Bavaria dated 21 January 1574: Jonas, Gienger and Gundel.[25] Dr Georg Gienger was a member of the Geheimer Rat, and Dr Philipp Gundel was a leading member of both the university and the Lower Austrian government.[26] It was Dr Jacob Jonas, however, who held the greatest authority, as Vizekanzler to Ferdinand I. That Jonas was also known by his contemporaries as a particularly vitriolic Romanist suggests that there may well have been a confessional edge to his patronage of an untried Eder, as well as mere recognition of potential.[27]

The court career of Eder also demonstrates, however, the type of service and loyalty to the dynasty required to maintain such high rank. In Eder's case, evidence of particular service to the dynasty is not easy to identify. The vagaries of Reichshofrat minute-taking make it almost impossible to say what Eder's precise role in Reichshofrat business was. The surviving Reichshofrat records, or Resolutionsprotokolle, offer little indication of Eder's particular duties or for which cases he bore particular responsibility. Lothar Gross has identified one instance in which Eder appears to personally have dealt with a case regarding a dispute over a mill at nearby Schwechat, but in the main the Protokolle indicate only the sessions at which Eder was present.[28] The same applies to records of Eder's earlier work in the Lower Austrian government. A published patent from 25 April 1559 lifting a ban on the purchase of cattle from Hungary, and another from 13 August 1563 concerning the status of those living in Vienna without a trade and without a master, both bear Eder's

---

24   Eder, *Catalogus Rectorum*, p. 73.

25   Schrauf (ed.), *Der Reichshofrath Dr Georg Eder. Eine Briefsammlung*, p. 78.

26   Gienger died on 14 January 1577 having served under both Ferdinand I and Maximilian II in the Geheimer Rat. He also reached the rank of Obersthofmarschal: see Fellner, Thomas and Kretschmayr, Heinrich (eds) (1907), *Die Österreichische Zentralverwaltung I Abteilung Von Maximilian I. bis zur vereinigung der Österreichischen und Böhmischen Hofkanzlei (1749)*, vol. 2, *Aktenstücke 1491–1681*, Vienna: Veröffentlichungen der Kommission für neuere Geschichte Österreichs, pp. 180–88. Gundel died on 4 September 1567 and had served in the Law Faculty of Vienna University including a spell as rector in 1540: see Locher, *Speculum*, vol. 1, p. 24. He was also known for his abilities as a humanist.

27   Thanks are due to Alexandra Kess for providing me with the following reference found through her own work on the Protestant historian Johann Sleidanus. Jonas Nidbruck, a Protestant Reichshofrat, wrote from Augsburg to Sleidanus on 3 July 1555 that the likes of Jonas was, along with Christoph Welsinger, chancellor of the Bishop of Strasbourg, one of the 'principal sources of all our misfortune'. Letter 147, in Baumgarten, Hermann (ed.) (1888), *Sleidans Briefwechsel*, Strasbourg, pp. 283–4.

28   Gross, Lothar (1936), 'Reichshofratsprotokolle als Quellen niederösterreichischer Geschichte', *Jb.f.Lk.v.NÖ*, 26, 119–23, especially 122. This case was dated 19 January 1564.

signature, but his is one name amongst many.[29] There does, however, remain evidence of one case in which Eder was involved early in his court career, and which displayed not only his legal talents but also his loyalty to the imperial authority. More significant still is that the case involved the formulation of a defence for the Emperor Ferdinand I himself, over a potentially explosive conflict with none other than the pope.[30]

By 1558 Habsburg-papal relations had reached a fresh low. The uncompromising Gianpietro Caraffa had been Pope Paul IV from April 1555, and since then tension had escalated between Rome and Vienna on several fronts. Association with his elder brother's past policies in the Italian lands, a son with increasingly dubious confessional leanings, and personal involvement in the construction of the Peace of Augsburg had all damaged Ferdinand's connection with the pope, but none of these more so than the circumstances of his election as emperor in 1558. Not only had his electors included Protestant princes, but to please them Ferdinand had taken his election as an opportunity to renew the Peace of Augsburg with its controversial terms. In a further slight, he had failed to welcome the papal nuncio at his coronation in Aachen in March. As a result, the pope and a number of his cardinals not only questioned the validity of an imperial election in which heretics had participated, but added that no Christian would have acted as Ferdinand.

The adequate defence of the emperor's position in this dispute was thus crucial for the maintenance of his authority, personal and imperial, not to mention the future peace of Europe. Eder's particular input into the formulation of legal arguments on behalf of the emperor is not entirely clear from the remaining documents. What survives is a manuscript of 57 folio pages, dated March 1558 and divided into three sections.[31] The first by Philipp Gundel, the second attributed to Gundel and 'Georgii Eder Camer Procuratoris VJ Doctorum' and the third by Gundel and Georg Gienger, the three pieces together set out a series of points in defence of the new emperor's position.[32] The section for which Eder was responsible

---

[29]   Patents reprinted in: Schuster, Richard (ed.) (1896), 'Regesten aus dem Archive des k.k. Ministeriums des Innern,' in Mayer, Anton (ed.), *Quellen zur Geschichte der Stadt Wien*, part 1 vol. 2, Vienna: Verlag und Eigenthum des Alterthums-Vereines zu Wien, pp. 1–94, no. 1464, p. 78 and no. 1497, p. 91, respectively.

[30]   The details of this incident have been succinctly outlined most recently in Sutter Fichtner, Paula (1982), *Ferdinand of Austria: The Politics of Dynasticism in the Age of the Reformation*, New York, NY: Columbia University Press, pp. 227–9.

[31]   This survives only in manuscript form at the Österreichische Nationalbibliothek, signature Bibl. Pal. Vind. Cod. 8727. It proclaims itself to be concerned with 'the business of the empire against the objections of the pope, and ... on behalf of the Emperor Ferdinand I against Pope Paul IV'. Gundel's section is followed by that on which he had collaborated with Eder, fols 34r–44r and not, incidentally, written in Eder's hand.

[32]   Much later in his career, Eder would take the Roman side of a conflict with his Wittelsbach patrons over secular involvement in ecclesiastical affairs: see pp. 124–5.

carries references from no less than 74 historical, legal and biblical sources and may well have formed part of the series of formal replies to the pope issued by the emperor's representatives over the following months.[33] Their relationship survived, but only just, and after a prolonged period of tension during which the pope withdrew his nuncio from the imperial court.

It would appear that Eder's role in the episode was so prized that the young jurist came to the attention of Ferdinand I himself. There survives a draft of a letter dated 3 March 1559 from Ferdinand I to Gundel, Stephan Hauptmann and Georg Eder, the last identified not only by name but also by the post to which Ferdinand had named him almost three years earlier, as Kammerprokurator to the Lower Austrian government.[34] The emperor was apparently pleased with his appointment: the letter of 3 March reveals Ferdinand's receipt of the reports concerning his conflict with Paul IV, while three further letters sent by Ferdinand to Eder between 3 May 1559 and 8 July 1559 over Hofkammer business indicate the continuation of the emperor's trust in his functionary.[35] Eder's subsequent appointment by Ferdinand I to the more prestigious post of Reichshofrat just four years later may well have been in response to the competence and service he demonstrated in defending imperial authority.[36]

Eder's rise at Vienna University can also be attributed to his ability to mount a defence against unwanted ecclesiastical encroachments on secular authority. Although he was the holder of two doctorates, one in law taken in 1551 and one in theology granted in 1571, Eder himself

---

[33]   One such response was delivered by the imperial ambassador to Rome, Martin Guzmán, who argued that indeed, an emperor could not be elected by heretics but that the honour had fallen to Ferdinand by default. To a similar end, the then Reichsvizekanzler Georg Sigismund Seld argued that the electors retained complete independence in secular affairs.

[34]   HHStA, Staatenabteilung Italien, Rom Varia 1551–59, Fasz. 2 (alt 1, 2), fol. 9r. Hauptmann's involvement in the conflict may be explained by his proficiency in canon law. He was also rector of Vienna University once in 1556 and again in 1559: see Locher, *Speculum*, vol. 1, p. 26.

[35]   HKA, Reichsakten, Fasz. 150/A, fols 351 r–v (3 May 1559), fols 353 r–v (5 June 1559), fol. 355r (8 July 1559). The first letter, sent from Augsburg and also addressed to Gundel, names both he and Eder as 'both doctors of law' possibly mere titles but also indicative of the fact that Eder's growing reputation was grounded in his legal skills. The two later letters are also addressed to Eder and Gundel as well as to Wilhelm von Wolkhenstain and Blasius Kuen.

[36]   Paula Sutter Fichtner notes that due to the Habsburgs' chronic financial problems, Ferdinand demanded detailed knowledge of the business of the Hofkammer. For example, its members were, amongst other stipulations, to send regular reports to the Geheimer Rat. Sutter Fichtner, *Ferdinand of Austria*, pp. 67–8. The letters to Eder noted here may have been part of merely routine business between Hofkammer and Geheimer Rat, but none the less reveal the importance of Eder to the workings of Ferdinand's growing bureaucracy.

never taught at Vienna University.[37] Hilde de Ridder Symoens has described the role of the early-modern university rector as simply the 'head of the institution'. As such, Eder carried the ultimate responsibility for education, discipline, finance and the overall management of the university.[38] His authority as rector is suggested in a number of Vienna University records. Again, their nature is such that Eder's particular input to decision-making is rarely clear, but he is listed as presiding at a number of councils such as that of the theology faculty on 17 October 1569 or at the consistorium of 7 December 1569. At the latter, for example, Eder oversaw the administration of a bequest to the university from the Archbishop of Gran, Nikolaus Oláh, for the establishment of two scholarships for such students 'who wish to be initiated in the holy rites and to be priests'.[39]

The exercise of authority would also have meant that Eder chaired all councils, including the academic court of justice, and would have led all ceremonies including doctoral promotions. The rector's role on such an occasion was in itself inherently portentous. Surrounded by the leading members of the university, he would accompany all the physical symbols of the promotion, such as the presentation of a scholarly book, and the placing of the doctor's cap on the head of the recipient, with a speech ostensibly about the graduate but as much reflective of the power of the university.[40] The following extract from the published version of Eder's

---

[37]   Paulus, 'Hofrath Dr Georg Eder', p. 17. For Eder's qualifications see Locher *Speculum*, vol. 1, p. 8 and p. 38. Although Eder is named as a professor of canon law from 1551 (Locher, *Speculum*, vol. 3, p. 22), this is not necessarily indicative of the holding of an active teaching post. Aschbach adds that Eder was absent from the lists of salaried teaching staff from 1552, 1554 and 1556: Aschbach, Joseph Ritter von (1888), *Geschichte der Wiener Universität. Die Wiener Universität und Ihre Gelehrten, 1520 bis 1565*, Vienna: Adolph Holzhausen. p. 169. It is worth noting, however, that the third volume of Locher's *Speculum* from 1775 refers to a legal manuscript of Eder's then housed in the university library that may have been used for academic purposes. Now apparently lost, Locher notes it as 'Ederi V.J. Doct. notata juridica', *Speculum*, vol. 3, p. 79.

[38]   Ridder-Symoens, Hilde de (1996), 'Management and Resources', in Ridder-Symoens, Hilde de (ed.), *A History of the University in Europe*, vol. 2, *Universities in Early Modern Europe*, Cambridge: Cambridge University Press, pp. 155–209, especially p. 173.

[39]   UAW, Th16 (1569–1666), microfilm 076, fol. 2r. Starzer, Albert (ed.) (1906) 'Fortsetzung' in Starzer, Albert (ed.), *Quellen zur Geschichte der Stadt Wien*, part I, vol. 5, Vienna: Verein für Geschichte der Stadt Wien, pp. 11–397, no. 5480, p. 128. The bequest imposed various restrictions on the geographical origins of the students to whom the grant could be awarded, as well as demanding certain levels of academic achievement on the part of the holders.

[40]   The right to grant such promotions actually belonged to the Kanzler, but as chairman of the proceedings, Eder as rector would have had the right to make the longest speeches and thus dominate the event. For an overview of such events see: Horn, Ewald (1893), 'Die Disputationen und Promotionen an den Deutschen Universitäten vornehmlich seit dem 16. Jahrhundert', *Elftes Beiheft zum Centralblatt für Bibliothekswesen*, Leipzig, pp. 1–126. It is also worth noting that the rector had the right to wear ceremonial robes that would have

conferment of the doctorate on one Alex Straus, formulaic as it is, reveals much of the symbolic weight of the moment and, by implication, Eder's status as the physical bestower of the dignity:[41]

> Finally, with that authority which this most celebrated [University] of Vienna first obtained both from the supreme pontiffs and emperors, and has subsequently retained by a very long-lived custom, I make, appoint and promote you, Alex Straus, licentiate, as a doctor in both branches of the law … and I hereby confer upon you all the privileges, honours, powers and immunities by which this profession has been honoured by the Christian princes, either by law or custom, so that you may enjoy and rejoice in them throughout the whole Christian world. This we declare in the name of the most holy and indivisible trinity of the Father, Son and Holy Spirit… . [42]

Eder was, furthermore, associated more than anyone else with the bestowal of such a dignity. The office of rector in the early-modern university was generally rotated between leading university figures on a semester-by-semester basis, with each faculty – philosophy, law, medicine and theology – taking turns to elect a member from among their own ranks every April for the summer semester and every October for the winter semester.[43] Eder's career, however, was unprecedented for the number of rectorates he held. In 1557 Eder received his first posting to the office of Vienna University rector, and filled this position no less than 11 times between 1557 and 1584.[44] To put this in perspective, within the

---

visually set him apart from others: see Ridder-Symoens, 'Management and Resources', p. 206.

[41]   On the significance of the title 'doctor' in the early modern period, see p. 68.

[42]   This text is from the climax of the ceremony. Eder, Georg (1581), *Quaerela Iustitiae, Lites nunc fieri omnio fere Immortales. In Coronatione Magnifici Nobilis & Clarissimi Viri, Domini Alexii Strauss, V.I. Doctoris Academiae Viennensis pro tempore Rectoris. Per D. Georg Ederum*, Vienna: Stephan Creuzer, fol. C4v.

[43]   Eder's first election at Vienna University was not as rector but rather as Prokurator of the German nation for the winter semester of 1552–53. Eder also acted five times as dean of the law faculty, once in 1571 as dean of the theology faculty and once in the winter semester of 1572–73 as Prokurator of the Hungarian nation. Eder was dean of the law faculty winter semester 1559–60, summer semester 1570, summer semester 1572, winter semester 1580–81, and winter semester 1582–83. Mühlberger, Kurt (1992), 'Bildung und Wissenschaft. Kaiser Maximilian II. und die Universität Wien', in Edelmayer, Friedrich and Kohler, Alfred (eds), *Kaiser Maximilian II. Kultur und Politik im 16. Jahrhundert*, Wiener Beiträge zur Geschichte der Neuzeit, vol. 17, Vienna: Verlag für Geschichte und Politik, pp. 203–31. On Eder's election as Prokurator of the Hungarian nation, see Locher, *Speculum*, vol. 1, p. 256.

[44]   For a summary of Eder's university career, see Mühlberger, 'Bildung und Wissenschaft', p. 224. Basing his figures on Locher, *Speculum*, vol. 1, Mühlberger lists Eder's rectorates: winter semester 1557–58, summer semester 1558, winter semester 1558–59, summer semester 1559, winter semester 1559–60, winter semester 1569–70, winter semester 1571–72, summer semester 1580, winter semester 1581–82, summer semester 1582, and summer semester 1584. On Eder's earlier 1552–53 election as Prokurator, see Locher, *Speculum*, vol. 1, p. 215.

span of Eder's career the highest number of rectorates held by any other individual at Vienna University was four.[45]

Eder's success in retaining rank at Vienna University can be attributed to the same two factors that led to his rise at the court: the presence of a small but influential group of fellow-Catholics, as outlined in Chapter 1, and the ability to defend the authority of both university and Habsburg ruler simultaneously.[46] One important such instance occurred early in Eder's career within Vienna University, during the period of his very first rectorship, between October 1557 and April 1558, when he defended university privileges against the encroachments of the Church. University materials from 1558 recount how Eder took forceful action against the city's Dominicans.[47] A monk by the name of Andronicus had fallen foul of his Dominican superiors and had been imprisoned by them within the cloister. The problem, however, was that Andronicus was also a university student, and Eder, having first gained the backing of the Lower Austrian government of which he was also a member, personally forced his way into the cloister to free his student. In so doing, Eder was not only yet again asserting the rights of secular powers over ecclesiastical powers, but was also being seen to defend the privileges of the university.[48]

The episode evidently had a decisive impact on Eder's career at the beleaguered university for the next several years. In spite of the system of rectorates rotating between faculties, Eder won the next four rectorial elections in a row: an unprecedented and highly visible vote of confidence

---

[45]   Hubertus Luetanus, with four stints as rector of Vienna University, came closest to Eder's record. See Locher, *Speculum*, vol. 1, pp. 26–9.

[46]   See pp. 34–7.

[47]   '[The Prior of the monastery of Dominicans] declared that the whole monastery had been profaned and the masters from the university had been excommunicated (even though, as he said, some could not have cared less), because our lord the splendid rector George Eder, doctor in both branches of the law, had along with his followers burst into the monastery with the utmost force, had smashed down an iron gate and some other barriers and had taken away ... brother Andronicus ...'. Details of this incident come originally from UAW: Rhein. Nat. Matrikel but have here been taken from the citation of this document in Aschbach, *Geschichte der Wiener Universität. Die Wiener Universität und Ihre Gelehrten*, p. 172.

[48]   The early-modern university retained from its medieval legacy certain exclusive rights: that of self-management including the administration of justice and discipline; exemptions from certain taxes, military service and court-quartering; and special protective laws that, for example, granted university members priority in the case of food shortage: Ridder-Symoens, 'Management and Resources', p. 164. These were not expressly denied by Ferdinand I, but his so-called Reformatio Nova of 1 January 1554 was another step in an increasing accrual of Habsburg authority over the university corporation.

indeed.[49] Equally impressive was the extent of Eder's hold on the post of Reichshofrat. During his own period of service therein, Eder encountered a total of 53 other members.[50] Some of these Reichshofräte were already there when Eder first entered the council in November 1563, others joined while he was in office, and some of this number remained after he left in September 1583. Only one, however, served longer than Eder, while few others even came close. Apart from Eder, Christoph Philipp Zott von Pernegg was the only other Reichshofrat to serve under the three emperors – Ferdinand I, Maximilian II and Rudolf II – and was also the only one to retain his post longer, outserving Eder by just six months.[51] Dr Johann Hegenmüller came closest to matching the length of service of these two men, acting as Reichshofrat from 1 March 1566 until July 1583.[52] Eder's longevity of service in this key post is all the more noteworthy in view of the markedly short careers of certain other members. Karl Rym, Herr zu Eckenbecke, for example, served in the Reichshofrat a mere four months while Gabriel Creutzer was first listed as a member on 6 August 1568, only to die on 1 December of the same year.[53]

The special nature of Eder's rise to prominence in sixteenth-century Vienna is also reflected in that he held a post as prestigious as that of Reichshofrat in tandem with equally high office at Vienna University. Between the 1550s and the 1580s, Eder was one of only three men who fulfilled such key functions in combination. To compound the rarity of Eder's feat, the two others, Melchior Hofmair and the Dr Christoph Pirckhaimer named above, only filled both positions in the 1580s, towards the end of Eder's career.[54] It is hardly surprising that as a result of the relatively small pool of talent available, certain figures did hold roles in both the court and university: Wolfgang Lazius and Hugo Blotius are two particularly notable examples. However, to be listed in

---

[49]   Eder thus became rector for summer semester 1558, winter semester 1558–59, summer semester 1559, and winter semester 1559–60.

[50]   This figure is drawn from a mixture of my own analysis of the Reichshofrat Protokolle and the invaluable research of Gschließer.

[51]   See Gschließer, *Der Reichshofrat*, pp. 99–100. Zott von Pernegg served from 19 January 1559 until 19 April 1579, when he died in office.

[52]   Ibid., pp. 119–21. The precise start date of Hegenmüller's career is unclear. He appears on the Reichshofrat paylist in March 1566 but not in the Protokolle until 19 October of the same year.

[53]   Ibid., p. 124 on Creutzer (also spelt Creuzer, Kreutzer, Kreuczer, or Kreiser). Rym (or Rieme, Rime, or Riemben) served between 8 March 1575 and July 1575: ibid., p. 132 for more.

[54]   Hofmair, also spelt Hofmayer, was rector in 1560, 1562 and 1570 while Pirckhaimer, also spelt Birckhaimer or Pürckhaimer, was only elected to the post in 1594. See Locher, *Speculum*, vol. 1, pp. 26–30. Hofmair was Reichshofrat from autumn 1584 until his death in August 1586, while Pirckhaimer held the position from August 1581 until August 1592. See Gschließer, *Der Reichshofrat*, pp. 145–6 and p. 142 respectively.

2.1 1558 woodcut depicting Eder. By permission of the British Library (shelfmark
731.e.8(3))

university or court registers as, to take the case of Lazius, dean of the
medical faculty and court 'Historiographus', does not necessarily imply
substantial activity in the posts stated. Eder's case is somewhat different.
The roles of Reichshofrat and rector both necessitated the fulfilling of
significant responsibilities on an almost daily basis, a fact that in itself
says much about Eder's will to serve and succeed in late sixteenth-century
Vienna.[55]

---

[55] As Reichshofrat, Eder would usually have been committed to working within the city
on an almost daily basis. Reichshofrat sessions took place at the Hofburg all year apart from
Christmas, Easter and Whitsun, and attendance at every one was a primary duty of office.
On the practical workings of the Reichshofrat, see Gschließer, *Der Reichshofrat*, pp. 77–9.
He notes that while in theory they were only to meet four times a week, in fact they often met

One intriguing question remains on the subject of Eder's rise at the Viennese court: what do the details of Eder's career and the means by which he rose to prominence tell us about his personality? In particular, was his apparent devotion to the secular authority a cynical effort at self-preservation and self-publicity? As has been seen, the available sources only permit reconstruction of the bare bones of key incidents in Eder's career. The intent of the man behind can in general only be inferred from such events, but there is a small amount of peripheral evidence that suggests Georg Eder was indeed a 'larger-than-life' personality, or at least someone who deliberately wanted to make his mark. Gall and Szaivert note, for example, that Eder was the first university rector to insert woodcuts of his own image into the university records, and was thus the originator of a tradition that increased throughout subsequent decades and rectorates.[56] This apparent wish to physically as well as figuratively stamp his own image on all he touched is also evident in the sections of Reichshofrat Resolutionsprotokolle for which Eder was responsible for minuting. Between 17 July 1577 and February 1578 Eder took his turn at noting down all Reichshofrat resolutions passed.[57] The other Reichshofräte who performed such a task, such as Dr Timotheus Jung and Dr Andreas Gail, remained fairly anonymous in such a position. The first page of Eder's script, however, is striking for its elaborate and bold title announcing: 'George Eder succeeded that noble and most illustrious man, Timotheus Jung, a doctor in both branches of the law ... the following are his deeds'.[58] Eder's opening page is also unique for bearing scriptural references, from the third and fortieth Psalms.

In addition, Eder, his hearers, or perhaps a mixture of both, ensured that no other rector who served at Vienna within the same period had nearly so many rectorial speeches published, and certainly none so many within such a short time frame. Five of Eder's speeches survive: that delivered on the doctoral promotion of Marcus Faschang on 1 October 1555, of Petrus a Rotis on 14 September 1557, of Laurenz Lehman on 19 January 1559, of Martin Puschman on 16 September 1568, and

---

five or six times, in the mornings and if necessary also in the afternoons. As many as a dozen cases could be discussed in each session.

[56]   Gall, Franz and Szaivert, Willy (eds) (1971), *Quellen zur Geschichte der Universität Wien. I Abteilung. Die Matrikel der Universität Wien*, vol. 3, 1518/II–1579/I and vol. 4 1579/II–1658/59, Vienna, Cologne, Graz: Publikationen des Instituts für Österreichische Geschichtsforschung, p. 115. See Figure 2.1, previous page. A copy of this woodcut was inserted in UAW, Hauptmatrikel IV, M4 1518 II–1594 I, microfilm 017, fol. 110b.

[57]   HHStA, Reichshofrat, RHR Protocollum rerum resolutarium XVI 42, fol. 387 and RHR Protocollum rerum resolutarium XVI 45, fol. 75. Eder's stint as scribe apparently ended on 7 February 1578, though his script does reappear on occasion throughout the months following.

[58]   HHStA, Reichshofrat, RHR Protocollum rerum resolutarium XVI fol. 387.

that quoted above, of Alex Straus on 13 September 1581.[59] The fact that the first three of these were also reprinted in abbreviated form in a compilation of Eder's speeches from 1559 adds further to the claim that in print as well as in fact, Eder's was one of the highest public profiles in the Vienna of his own day.[60]

Eder's prominence was further enhanced by his deliberate and carefully managed association with the humanist culture of the Viennese court and university in the late sixteenth century.[61] Overlooking any confessional differences, Eder worked closely with such figures in a series of projects that further glorified the image of the university while publicly portraying Eder as a central part of the imperial coterie. It was Eder, for example, who as rector involved himself heavily with the revival of the Latin oration as cultural event within the university; it was also Eder who was the main force behind the production of the first ever history of Vienna University. As a result, Eder not only enhanced his own reputation in Vienna but associated himself with the humanism of the court and all that it stood for. Secondly, and in large part thanks to his skill in such areas, it was also Eder who was called upon to make a number of speeches at pivotal moments in Viennese public life. As a result, it was again Georg Eder who managed more than anyone to associate himself closely with the culture and authority of the imperial court and dynasty.

Whether this was Eder's main intention is a moot point, for ostensibly at least, Eder's project in these years was primarily designed to revive Vienna University's flagging fortunes. Recognising the wealth of talented scholars then in the employ of the court and the university, Eder and three men already mentioned, Paulus Fabricius, Andreas Dadius and Petrus a Rotis, took the lead in organising a revival of the 'quodlibetanischen Disputationen' and the Dichterkrönungen, or, the crowning of a poet

---

[59] See p. 48, note 42.

[60] These five speeches reflect only those that were published and that have survived: it may reasonably be assumed there were many more never published or which have not survived. The first, 'Politicum ordine etiam in ecclesia retinendum esse, & quid ad rem conferat Iurisprudentia: habita Vien: in aedibus D. Stephani dum clariß: viro D. Marco Faschang Doctoream dignitatem in V.I. conferret. I Octobris Anno M. D. LV.' remains only in an abbreviated form in a later compilation: 1559's *Orationes sex*. This speech is also unusual in that Eder was not actually rector when it was delivered in October 1555. Another from September 1557 on the promotion of Petrus a Rotis was also reprinted in *Orationes sex* as well as alone under the title of *Ius Non Opinione Inductum*. A third from 1559, 'De Maiestate legum & ordinum sive gradu dignitate & usu, Qua Excellentiss: viro D. Laurentio Leemanno Grecarum literarum professori Doctorea dignitas in VI. ab Authore in tertio Rectoratu suo collata fuit. XIX. Ianuarii Anno M.D.LIX' again exists only in *Orationes sex*, while the fourth, 1570's *Ad Rubricam Codicis De Summa Trinitate*, was published separately.

[61] Eder's wide range of intellectual interests and active legal career meant that he seems never to have fully devoted himself to humanist scholarship as an end in itself.

laureate.[62] This project was significant in itself, as such disputations had not been held in the University of Vienna since 1525.[63] Eder's move was thus an attempt to hearken back to the university's pre-siege glory days, and indeed, on 15 September 1558 the Dichterkrönungen was celebrated afresh in the presence not only of scholars but also numerous members of the nobility. A welcome by-product for Eder was the ostentatious praise he subsequently received from those so honoured. As this came from the most notable humanist scholars Vienna could boast, and as it came in published form, Eder's profile gained not only from the fact that he had physically presided over a grand, court-sanctioned occasion, but that his role in this would be preserved in eloquent print for years to come. The key piece of evidence in this regard is the *Laurea poetica*, a work of at least 40 folio pages containing the text of the speeches delivered in connection with the award of the laureate titles.[64] In it, Eder is the recipient of copious praise from the three poets in receipt of the award, Elias Corvinus, Johannes Lauterbach and Vitus Jacobaeus, as well as such court luminaries as Wolfgang Lazius.[65] Further, later works added to the growing corpus of praise in print for Eder, the nominal source of such honours.[66]

---

[62]   Since his doctoral promotion in 1557, a Rotis also held the post of professor of law at Vienna University. This was also Eder's faculty, but it is worth reiterating the fluidity of intellectual pursuit in the early modern period which did not restrict individuals to activity in just one particular field. In addition, it may be telling that Dadius and a Rotis were both fellow-Catholics.

[63]   Conrad Celtis had been one of those so honoured.

[64]   Eder, Georg (1558), *Laurea poetica, ex caesareo privilegio in celeberrimo archigymnasio Viennensi tribus nuper viris eruditiss...*, Vienna: Raphael Hofhalter.

[65]   For example, fol. A vi verso contains the following from Lazius to Eder: 'You, Rector Eder, are elevating your school to the skies.' Eder's praise from Jacobaeus was equally unrestrained: 'you will be greeted with such a triumph, so that honour may closely accompany your virtue ...', fols Kii r–Kiii r. On Corvinus and Jacobaeus, see Aschbach, *Geschichte der Wiener Universität. Die Wiener Universität und Ihre Gelehrten*, pp. 159–60 and pp. 196–7 respectively. Jacobaeus later became a poet laureate.

[66]   References to Eder occur in a number of printed speeches from others in receipt of his or at least his university's benevolence. These works are not easy to trace, and the physically fragile nature of such documents mean that few will have survived over four centuries. Titles from much older bibliographies such as Denis, Michael (1782 and 1793), *Wiens Buchdruckergeschicht bis M.D.L.X.*, 2 vols, Vienna: Wappler, and to a lesser extent Mayer, Anton (1883), *Wiens Buchdrucker–Geschichte*, vol. 1, *1482–1682*, Vienna: Verlag d. Comites z. Feier d. vierhundertj. Einführung d. Buchdruckerkunst in Wien do however point to these further telling hints at Eder's prominence. At least six such works are named and one that has survived gives a hint of the praise Eder enjoyed. Rocco Boni's 1559 *Austriados Libri Quatuor ad invictissimvm Ro. Imperatorem Ferdinandum primum, & Serenissimum Bohemiae Regem D. Maximilianum suae Maiest. Filium, carmine heroico descripti & approbati à Magnifico Viro D. Georgio Edero I.C. Caesareo Rectore dignissimo & Collegio Poëtico celeberrimi Archigymnasii Viennensis; Quod poema inscribitur Oraculum*, Vienna: Michael Zimmermann, concludes with the following: 'in praise of that splendid man ... Georg Eder ... his talents flourish, he is second to none in his ability, and deserves to live

That Eder may well have anticipated such a result is suggested by the fact that he also orchestrated a connected project – the production of the first ever history of Vienna University – which reads equally as a public, permanent testimony to his own greatness. What survives today is in fact only Eder's contribution, originally intended as a mere appendix to a poem in praise of the university by Vitus Jacobaeus, one of the newly crowned laureates.[67] Although this poem was evidently in production by 1559, no record survives of it ever being published or even of its survival in manuscript form.[68] Not surprisingly, however, Eder's part of the project was indeed published and within its apparently 'historical' claims lie even more strands of evidence pointing to the nature of Eder's prominence in the Vienna of his own day, and how he achieved the same. Predictably, he dedicated the work to his patron and protector, the above-named and highly influential Georg Gienger. By offering 1237 as the year of foundation for the university rather than the correct date of 1365, Eder also ingratiated himself with the court historian Wolfgang Lazius who first used the incorrect date in his own work on the history of the city of Vienna.[69] Yet in his composition of such a work Eder also closely associated himself with Vienna University's glorious past. Eder's *Catalogus Rectorum* is essentially a 106-page table indicating who was rector in what year and what the notable events were of each rectorate. As Eder himself was rector in 1559, the year the work was published, the nature of the document allowed his name to conclude the work as the pinnacle of centuries of achievement. Eder himself included nothing to dissuade the reader: he was careful to outline, for example, that the tradition of public oration and disputation was revived under his rectorate and the *Catalogus Rectorum* even includes the first published picture of Eder, on the back of the title page.[70] To add

---

as long as Nestor ... He has entered the fields where Socrates dwelt, and the grassy swards of wisdom, where the young pluck gilded apples with their hands. Will the present age, or posterity long after, be able to forget so great a man?', fol. Iiii v.

[67]   Eder, Georg (1559), *Catalogus Rectorum Et Illustrium Virorum Archigymnasii Viennensis*, Vienna; Raphael Hofhalter.

[68]   Ibid., pp. 91–2. Eder wrote: 'in order to rescue it from this most unfair scorn, I began to draw up from each of the documents of the academy, almost all of which I have perused, an all-embracing account, I might almost say, of this most ancient and famed school; which Vitus Jacobaeus, the poet laureate expressed at my prompting in a poem written ... to defend the honour of the academy ...'.

[69]   Wolfgang Lazius (1546), *Vienna Austriae. Rerum Viennensium Commentatii in quatuor libros distincti, in quibus celeberrimae illius Austriae civitatis exordia, vetustas, nobilitas, magistratus, familiaeque ad planum (quod ajunt) explicantur*, Basle.

[70]   Eder's rectorates in 1557 and 1558 are numbered 362, 363 and 364, pp. 89–91. Copies of the woodcut of Eder used in his *Catalogus Rectorum* (identical to that in Figure 2.1) would also have, it has been suggested, been distributed by Eder to his patrons and friends 'according to good humanist custom'. Gall and Szaivert (eds), *Quellen zur Geschichte der Universität Wien. I Abteilung. Die Matrikel der Universität Wien* vol. III, p. 115.

a piece of telling if anecdotal evidence, in the Austrian National Library there survives today a copy not only bound with eight other works all by Eder, Fabricius, Corvinus, Jacobaeus, and Dadius, but also bearing what appears to be a hand-written dedication from Eder to Dadius at the bottom of the title page of the *Catalogus Rectorum*.[71] This in itself hints that Eder's foray into university history was yet something else he could use to heighten his profile among the influential.

Eder's status in the intertwined spheres of Vienna's court and university in turn provided him with the means to make his own mark on the civic culture of late sixteenth-century Vienna and another vehicle in which to proclaim his dynastic allegiance. No doubt in view of his growing reputation and increasingly public humanist connections by the late 1550s, it was Eder to whom it fell to make speeches at key moments in Viennese civic life. Four speeches survive in their published form: Eder may well have spoken at other important occasions, but it would be hard to imagine situations more significant than those from which the text survives. The first oration had come much earlier than the others in Eder's career, in 1551. Indeed, such an early date, before Eder would have been able to make many influential friends in Vienna, may point to the fact that he was a competent Latin orator in his own right, not entirely reliant on though undoubtedly helped by later patrons. Certainly the occasion of what must have been one of Eder's first public orations in Vienna was at a particularly poignant moment in the city's history. On 8 January 1551 Vienna saw a memorial service for none other than Nikolaus von Salm, the man who had led the defence of Vienna in the Turkish siege of 1529.[72] In his speech, Eder not only took the chance to display his own talents as an orator but also to demonstrate his personal connections to such a local hero, by thanking the dead man's family for their support before his arrival in Vienna.[73]

The three other speeches of which copies survive were all used to mark Vienna's recognition of key moments in the life of the imperial dynasty, and under such circumstances Eder's orations would also have added immensely to his personal prominence as a supporter of the Habsburg authority. Perhaps the most dramatic such occasion was that of 1558 when Ferdinand I returned to Vienna as newly elected Holy Roman Emperor and the university took part in the celebrations. As rector, Eder headed the delegation sent out to meet the new emperor. The group, including a Rotis, Fabricius, Jacobaeus and court historian Johannes Sambucus,

---

[71]   ÖNB, 257.650–B.Fid. (=76–142).

[72]   See p. 43, note 22 for details.

[73]   '... the most lavish benefits and divine grace were bestowed upon myself and my studies; you embraced me with these advantages with such enormous kindness from the time when I was placed in charge of instructing the young men ...', Eder, *Georgii Eder De Illustriss. Principis et D.D. Nicolai Comitis a Salm & Neuburg ad Oenum*, fol. Aii r.

travelled along the Danube as far as Klosterneuburg on a lavishly decorated boat from which Eder delivered a speech of congratulations and loyalty on behalf of the university to the ruler. This too was published in two versions: one on its delivery in 1558 and another in abbreviated form in Eder's *Orationes sex* the year after.[74] Eder's very public and prestigious role in an event of such symbolic importance may well have been connected to his simultaneous defence of the new emperor against Paul IV, already discussed in this chapter. Whatever the case, it did no harm to his public profile and on 19 February 1559 Eder also produced a speech to mark the funeral of Ferdinand I's brother, the former Emperor Charles V.[75] Again accompanied in this by Jacobaeus and Fabricius, such a role would have increasingly consolidated Eder's position as the public face of Vienna University and indeed Vienna's humanist community, to the influential of Vienna and in particular to members of the dynasty. The final speech which survives would have reinforced this impression: Eder also spoke in public praise of the newly crowned King of Hungary, the Emperor Maximilian II's son Rudolf, on 21 September 1572.[76]

Georg Eder was, it seems, an ambitious but highly able man who quickly became one of Vienna's most prominent court, university and civic figures. He certainly knew how to play the politics of the day, but there was much more to Eder than self-serving court functionary. The years 1550–73 saw Eder simultaneously devote his talents and considerable energy to the cause of Catholic reform. This was, admittedly, an aulic Catholic reform that remained carefully within the parameters of what was then acceptable to Habsburg authority. None the less, Eder achieved much for the faith, a feat all the more remarkable in view of the fact that he remained a layman throughout his life.

---

[74] Eder, Georg (1558), *Triumphus D. Ferdinando I. Ro. Imperator*, Vienna: Raphael Hofhalter.

[75] Eder, Georg (1559), *Luctus Archigymnasii Viennen: Pro Funere D. Caroli Quinti*, Vienna: Raphael Hofhalter.

[76] Eder, Georg (1573), *Orationes II. Gratulatoriae, Ad Rudolphum Sereniss*, Vienna: Stephan Creutzer.

CHAPTER 3

Service to the Church, 1550–73

Up to 1573, Georg Eder served both his emperor and his faith simultaneously in Vienna. The two were not mutually exclusive: Eder thrived in Vienna between 1550 and 1573, not just as a nominal Catholic but as a man with very public zeal for the preservation and restoration of his religion. This chapter acts as a partner to the one before, with the focus here on Eder's spiritual rather than his political life. It will reinforce, in part, a theme raised in the preceding chapter: Catholicism, even of the active variety as lived by Eder, was in no way a barrier to success in the court and city of late sixteenth-century Vienna, as long as the imperial authority was treated with reverence.

This examination of Eder's Catholicism also raises a further theme that goes far beyond the specific field of Austrian-Habsburg history. Georg Eder displayed a close involvement in the work of Catholic reform, both inspired by and approved of by members of the Society of Jesus, yet remained a layman throughout his life. Eder's relationship with the Jesuits went back to his youth, and was based throughout on personal ties, mainly through the apparently lifelong relationship he developed with Peter Canisius at university in Cologne. It was, furthermore, a relationship that lasted over four decades: right up to the end of Eder's life, the Jesuits extended their support and patronage to their lay co-worker in Vienna. This chapter therefore also acts as a first case study of the ability of a layman to participate fully in Catholic reform in the later part of the sixteenth century.

Cologne matriculation registers indicate that 'Georg Eder, Frisingensis, Bavarus' entered the university in December 1543.[1] It was to be this single event that had the greatest influence on Eder's life, for Cologne in the 1540s was a hotbed of Jesuit activity. The order was still very young: it had only received formal approval in Rome on 27 September 1540 through the bull 'Regimini militantis ecclesiae' of Pope Paul III. John O'Malley has noted that in the 1540s, on the whole, 'Jesuit presence in Germany was sparse indeed, and outside Cologne, practically non-existent.'[2] This is not, however, to understate the significance of Cologne in this formative decade. It was there that in 1544 saw the foundation of

---

[1]   Keussen, Hermann (ed.) (1979), *Die Matrikel der Universität Köln*, vol. 2, Düsseldorf: Droste, p. 982.

[2]   O'Malley, John W. (1993), *The First Jesuits*, Cambridge, MA: Harvard University Press, p. 273.

the first Jesuit college in the German-speaking lands, and it was Cologne that was, by 1562, home to the largest Jesuit community north of the Alps with 45 Jesuits and a strong reputation for winning new members.[3]

Subsequent Jesuit myth-making may be a factor, but it does appear that the personalities of the handful of Jesuits who began the work in Cologne were vital to the order's success in the area. Peter Faber or Pierre Faure from Savoy was the first Jesuit to operate in the German lands, arriving in Cologne at the beginning of 1543 at the age of 37. Faber was highly praised by a contemporary at Cologne for his piety and authority as a teacher of 'correct' theology; that this praise came from none other than Peter Canisius says much not only about Faber, but about the overall calibre of men based in Cologne in the 1540s.[4] It was Faber who led the 20-year-old Canisius, then a Cologne University student, through the Spiritual Exercises. Two years later, in 1543, Canisius joined the order, thus beginning a 54-year career of Jesuit service in the German-speaking lands that included the composition of his series of famous Catholic catechisms and concluded after death with his canonisation in 1925.[5] Nor were these two men alone: Faber reported in a letter of 10 May 1544 that he was staying in a rented house in Cologne with seven other Jesuits including Ämilian Loyola, a nephew of the order's founder.[6] Together they worked hard to combat religious misbelief in the Cologne of the apostate archbishop, Hermann von Wied, while simultaneously

---

[3]   Ibid., p. 55. As Po-Chia Hsia also notes, 'from a modest beginning of half-a-dozen Jesuits in the college at Cologne, the Society had grown to five provinces by 1630 ... with close to 3000 members', Po-Chia Hsia, R. (1998), *The World of Catholic Renewal 1540–1770*, Cambridge: Cambridge University Press, p. 77.

[4]   Soon after he left Cologne, Canisius wrote of Faber, 'if at all he is a mere man and not, more likely, an angel of the Lord; I have never met such a learned and deep theologian, never heard or seen such a man of such excellent virtue ...'. Duhr, Bernhard (1907), *Geschichte der Jesuiten in den Ländern deutscher Zunge*, vol. 1, *Geschichte der Jesuiten in den Ländern deutscher Zunge im XVI. Jahrhundert*, Freiburg im Briesgau: Herder, p. 10, citing Braunsberger, Otto (ed.) (1896), *Beati Petri Canisii, Societatis Iesu, Epistulae et Acta*, vol. 1, Freiburg im Briesgau: Herder, p. 76.

[5]   Canisius' first version of the catechism, the *Summa doctrinae christianae ... in usum Christianae pueritiae* was first published in 1555 and was the largest he would produce. It was intended for university students and advanced grammar school students, unlike his *Summa ... ad captum rudiorum accommodata* of 1556 which was aimed at very young children. Canisius' *Parvus Catechismus Catholicorum* of 1558 was an intermediate text. These were hugely successful: the *Summa doctrinae christianae* alone was reprinted more than 130 times before the end of the sixteenth century. Greengrass, Mark (1998), *The European Reformation c. 1500–1618*, London: Longman, p. 252.

[6]   Cited in Duhr, *Geschichte der Jesuiten in den Ländern deutscher Zunge*, vol. 1, p. 35. According to James Brodrick, the rent on this house was paid by Canisius out of the remains of his inheritance: Brodrick, James (1935), *Saint Peter Canisius, S.J. 1521–1597*, London: Sheed & Ward, p. 53.

performing works of charity.[7] Canisius and another Jesuit housemate, Alvaro Alfonso, even put aside their own studies to visit hospitals or tend the sick they had taken in under their own roof.

It is impossible that such an example would have been lost on the young Bavarian Catholic who happened to be studying in Cologne at precisely the same moment. The evidence available, however, is much more than circumstantial. Eder's particular friend in the order appears to have been its rising star, the young Canisius. Canisius referred to Eder in several letters written predominantly from Cologne between 1544 and 1548. The timing of the first such mention is particularly telling. Written by Canisius to Faber on 30 December 1544, just one year after Eder would have first arrived in Cologne, Canisius already felt able to refer to him in warm terms.[8] Eder's development was similarly mentioned in passing in letters written by Canisius in 1545, 1547 and 1548. In one of these, written on 17 June 1547, Canisius wrote to Leonardo Kessel, later rector of the Jesuit college at Cologne, about an apparent change in the plans of the young Eder: 'If what you write about the famous Georg's intention to become a Carthusian is true, I cannot but wonder at the change on the occasion at the right hand of the Almighty.'[9] Whether this suggests that Eder had now decided against being a Carthusian, or whether Eder had now decided he should join the Carthusian order, is unclear. Whatever the case, it seems such plans came to nought and just over a year later Canisius was able to write in moving terms of his fondness and hope for his protégé. In this, dated 12 August 1548, Canisius asked Kessel and Adriani to 'cherish Georg', as he was a young man dear to him in the Lord, and the holder of great prospects.[10]

---

7   Von Wied's foray into heresy manifested itself at the very same time as the Jesuits' early activity in Cologne: for example, it was Easter Sunday 1543 that von Wied said Mass in German at Bonn, and afterwards distributed communion in both kinds. And it was 1543 that Wied commissioned Melanchthon and Bucer to write a reformed order governing worship in the city: (1543) *Von Gottes gnaden unser Hermans Ertzbishoffs zu Coln unnd Churfürsten &c. einfaltigs bedencken, warauff ein Christliche … Reformation und Lehr brauch der Heyligen Sacramenten und Ceremonien, Seelsorge, und anderem Kirchendienst verbesserung … auzurichen seye.* Bonn: Laurentius von der Mullen. Thanks are due to Michael Springer for this reference.

8   'You are greeted in particular by … the Provincial of the Carmelites, Philip Bacchalaureus, … and Georg', Braunsberger (ed.), *Beati Petri Canisii*, vol. 1, p. 126. Eder's surname is never given, but Braunsberger is happy to identify 'Georgius' as such. In view of the small size of the Cologne group of Jesuits and their adherents, plus all the other evidence pointing to a close connection between Eder and Canisius formed in these years, it does seem reasonable to concur that it is Eder to whom Canisius is referring in these letters. In another letter to Faber dated 12 August 1545, Canisius again includes 'Georgius' in his list of greetings from Cologne. Ibid., pp. 158–63.

9   Ibid., pp. 250–52.

10   Ibid., pp. 281–6.

Eder himself later publicly recalled the value of this early association with the Jesuits at Cologne. Canisius was, according to Eder, one of a number who had helped support him financially through almost seven years of study.[11] It is certainly true that Canisius was from an affluent background: his father had been a wealthy Dutch Burgomaster. His influence on Eder evidently went further than bolstering his young friend's finances. Eder's first degree at Cologne was taken in the faculty of philosophy; he then received a master's degree from the faculty of arts, and it was also at Cologne that Eder began to study for his doctorate in law, awarded in 1551 after his move south to Vienna. In these years at Cologne he did, however, sit under the informal tutelage of Canisius in theological studies, the source of the jurist's later erudition on such questions.[12] There is, furthermore, an unquantifiable aspect to Canisius' influence on Eder in this period. Eder would have not only heard Canisius preach sermons famous amongst contemporaries for their high quality, but would have seen him evolve through the various offices of the Church, from disciple to Jesuit to a fully ordained priest.[13] It is entirely credible that the example of living devotion was not lost on the young Bavarian.

It may even be the case that Eder's move to Vienna in 1550 was in order to follow the fledgling Jesuit community recently founded there. Eder was only employed by the court after his arrival in Vienna. It is just as feasible that he went to Vienna at least in part with the intention of aiding the order there, as that he went explicitly hoping for court employment.[14] Jesuits had been represented in Vienna since the arrival of the Spaniard Nicolaus Bobadilla there in 1542, and under Claude Le Jay the city became the setting for one of the first Jesuit colleges in the empire, founded in 1551. These were, however, difficult years for the order in Vienna. By 1552 the city had 25 Jesuits active within its walls, but most of these spoke no or severely limited German.[15] The establishment of the college was in itself the first episode in what would be a long-running feud between the order and Vienna University, long struggling to maintain steady matriculation

---

[11]   'In order to show my gratitude I most willingly confess and acknowledge that for up to almost seven years I was brought up by alms provided by ... Doctor Peter Canisius', Eder, Georg (1559), *Catalogus Rectorum*, p. 10.

[12]   Wiedemann, Theodor (1880), *Geschichte der Reformation und Gegenreformation im Lande unter der Enns*, Prague: Tempsky, vol. 2, p. 144.

[13]   Canisius preached his first sermon in Cologne in September 1544, and was ordained in 1546, both events at which Eder may well have been present. According to Brodrick, Canisius' oratorical skills were such that when he participated in any public disputation, all the professors of the arts and philosophy faculties at Cologne University also used to attend. Brodrick, *Saint Peter Canisius*, p. 63.

[14]   It is also possible, however, that Eder went knowing he might find a patron there, as he evidently did: see pp. 42–4. The need for an influential patron appears to have marked much of Georg Eder's career.

[15]   Duhr, *Geschichte der Jesuiten in den Ländern deutscher Zunge*, vol. 1, p. 275.

rates.[16] Even finding living and teaching accommodation was a trial: in 1551 the Viennese Jesuits moved into a disused wing of the dilapidated monastery of St Dominic. Despite the presence of only a few remaining friars, the Dominicans resented the Jesuits' presence and the Archduke Ferdinand himself had to intervene and guarantee their rent.[17] Within three years the Viennese Jesuits had to move both accommodation and college again, this time to an almost empty Carmelite monastery near the city centre. Yet again, their hold here was insecure: in December 1558 the Carmelites tried to reclaim their property, but were again stopped from doing so by Ferdinand.[18]

Surviving records reveal nothing specific of Eder's assistance to the floundering order in these early years in Vienna. That he was their close associate and valued supporter may however be inferred from a number of sources. Vienna was, for one thing, the home of Eder's old friend Canisius between 1552 and 1556.[19] In these years Canisius greatly boosted the ailing branch in Vienna. Immediately on his arrival he began to preach his famous sermons in a language and a style that the Viennese could comprehend.[20] He performed many works of mercy, including visits to those in prison and the sick, while the outbreak of plague in the city just six months after Canisius' arrival would only have enhanced his and his order's local reputation for pious charity.

It is unthinkable that Eder would not have been involved at least in part with his mentor Canisius' ministry in Vienna. The two definitely

---

[16]   It would be many years before Jesuits or those educated by Jesuits could receive degrees from Vienna University. The Jesuits also opened a school for younger pupils in May 1554: before long it boasted 120 pupils, and by 1558 had over 500 enrolled. Bittner, Ludwig (1936), *Inventare des Wiener Haus-, Hof- und Staatsarchivs*, vol. 5, *Gesamtinventar des Wiener Haus-, Hof- und Staatsarchivs*, vol. 4, Vienna: Verlag A. Holzhausens Nachfolger, p. 518; Spielman, John P. (1993), *The City and the Crown. Vienna and the Imperial Court 1600–1740*, West Lafeyette, IN: Purdue University Press, p. 24.

[17]   Ferdinand gave the Society an endowment of 1200 florins per year. Brodrick, *Saint Peter Canisius*, p. 199.

[18]   The patronage of Ferdinand I was largely responsible for keeping the Viennese branch of the order afloat in its early years. It was also he who financially backed the Jesuit college's new printing press, set up 'Am Hof' in 1559, with an annual sum of 300 Talern as well as the grant of an imperial printing privilege. On this press see Grolig, Moritz (1909), 'Die Buchdruckerei des Jesuitenkollegiums in Wien (1559–1565)', *Mitteilungen des Österreichischen Vereins für Bibliothekswesen*, 13, 105–20, 108.

[19]   In 1556 Canisius was made first superior of the German province of the Society of Jesus, with new responsibilities that saw him travel extensively throughout the German-speaking lands. He was thus no longer so heavily based at Vienna.

[20]   A particular problem in Vienna was that many of the Jesuits there were originally from Italy: the Viennese could neither understand them, nor warm to what they perceived as an overly dramatic style of oratory. Within a year of his arrival in Vienna Canisius became the regular preacher at the church of St Mary by the River, one of many parishes without a priest. He was also preacher to Archduke Ferdinand.

remained in contact at least until 12 October 1577, the date of the final surviving letter in which Eder refers to his connection with Canisius.[21] That Eder was involved to a considerable extent with Canisius' work in Vienna is suggested by the regard in which Eder appears to have been held by the Viennese Jesuits, not just throughout his life but even after his death. One such example lies in the fact that it was Eder's connection with the Jesuits that enabled his eldest son, Bernhard, to attend the German College in Rome. Eder himself could not have afforded the expense of sending his son to the college: one of the most constant refrains in his private correspondence is that his employers, the Habsburgs, have yet again fallen into serious arrears with payments of his salary.[22] Such was Eder's relationship with the Jesuits, however, on 28 October 1573 he felt able to broach the subject of his son's training with no less than Mercurian, general of the order itself.[23] That such confidence was justified is reflected in the fact that a slightly earlier letter, this time from the Jesuit Provincial in Vienna, Johann Magius, contained a glowing recommendation for Eder, father and son.[24] Their backing, plus some financial aid administered by Gregory XIII, meant that Bernhard stayed in Rome for 12 years between 1573 and 1585. A doctor of civil and canon law, like his father, on leaving Rome Bernhard was made canon of Breslau and Olmütz by Gregory XIII.[25] According to Eder, it was also to Olmütz that he sent one of his younger sons: predictably, it was to the Jesuits there that he entrusted the boy's care.[26]

---

[21]   Eder wrote to Duke Albrecht of Bavaria that he wished that Canisius could see a manuscript of the book of which he was then working, *Das guldene Flüß Christlicher Gemain Und Gesellschaft*, published 1579. Schrauf, Karl (ed.) (1904), *Der Reichshofrath Dr Georg Eder. Eine Briefsammlung. Als Beitrag zur Geschichte der Gegenreformation in Niederösterreich*, Vienna: Adolf Holzhausen, p. 123.

[22]   For example, on 28 August 1574, just a year after Bernhard left for Rome, Eder complained to Duke Albrecht of Bavaria that he had now gone for five years without notification of his salary or any other provision. Ibid., p. 88.

[23]   ARSI, Epistolae Germaniae 153, fols 293r–294r.

[24]   On 4 October 1573 Magius had described Eder senior to Mercurian as a spirited defender of Catholicism and enthusiastic supporter of their order who was already known to him, ibid., fols 235r–v.

[25]   Gall and Szaivert note that beside his name in the matriculation records of Vienna University, 'nunc canonicus Olomucensis et Wratislauiensis' has been added. Gall, Franz and Szaivert, Willy (eds) (1971), *Quellen zur Geschichte der Universität Wien. I Abteilung. Die Matrikel der Universität Wien*, vol. 3, 1518/II–1579/I and vol. 4 1579/II–1658/59, Vienna, Cologne, Graz: Publikationen des Instituts für Österreichische Geschichtsforschung, p. 258. Bernhard Eder died in 1619. For more on his career, see Steinhuber, Andreas (1895), *Geschichte des Collegium Germanicum Hungaricum in Rom*, vol. 1, Freiburg im Breisgau: Herder, pp. 304–305.

[26]   Eder to Duke Albrecht of Bavaria, 24 May 1577, Schrauf (ed.), *Der Reichshofrath Dr Georg Eder. Eine Briefsammlung*, p. 100.

The esteem in which Georg Eder was held by the Viennese Jesuits extended much further, however, than the writing of references for his son. On 1 October 1571, for instance, when Eder was made an honorary doctor of theology at Vienna University, his promotion was sponsored by a Jesuit, the Scottish-born Jacob Gordon.[27] Perhaps even more significant, however, is the way in which Eder was remembered after his death. News of Eder's demise and his faithfulness were noted in the Viennese Jesuits' Hauschronik for 19 May 1587.[28] His contribution to the order in Vienna was, furthermore, remembered long after this date. At a memorial held at Vienna University in 1648, by then itself under Jesuit control, Eder's role was still being commemorated in a very public fashion, in which he was named as a 'particular defender of the immaculate mother of God' alongside equally effective churchmen and his lifelong ally, Canisius.[29] In two separate Jesuit histories of Austria and of Vienna University, both composed a full two centuries after Eder's birth, he was still being noted for his services to the Society of Jesus.[30] Antonius Socher in particular credited Eder with the early success of the order not only in Vienna but in all Austria.[31]

How, then, did this deep relationship with the Society of Jesus impact on Eder's life in Vienna? It is easier to answer this by establishing firstly what it did not do. It did not mean that Eder actually joined the Jesuits, or indeed any order: he remained a lay person throughout his life. Eder's Jesuit connections did not prevent him from forming important connections with other Catholics outside the order. Nor did Eder's association with the Society of Jesus conflict with his position at the Habsburg court – at least not until the *Evangelische Inquisition* incident of 1573, to be discussed in Chapter 4.

---

[27]   UAW, Theol. Akten, Th4 (1567–1644), microfilm 075, fol. 11.

[28]   'On 19 May 1587 our noteworthy friend, the most illustrious Dr Eder, died. Eder had a share in all the good things of our society, and was a diligent bulwark and promoter of the Catholic faith', ÖNB, Cod. 8367, fol. 35r, cited in Wiedemann, *Geschichte der Reformation und Gegenreformation*, vol. 2, p. 145.

[29]   Mitterdorffer, R.P. Sebastiano (1724), *Conspectus historiae universitatis Viennensis ex actis veteribus que documentis erutae atque a primis illius initiis ad annum usque 1701 deductae. (etc.)*, vol. 2, Vienna: Schwendimann, p. 250.

[30]   Ibid., and Socher, Antonius, S.J. (1740), *Historia Provinciae Austriae Societatis Jesu Pars Prima*, Vienna: Kurtzböck.

[31]   'He fostered this province in its infancy in Vienna, as well as throughout all Austria, with his perpetual kindness', Socher, *Historia Provinciae Austriae Societatis Jesu*, pp. 125–6. See too Mitterdorffer *Conspectus Historiae Universitatis Viennensis*, vol. 2, p. 55 for similar comments on Eder: 'a man most highly esteemed by all good men ... because of his strengthening of the devotion and piety of the Church and because of his services to the Society of Jesus, which he furthered with every assistance and words of praise when it was growing in Vienna ...'.

In view of the nature of Eder's relationship with the likes of Canisius, it is at first sight hard to understand why Eder remained a layman. In part, this difficulty is a product of centuries of post-Tridentine Church teaching and historiography in which the role of the laity has been consistently distinguished from that of the clergy, and then minimised. Adriano Prosperi's 1988 essay on Carlo Borromeo makes this point well:

> It may be said summarily that the dominant preoccupation in the pre-Tridentine age had been that of reacting to a process of secularisation that tended to cancel the distinction between the clerics and layfolk; in the church of the succeeding period there is in some ways an inverse process, one of domination according to clerical models and values by an ecclesiastical body preoccupied with the defence specifically of its dignity and generally of its elevated social status.[32]

Po-Chia Hsia adds that this was particularly the case within the Jesuits: 'fundamental to the meaning of the Society of Jesus was the attempt to reassert sacerdotal authority and to re-establish the cosmic hierarchy wherein the clergy stood superior above the laity, interceding on their behalf with the Almighty'.[33]

The case of Georg Eder, however, appears to contradict such a movement. His position as a layman is in no doubt. Eder was a twice-married father to at least eight children. A tablet erected at Stephansdom by Eder to the memory of his first wife Katharina Reicher from Halle, indicates that he was widowed for the first time on 1 August 1559 and that by then he had also lost three sons.[34] Another stone erected by Eder at Stephansdom, this time in memory of his second wife, appears not to have survived the bombs of the Second World War. For details it is necessary to rely on the notes taken by Karl Schrauf at the end of the nineteenth century, who recorded that Eder's second wife was a Rosina Gerchinger of Augsburg.[35] Herself previously married to a 'Doctor Egydi Neubeckhens', by her death on 18 June 1573 she had mothered or step-mothered another five of Eder's children into adulthood. Evidence

---

[32]   Prosperi, Adriano (1988), 'Clerics and Laymen in the Work of Carlo Borromeo', in Headley, John M. and Tomaro, John B. (eds), *San Carlo Borromeo. Catholic Reform and Ecclesiastical Politics in the Second half of the Sixteenth Century*, London: Associated University Presses, pp. 112–38, p. 124.

[33]   Po-Chia Hsia, R. (1984), *Society and Religion in Münster, 1535–1618*, New Haven, CT: Yale University Press, p. 74.

[34]   This may still be seen today, on the portico of the north tower. It is unclear from which 'Halle' Reicher came.

[35]   UAW, Schrauf, Karl, Konvolut, Altes Biographisches Material-Eder, fol. 70r. This stone was apparently erected after Eder's own death, as according to Schrauf's notes the inscription ends with the date of his demise.

remains of four of these children: one daughter, Regina, and three sons, the aforementioned Bernhard, as well as Maximilian and Adam.[36]

As a husband and father, Eder could not have joined the Jesuits, even as a 'temporal coadjutor' or lay Jesuit, and a man with his views on Catholic reform would not have contemplated a life within the Church in any capacity with a family in tow.[37] It is possible that Eder's decision to marry rather than follow the lead of his friends at Cologne was made for practical reasons. It has already been established that Eder was reliant on the financial help of others to continue his studies at Cologne: later in life he commented that he had very little money.[38] This may indicate that at least one of Eder's marriages had been made for financial betterment. It is also possible that Eder remained a member of the laity for strategic reasons. Jesuits were not permitted to work in such offices as that of Reichshofrat, and it is not beyond belief that Eder was encouraged to serve as a layman in order to infiltrate such a post. Such courting of those in high position would be consistent with the emphasis laid by the Jesuits on gaining influence with the powerful as a means of furthering their own cause.

Such theories are however unnecessary in the light of a much more simple reason why Georg Eder remained a member of the laity. His case suggests that in his own day, lay status did not automatically imply inferior

---

36   In a letter to Duke Albrecht of Bavaria dated 28 August 1574, Eder commented that he had to consider the welfare of his five children: Schrauf (ed.), *Der Reichshofrath Dr Georg Eder. Eine Briefsammlung*, p. 87. On the significance of Regina Eder's marriage in 1581, see p. 101. Eder's three sons were all educated at Vienna University. On the boys' education, see Gall and Szaivert (eds), *Quellen zur Geschichte der Universität Wien* vol. 3, p. 158, for an entry concerning 'Maximilianus Eder filius rectoris Vienn(ensis) 1571 ...' and p. 258 on 'Bernhardus Eder filius rectoris Vienn(ensis) 1571 ...'. Page 168 of the same volume also refers to 'Adam Eder' having matriculated in 1575. It is not specifically stated that he is also Eder's son, but the date makes it reasonable to guess he may have been a younger brother of the other two. In addition, Eder was not a common surname in sixteenth-century Vienna. Only one other 'Eder' family is listed as living in Vienna when a Hofquartier survey was taken in 1566: that of a 'Hanns Eder, distiller', who lived at number 869 Annagasse. This information comes from Camesina Ritter v. San Vittore, Albert (ed.) (1881), *Urkundliche Beiträge zur Geschichte Wien's im XVI. Jahrhundert*, Vienna: Alfred Hölder, p. 35.

37   According to John O'Malley, 'temporal coadjutors' were fully-fledged members of the Society but did not go on to take sacred orders. In the sixteenth century they constituted approximately 25 per cent of the order's total membership. They also took a vow of chastity, a fact that would automatically exclude twice-married Eder: *The First Jesuits*, p. 60. Eder made his views on Catholic clerics with families known in his Bavarian correspondence. On 4 October 1578 he wrote to Duke Albrecht of Bavaria that he didn't believe that there remained more than two prelates in the whole land who had remained true to the faith, noting with particular displeasure that 'they almost all have wives ...'. Schrauf (ed.), *Der Reichshofrath Dr Georg Eder. Eine Briefsammlung*, p. 232.

38   Eder to Duke Albrecht of Bavaria in a letter dated 7 September 1577, Schrauf (ed.), *Der Reichshofrath Dr Georg Eder. Eine Briefsammlung*, p. 111.

service to the Church, but merely non-clerical service. This would have been no issue at all with regard to Eder's relationship with the Jesuits.[39] As John O'Malley's excellent study of the origins of the order reveals, their motto was 'the world is our house' and their rapid success at gaining converts, members and schools indicates their efficacy in 'the world'.[40] Within such a context, it is not surprising that Eder felt able to describe himself as a Jesuit in spirit if not in fact. In a particularly noteworthy letter of 5 May 1573, Eder wrote to Magius that he was writing as one Jesuit to another, 'in a strictly Jesuitical frame of mind'.[41] Furthermore, within the broader picture of Catholic reform, lay confraternities had a long and distinguished reputation throughout Catholic Europe, and it has also been noted by a historian of education that a possessor of a theology doctorate such as Eder would have been held in as high esteem as a bishop.[42]

Just as it needs to be established that Eder's service to the Church in Vienna was as a layman, no matter how strong his connections with the Jesuits, so too it must be noted that Eder was not exclusively linked to that one order. Even in Cologne, Eder had been influenced by members of other orders as well as by members of the secular clergy. Aside from

---

[39]   In this context, a quotation from Monsieur de Caradeuc de La Chatolais in the mid-eighteenth century *Compte rendu des constitutions des jésuites*, is particularly telling: 'There are still, following the Bull of Paul III, persons living in obedience to the general who enjoy exemptions, powers and rights which would seem to remove them from his authority, and of whom Pope Paul III declares that the general will conserve full and entire jurisdiction. Who are these people? Are they the anonymous Jesuits, living with their families, who do not wear a religious habit, but dress respectably, in conformity with the custom of the place where they live, and who are never loath, as the Constitutions provide, to profess poverty? Are they the invisible Jesuits who have been talked about for two centuries? ... They have male and female affiliates, whose existence is not in doubt'. Cited in Châtellier, Louis (1989), *The Europe of the Devout: The Catholic Reformation and the Formation of a New Society*, Cambridge: Cambridge University Press, pp. 190–91.

[40]   John O'Malley, *The First Jesuits*, Chapter 1.

[41]   ARSI, Epistolae Germaniae 153, fol. 56r–58v. The Jesuit historian Socher confirms that Eder used to 'profess himself a Jesuit no less than the Jesuits themselves' and openly described himself as a Jesuit in letters. Socher adds: 'I should certainly not hesitate to call Georg one of our number: he used to show himself as such openly more than once in his writings', Socher, *Historia Provinciae Austriae Societatis Jesu*, p. 359.

[42]   Frijhoff, Willem (1996), 'Graduation and Careers' in Ridder-Symoens, Hilde de (ed.), *A History of the University in Europe*, vol. 2, *Universities in Early Modern Europe*, Cambridge: Cambridge University Press, pp. 355–415, pp. 366–70. It is possible that Eder himself was a member of a confraternity, but no evidence of this survives. For an example of the workings of a confraternity in an urban environment, see Terpstra, Nicholas (1995), *Lay Confraternities and Civic Religion in Renaissance Bologna*, Cambridge: Cambridge University Press; also see John Patrick Donnelly (ed.), (1999), *Confraternities and Catholic Reform*, Kirksville, MO: Truman State University Press. In Châtellier's 1989 study, *The Europe of the Devout: The Catholic Reformation and the Formation of a New Society*, frequent mention is made of confraternities in Baroque Vienna.

the fact, noted above, that as a young man Eder seems to have at least flirted with the idea of joining the Carthusian order, he later paid tribute to various non-Jesuit Church patrons. Looking back on his days in Cologne, in 1568 Eder publicly recorded his gratitude to the likes of Tilman Siberg, a Dominican prior, and canons Andreas Bardwick and Matthias Aquensis.[43] The last two also number alongside Canisius as those who helped Eder financially during his studies at Cologne.[44]

In Vienna too it seems Eder benefited from the patronage of non-Jesuits. In 1568 again, Eder used the preface of one of his theological works to acknowledge the help of Bishop Urban of Gurk and Matthias Wertwein who had acted as Bishop of Vienna between 1552 and 1553.[45] Such involvement with Catholics from all branches of the Church appears to have remained a feature of Eder's life throughout his time in Vienna. Theodor Wiedemann records the story of the gift Eder received from the Archbishop of Salzburg on the occasion of his second marriage in 1559.[46] Later work by Dirk Jacob Jansen also places Eder in the social company of Dominicans and the Bishop of Györ at some point before 1568.[47]

---

[43]   Eder, Georg (1568), *Partitiones, Catechismi, Catholici*, Cologne: Gervinus Calenius and Johanne Quentel, fol. A*4v.

[44]   See p. 62.

[45]   Eder, Georg (1568), *Oeconomia Bibliorum,* Cologne: Gervinus Calenius and Johanne Quentel, fol. *c1v. On Wertwein see Krexner, Martin and Loidl, Franz (1983), *Wiens Bischöfe und Erzbischöfe*, Vienna, pp. 36–7.

[46]   Wiedemann, Theodor (1886), *Geschichte der Reformation und Gegenreformation im Lande unter der Enns*, Prague: Tempsky, vol. 5, p. 509. On 20 September 1559 Archbishop Michael of Salzburg asked the then Passau Offizial Christoph Hillinger to send Eder the sum of ten Doppeldukaten as a wedding gift. Such a gesture may well have been mere protocol as Eder was the rector of Vienna University. It does however still point to Eder's connections and involvement with the secular clergy.

[47]   In a letter of 2 February 1581 Strada wrote to Jacopo Dani, secretary of the Grand Duke of Tuscany, recalling entertainment for Riccardo Riccardi, a young Florentine gentleman Dani had recommended. In attendance at the banquet were Georg Draskovich, Bishop of Györ, two Dominican friars, court preacher Citardus and a 'Doctor ... a gentleman that had very learned conversation with men who spoke Italian and were very knowledgeable in the arts and sciences'. Jansen suggests this unnamed gentleman was probably Eder. 'Citardus' was Ferdinand I's Dominican court preacher, Matthias Esche of Sittard. This letter must, however, have been written retrospectively and refers to an occasion that evidently took place before the end of 1568. It could not have happened after that date, as one of the guests, Citardus, died in the autumn of that year. Jansen, Dirk Jacob (1992), 'The Instruments of Patronage. Jacopo Strada at the Court of Maximilian II: A Case-Study', in Edelmayer, Friedrich and Kohler, Alfred (eds), *Kaiser Maximilian II. Kultur und Politik im 16. Jahrhundert*, Wiener Beiträge zur Geschichte der Neuzeit, vol. 17, Vienna: Verlag für Geschichte und Politik, pp. 82–202, pp. 200–201. For more on this, see too Louthan, Howard (1997), *The Quest For Compromise: Peacemakers in Counter–Reformation Vienna*, Cambridge: Cambridge University Press, p. 125.

Yet it was another figure in Vienna, Martin Eisengrein, with whom Eder had the closest non-Jesuit association.[48] Eisengrein (1535–78) was originally from a wealthy Lutheran family from Stuttgart, and was himself still a Protestant when he arrived in 1553 to continue his studies in the arts and law faculties of Vienna University. Sometime in 1558 or 1559 Eisengrein was, however, converted to Catholicism and immediately dropped his studies to take up theology. Ordained in 1560, Eisengrein quickly became cathedral preacher in Vienna's Stephansdom where he remained for two years. It was Eder and the Viennese Jesuits who Eisengrein credited with this rapid conversion, and although Eisengrein himself spent most of the remaining 16 years of his life based at Ingolstadt, he and Eder remained in regular contact.[49] Particularly poignant is Eder's reaction to news of his friend's death. In a letter to Duke Albrecht of Bavaria dated 17 May 1578, Eder wrote in a terse postscript: 'It is said that Eisengrein is dead; my heart is heavy if that is so'.[50]

Despite the extent of Jesuit influence on his life, Georg Eder therefore showed himself willing to work with all Catholics to achieve religious change. There may well have been potential for inter-order disputes: the hostility of the Carmelites and Dominicans to the Jesuits' use of their property in Vienna is a case in point, as was Eder's clash with the Dominicans over the fate of his student, Andronicus.[51] Nor were relations between the secular and the regular clergy always good. Yet Eder's case does demonstrate the reality of the struggle for Catholic survival and reform in the latter half of the sixteenth century: it did not necessarily operate on a clear-cut, orderly basis but was rather the result of local contacts and personal ties.

It is also the case that Eder suffered on occasion for his religious stance. In a letter of 1 April 1573 sent to the Jesuit Provincial, Magius, Eder complained of his image at court: 'I run about, hither and thither, to Trautson, to the Spanish legate, to others, that we may seek remedies ... on account of which I seem a fool at court.' He later added that he knew

---

[48]   There has been a significant body of writing produced on Eisengrein. See in particular Soergel, Philip (1993), *Wondrous In His Saints: Counter-Reformation Propaganda in Bavaria*, Berkeley, CA: University of California Press, and the much older Pfleger, Luzian (1908), 'Martin Eisengrein (1535–1578). Ein Lebensbild aus der Zeit der katholischen Restauration in Bayern' in Pastor, Ludwig (ed.), *Erläuterungen und Ergänzungen zu Janssens Geschichte des deutschen Volkes*, vol. 6, Freiburg im Breisgau.

[49]   Pfleger, 'Martin Eisengrein', pp. 9–10. Eisengrein spent part of his time in Vienna lodging at the home of Jacob Jonas, the Catholic Vizekanzler who had been instrumental in advancing Eder's career. It may well be that he too influenced Eisengrein to bring about his conversion. Eight letters in which Eder refers to his friendship with Eisengrein are included in the collection, Schrauf (ed.), *Der Reichshofrath Dr Georg Eder. Eine Briefsammlung*.

[50]   Ibid., p. 169. Eisengrein had died on 4 May.

[51]   On Eder's intervention as university rector over the case of Andronicus, see p. 49.

that there were Catholic bishops and even a cardinal who regarded him as 'superstitious'.[52] The sources also suggest that Eder actually masked his true attitude to the Jesuits while in his role as university rector. In a letter of 2 January 1560 from the rector of the Jesuit college in Vienna, Joannes de Victoria, to Peter Canisius, Victoria comments: 'We had clearly understood that Eder had a far different attitude to the Society or the college of Vienna than he indicated by certain exterior signs'.[53]

Exactly what these signs were is not clear, but it is true that Eder and like-minded members of Vienna University could not always enact the anti-heresy legislation they would have most desired. Shortly after his arrival in Vienna, Canisius headed a commission to reform the university and student lodgings, with the ultimate intention of eradicating false doctrine therein. According to two 1569 reports by the Papal nuncio, Biglia, Eder was also concerned by the promotion of Lutherans within Vienna University.[54] This concern, however, put men such as Eder in the minority and counted for little against the determination, particularly of Maximilian II, to maintain confessional harmony. As noted in Chapter 1, in 1564 Maximilian passed a law stating that doctoral candidates at Vienna University had only to swear that they were members of the Christian Church, as opposed to the Roman Catholic Church.[55] The emperor reinforced this four years later with a decree stating that affiliation to the Confession of Augsburg would be no barrier to promotion within the university.[56]

As has also been established, however, Maximilian II was equally keen to promote Catholic reform where possible, and as a result Eder was not only able to pursue many of his own efforts to revive the Church, but also to find officially sanctioned means of doing so.[57] On occasion, perhaps

---

[52]   Extracts from this letter are printed in Socher, *Historia Provinciae Austriae Societatis Jesu*, pp. 360–61. 'Trautson' refers to Hans Trautson, a member of the Geheimer Rat as Obersthofmeister and Obersthofmarschall under both Ferdinand I and Maximilian II.

[53]   Braunsberger, Otto (ed.) (1898), *Beati Petri Canisii, Societatis Iesu, Epistulae et Acta*, vol. 2, Freiburg im Briesgau: Herder, pp. 573–4.

[54]   Report number 149, dated 28 July 1569, and report dated 9 December 1569: Dengel, Ignaz Philipp (ed.) (1939), *Nuntiaturberichte aus Deutschland 1560–1572*, part 2, vol. 6, Vienna: Adolf Holzhausen, p. 327. The paraphrase is Dengel's.

[55]   See p. 29. This was tested by Sigismund Eisler who, despite his refusal to swear allegiance to the Roman Catholic church, nonetheless gained a doctorate, became a professor, rose to the rank of Dekan of the law faculty and in 1576 was elected rector. See Mühlberger, Kurt (1992), 'Bildung und Wissenschaft. Kaiser Maximilian II. und die Universität Wien', in Edelmayer, Friedrich and Kohler, Alfred (eds), *Kaiser Maximilian II. Kultur und Politik im 16. Jahrhundert*, Wiener Beiträge zur Geschichte der Neuzeit, vol. 17, Vienna: Verlag für Geschichte und Politik, pp. 203–31, p. 218.

[56]   This decree was dated 4 February 1568.

[57]   The Jesuits' unwillingness to compromise may have run counter to his confessional politics, but Maximilian II did allow his sons Rudolf and Ernst to be educated by Jesuits in Spain.

out of respect for his father's fondness for the new order, Maximilian permitted the findings of the Klosterrat to work in the Jesuits' particular favour. In July 1571, for instance, a Klosterrat evaluation noted that the Klarissenkloster of St Anna remained a wealthy house but was inhabited by only one nun. The Klosterrat subsequently advised the emperor to incorporate the Klarissenkloster into that of St James, but the Jesuit Provincial Magius seized the chance to ask the emperor rather to use the Klarissenkloster to enlarge the material income of the Jesuit college. This Maximilian did, albeit slowly.[58] It was also under the authority of Maximilian II that the Carmelite property in which the Jesuits had been based since 1554 was formally handed over to the Society of Jesus. On 15 October 1568 the Reichskanzlei entrusted the administration of the exchange to Jakob Öchsel and to Georg Eder himself, another suggestion of Eder's known association with the Jesuits.[59]

Such generosity to the Catholic Church in a political climate of confessional peace-keeping bears witness to what must have been painfully apparent to Eder and emperor alike: that the religious state of Lower Austria and of Vienna was in a perilous situation and desperately in need of change. At the heart of the problem was the sheer lack of clergy, regular and secular, in quantity and in quality. A survey of 1568 by the Hofkammer listed the largest religious house in Vienna as consisting of only 12 Observant Franciscan monks, while the largest female house was the nine-strong house of St James.[60] The supply of secular priests for Vienna was to a large extent dependent on the theology faculty of the university, and this had also been long in decline: between 1529 and 1539, the faculty had only two professors, and had none at all for a short period after 1549. According to the Bishop of Laibach, writing in the late 1540s, not a single priest had been ordained in Vienna in two decades.[61] Those who did minister in Vienna were also far from acceptable. In the mid-sixteenth century, one observer wrote that 'the seven deadly sins have become as the daily bread of our clergy here', while the convert from Protestantism, Friedrich Staphylus, reported to the then-Emperor Ferdinand that there were more sects than there were parishes, and that hardly one priest in a hundred denied himself a concubine.[62]

---

[58]   Bittner, *Inventare des Wiener Haus-, Hof- und Staatsarchivs Bd. V*, vol. 4, pp. 519–21.

[59]   As it turned out, Eder and Öchsel had to travel to Pressburg on the important dates of the transfer and substitutes had to be found for them. Ibid., p. 526. For further instances of Maximilian II's gestures of support to the Jesuits in Vienna, see Sutter Fichtner, Paula (2001), *Emperor Maximilian II*, New Haven, CT: Yale University Press, p. 192.

[60]   Geyer, Roderick (1956), 'Dr Johann Caspar Neubeck, Bischof von Wien, 1574–1594', unpublished Doktorarbeit, University of Vienna, p. 42.

[61]   Brodrick, *Saint Peter Canisius*, p. 170.

[62]   Ibid., p. 170. The translation is by Brodrick.

By the latter half of the sixteenth century, the effects of this on the next generation were clear to be seen. In a letter of 10 June 1568 the Papal nuncio Biglia reported the statistics of participation in communion for Easter of that year, for both within and without the city walls of Vienna. Biglia also divided his list according to those who took communion *sub una* and *sub utraque*. The number of those who participated according to Catholic rites within the city walls was only 5704 with, tellingly, the vast majority of these receiving communion from the Jesuits.[63] To put this in perspective, the total population of the 'inner' part of Vienna by the middle of the sixteenth century was between 25 000 and 30 000. The statistics are bleaker still for the nature of participation beyond the city walls. Here the impact of the Auslaufen to Lutheran services was much in evidence: 4618 took communion in both kinds outside the city walls. [64]

To compound such problems a further difficulty was that of finding a candidate, suitable or otherwise, willing to take the role of Bishop of Vienna. The bishopric of Vienna was a relatively recent creation, and hardly an alluring one. Aside from the spiritual torpor of clergy and laity, plus the minefield of imperial politics, the bishopric itself was not an impressive gain. Only created in 1469, it was small and poorly endowed, particularly in comparison to that of the neighbouring Bishop of Passau. As a result, the post had no incumbent at all between 1555 and 1558, and between 1568 and 1574, while between 1563 and 1568 Urban Sagstetter acted only as administrator.[65]

Eder therefore had great motivation to take action, and this he did within the parameters outlined above. He acted as a layman, he co-operated with all members of the Catholic community, and he was able to work within the constraints of imperial service, in order to serve his faith. In all of this Eder remained overwhelmingly influenced by the Jesuit 'way of proceeding', revealed both explicitly in his words and implicitly in his actions.[66]

---

[63]   3600 parishioners are recorded as having received communion sub una from the Jesuits at Easter 1568. The highest figure after this is 1022 for Stephansdom; 2369 took communion in both kinds within the city walls, a smaller number but still a significant minority. Biglia to Alessandrino, Dengel (ed.), *Nuntiaturberichte aus Deutschland 1560–1572* part 2, vol. 6, p. 153. On Vienna's population, see Spielmann, *The City and the Crown*, p. 30.

[64]   By contrast, only 1674 took communion according to the Roman rite. Biglia to Alessandrino, Dengel (ed.), *Nuntiaturberichte aus Deutschland 1560–1572* part 2, vol. 6, p. 153.

[65]   Anton Brus was Bishop of Vienna between 1558 and February 1563. The bishopric was then administered by Urban Sagstetter until June 1568, but he was not present in the early years. The post remained wholly unfilled until the appointment of Johann Neuböck in 1574. For more on this situation, see Krexner and Loidl, *Wiens Bischöfe und Erzbischöfe*, pp. 40–45.

[66]   O'Malley, *The First Jesuits*, p. 11. This phrase was commonly used in Jesuit writing to describe their ministry.

Evidence for Eder's service to the Church during his first decade in Vienna, in the 1550s, is very limited. What does survive, however, suggests that Eder was deeply influenced by the work of his friend Canisius for the Church in Vienna. It has already been noted that during the period of his residence in Vienna, between 1552 and 1556, Peter Canisius performed a highly active ministry, particularly of preaching; as a result, he was headhunted on several occasions to take on the unenvied post of Bishop of Vienna. Canisius was unwilling to do so, possibly out of devotion to his own order but also a fear that the additional duties would distract him from the task of winning souls. He had therefore to turn down repeated requests from the Emperor Ferdinand himself to accept the Vienna bishopric, and was even compelled by Pope Julius III to at least act as its administrator for a year between 1554 and 1555.[67]

The impact of his example was, however, not lost on his younger friend Eder. In 1574 Eder made a telling claim to the Duke of Bavaria about the nature of his past service to the Church in Vienna. He asserted that Martin Eisengrein and others would report that in the time the Vienna bishopric was vacant, he did so much that it was as if a bishop were there.[68] The editor of this letter, Karl Schrauf, suggests that this vacancy refers to a period between 5 June 1561 and 1563, from the time of Anton Brus's call to be Archbishop of Prague, to the beginning of the administration of Urban Sagstetter.[69] This could be correct, though Eisengrein could only have borne witness to the first half of this activity as he left Vienna for Ingolstadt in 1562. Eisengrein was, however, in Vienna throughout the much more substantial years of vacancy between 1555 and 1558, and it may well have been the case that during this earlier period Eder assisted Canisius in his work, or at least saw the necessary skills in action to perform effectively in the role of bishop. Whatever the case, by the 1560s and 1570s Georg Eder had evidently gained, most likely from Canisius, a strong grasp of the qualities needed to make a competent bishop: a concern for the imposition of clerical discipline and morality, the encouragement of high-quality preaching, and the proper education of the faithful. Like the Jesuits, Eder pressed this agenda as a means of bolstering the existing local ecclesiastical structure without

---

[67]   Matthias Wertwein died in 1553 after just one year in office. The post remained vacant until 3 November 1554 when Canisius was compelled to act as administrator.

[68]   Eder to Duke Albrecht of Bavaria, 28 August 1574, Schrauf (ed.), *Der Reichshofrath Dr Georg Eder. Eine Briefsammlung*, p. 89. By 1574, Martin Eisengrein was a highly respected Ingolstadt theologian, and would have been well known to the recipient of Eder's letter.

[69]   Ibid., p. 89.

actually joining it himself.[70] Also like the Jesuits, Eder worked toward such goals with great energy.

One way in which Eder acted as a 'surrogate bishop' in the 1560s and early 1570s was through his efforts to impose clerical discipline and secure competent, theologically correct preachers for vacant pulpits. This Eder was able to do because of, rather than in spite of, his posts at the imperial court. With his known concern for Catholic reform, Eder was a natural choice to participate in some of the Klosterrat activities.[71] Details of three cases survive, the first of which reveals Eder's role in the selection of a suitable preacher for the vacant position at Vienna's church of St Michael. On Whit Monday, 1572, Eder was among those who heard a sermon preached at St Michael's by one Georg Puelacher. The experience was evidently not a good one: with Eder's supervision the post was filled on 5 August not by Puelacher but by a Martin Radwiger, 'because his sermon was pleasing'.[72]

Eder's service to the Church in Vienna was further exercised through his participation in Klosterrat activities which curtailed the immoral lifestyles enjoyed in certain monasteries under investigation. Evidence survives of Eder's and fellow-Catholic Reichshofrat Johann Hegenmüller's involvement in an assessment of the Chorherrenstifte St Dorothea. On 14 November 1571 the two men reported that the life of the inhabitants was 'very irritating' and 'thoughtless'.[73] This seems tame, however, in comparison with Eder's investigation of the convent of St James, mentioned above. In a report dated June 1573, Eder, city counsellor Caspar von Lindegg zu Lisana,

---

[70]   This function of the Society of Jesus is noted by John O'Malley in his 1993 essay: O'Malley, John W. (1993), 'Was Ignatius Loyola a Church Reformer? How to look at Early Modern Catholicism', in O'Malley, J.W. (ed.), *Religious Culture in the Sixteenth Century*, Aldershot: Variorum XII, pp. 177–93. For the Jesuits' role in supporting local Catholic worship in a different context see Gentilcore, David (1994), 'Adapt Yourselves to the People's Capabilities: Missionary Strategies, Methods and Impact in the kingdom of Naples, 1600–1800', *JEH*, 45, 269–96.

[71]   I am hesitant to describe Eder as a 'member' of the Klosterrat, though it is arguable that by virtue of his various court offices, 'membership' would not necessarily be a prerequisite to participation in Klosterrat proceedings. It is true that the only records of Eder's input into the finding of preachers for vacant parishes are dated after 1568, when the Klosterrat was first established. It is also true that the cases in which Eder was apparently involved deal with exactly the issues of discipline and morality with which the Klosterrat was most concerned. In no source, however, is it ever explicitly stated that Eder worked as part of the monastery commission, and later in life he expressed displeasure at its operation: see p. 124. Most of all, however, to describe Eder as a member of such a body is to de-emphasise the driving force behind his work for reform, which was his connection with the Society of Jesus. Any participation by Eder in Klosterrat operations was supplementary to his other efforts toward bringing Catholic reform.

[72]   Wiedemann, *Geschichte der Reformation und Gegenreformation im Lande unter der Enns*, vol. 2, p. 132.

[73]   Ibid., p. 127.

and the Bishop of Gurk's representative, Kaspar Christiani, outlined their findings. Amongst a litany of other moral and disciplinary outrages, it was found that the canon Matthias Spasmus had fathered two children with one of the nuns. Eder and his colleagues also found that the convent housed the equivalent of 50 buckets of wine, more than necessary for any number of eucharists, while one of the nuns, Susanna von Püchheim, was memorably described by Eder himself as a 'chatterbeak' who loved nothing better than to travel into the city and gossip.[74] This particular investigation ended with the punishment of many in the convent: the two illegitimate children were removed from the premises, the abbess was imprisoned in a convent far from Vienna, and the head of the convent of St Laurence was placed in administrative charge of the shamed convent of St James.[75]

Eder did not restrict his service to the Church to the supervision of the standards and teaching of others, however. There survives one known case of his own preaching, though such is the nature of the sermon as evidence that Eder may well have preached more than survives in print. As with his work for the Klosterrat, Eder preached his sermon as a layman and did so in his official capacity, this time as university rector, under the guise of an oration at a doctoral promotion. Published two years after its delivery in 1570 under the title *Oratio Pro fide catholica*, the subject of Eder's speech had been the truth of the Catholic Church and the necessity of a decisive renunciation of heresy.[76]

It was however towards the medium of print that Eder appears to have most heavily directed his concern for the correct education of the Catholic faithful. In each of the three consecutive years between 1568 and 1570, Eder published at least one new volume aimed at the instillation of orthodox Catholic doctrine into the minds and souls of his readers. The year 1568 saw the publication of his first two such works, the *Oeconomia Bibliorum* and the *Partitiones, Catechismi, Catholici*. Although many surviving copies appear to have been bound together, these were individual books with different audiences in mind.[77] The first edition of the physically heftier *Oeconomia Bibliorum* contained 714

---

[74]   Ibid., p. 130.

[75]   For more on sixteenth-century visitations in Vienna, see Vocelka, Karl (2003), 'Kirchengeschichte', in Vocelka, K. and Traninger, A. (eds), *Wien. Geschichte einer Stadt*, vol. 2, *Die frühneuzeitliche Residenz (16. bis 18. Jahrhundert)*, Vienna, Cologne, Weimar: Böhlau, pp. 311–64, especially pp. 319–21.

[76]   The preface to the reader by Martin Winclerus establishes the theme of heresy arousing Catholics to reveal the truth afresh: '... heretics are of benefit to us, not by teaching the truth, which they do not know, but by rousing Catholics to seek and reveal the truth', Eder, Georg (1570), *Ad Rubricam Codicis De Summa Trinitate*, Bautzen: Johannis Vuolrab, fol. A3r.

[77]   See pp. 11–13.

folio pages of what was essentially a book-by-book introduction to the Bible for Catholic priests. Presented in the form of charts and tables rather than undiluted Latin prose, it works methodically through the history, content and theology of each book of the Bible, with references from a wide range of sources: the Church Fathers, the councils, and Eder's own contemporaries.

The 119-page *Partitiones* was also in folio format but aimed at a younger readership. Dedicated to the University of Cologne, the work contained extracts from the key passages of the two-year-old *Catechismus ex Decreto Concilii Tridentini ad parochos* that had been produced as a result of the Council of Trent. The original version had been addressed specifically to parish priests who were then to provide oral explanation of the doctrine therein to their parishioners; Eder's re-working was intended primarily for use within schools. Like the Tridentine work on which it was based, Eder's *Partitiones* was divided into four pieces of condensed theology: the Creed, the Sacraments, the Decalogue, and the Lord's Prayer. Unlike the original, but like Eder's *Oeconomia Bibliorum*, the *Partitiones* utilised diagrams and charts to provide a more educator-friendly presentation of the complex doctrines to be communicated.[78]

Eder's one publication from 1569, the *Catechismus Catholicus* was, like the *Partitiones* of the previous year, a simplified version of the Tridentine catechism aimed at the education of younger Catholics.[79] Appropriately dedicated to Duke Ernst of Bavaria, made Bishop of Freising five years earlier at the tender age of eleven, the *Catechismus Catholicus* followed exactly the same pattern of the *Partitiones*, from the employment of charts and tables to communicate complex ideas, to the fourfold structure of the Creed, Sacraments, Decalogue and Lord's Prayer. This was, however, a physically smaller work than the two of the previous year: it consisted of 463 pages but was bound as an octavo.

The year 1570 saw the publication of one further pedagogical work composed by Eder: the *Compendium Catechismi Catholici*. Like the *Partitiones* of 1568 in structure and aim, and like the *Catechismus Catholicus* of 1569 in its dedication and physical dimensions, there were two important additions to the version of 1570.[80] A 143-page section entitled *Confessio Catholica Concilii Tridentini* was appended at the back, comprising a list of key doctrines of the Catholic Church, with a short

---

[78] Eder's employment of such charts was not new: Martin Luther's 'Shorter Catechism' had appeared in a similar format in 1528, and the style had medieval precedents.

[79] Eder, Georg (1569), *Catechismus Catholicus*, Cologne: Gervinus Calenius and Johanne Quentel.

[80] Eder, Georg (1570), *Compendium Catechismi Catholici*, Cologne: Gervinus Calenius and Johanne Quentel.

explanation of each.[81] The main body of the *Compendium* itself bore the greater departure: for the first time, a work of Eder's was complete with numerous illustrations designed to enhance the reader's comprehension of the text. Some of these are woodcuts that simply depict a scene relevant to that section of the work. In the first part, for example, on the Creed, a woodcut of the crucifixion scene complements the line: 'Suffered under Pontius Pilate'.[82] Others are designed to enhance understanding of more abstract notions: at the outset of the section of the sacraments is a picture of Christ on the cross surrounded by images of each of the sacraments in practice.[83]

The physical and intellectual processes behind the production of such works again reflect those features of Eder's service to the Church already identified in this chapter. The composition of such substantial works interfered neither politically nor physically with Eder's court career. His religious writings were all specifically aimed at strengthening the Catholic Church, a goal in harmony with the religious policies of Maximilian II: indeed, the *Oeconomia Bibliorum* of 1568 was dedicated to the pope and the emperor.

Eder's writing of Catholic pedagogical works also reflects the continued influence of the Society of Jesus. Education was a key part of the Jesuits' ministry, from the sermons they preached on the streets, to the colleges they established in the cities to which they were sent.[84] Peter Canisius was a particular proponent of the catechism as pedagogical tool: the significance of his trilogy of Catholic catechisms from the 1550s has already been noted.[85] Of Canisius, John O'Malley has added that 'to a degree unusual for Jesuits in other parts of the world, he laboured more directly for the implementation of the Tridentine decrees, beginning in 1565 with his appointment by the pope as his special envoy to carry them to the German bishops.'[86] In view of the extent of Canisius' influence over Eder, it seems no coincidence that the younger man focused his own writing on the distillation of the Tridentine decrees into catechetical form, thereby following Canisius in both style and content of pedagogical work.

---

[81]   *Confessio Catholica Concilii Tridentini, de praecipuis christianae religionis Articulos, hoc potissimum seculo controversis.*

[82]   Eder, *Compendium Catechismi Catholici*, fol. C4r.

[83]   Ibid., fol. G2v.

[84]   John O'Malley notes that the Formula of the Society of Jesus listed the 'instruction of young and uneducated persons in Christianity' as a specific ministry of the Society. He adds that all Jesuit documents from the order's early period clearly refer to catechism, not the schools for which the Jesuits became better known. O'Malley, *The First Jesuits*, p. 116.

[85]   See p. 60, note 5.

[86]   O'Malley, *The First Jesuits*, p. 276.

On this subject, 1567 had seen a curious incident which points simultaneously to Eder's closeness to the Jesuits, in spirit and in fact, and a stunning lack of communication which had led to a considerable amount of wasted effort on the part of layman and order. On 23 July 1567 Peter Hoffaeus, rector of the Jesuit college in Munich, wrote to the general of the order, reporting that Eder's friend, Martin Eisengrein, had told him that in Vienna, 'the imperial counsellor Doctor Eder, a great friend of the Society', was currently working on a translation of the Tridentine catechism from Latin into German.[87] Unfortunately, Hoffaeus himself had been doing exactly the same, and he asked his superior for advice on how best to proceed. The then-general Francis Borgia replied on 23 September relaying the news that the pope wished the translation by Hoffaeus to proceed. Hoffaeus' German translation of the Tridentine catechism was subsequently published at Dillingen in the following year. To add to the confusion, however, in the dedication to what was apparently his second choice of project – the diagrammatic version of the Latin catechism that was the *Partitiones Catechismi Catholici...ad parochos* – Eder noted that it was his 'teacher in theology and particular patron, Peter Canisius' who had beaten him to the original task.[88]

The reason for the pope's choice of the Jesuit Hoffaeus' translation as opposed to that of Eder may well lie in Eder's continued status as a layman. Translations of the Tridentine catechism to languages other than Latin or Italian were entrusted primarily to members of the Society of Jesus, no doubt to ensure the accuracy of such important teaching. Eder's status therefore explains why his pedagogical writings remained firmly rooted in Latin versions of the catechism of the Council of Trent, and why they were all so closely derived from each other.[89] Just as the content of the 1568 *Partitiones Catechismi Catholici* is based almost entirely on that of the *Catechismus ex Decreto Concilii Tridentini ... ad parochos*, so too Eder's *Catechismus Catholicus* of 1569 and *Compendium Catechismi Catholici* of 1570 all rely heavily on each other in style, structure and verbatim content.

This is not to say, however, that Eder's contribution as a layman to Catholic pedagogy was regarded in any way as inferior.[90] On the contrary, Eder's Catholic writings attracted the praise of many within the hierarchy of the Church, including the pope himself. Even more significant is that

---

[87]   Duhr, *Geschichte der Jesuiten in den Ländern deutscher Zunge*, p. 782.

[88]   Eder, *Partitiones, Catechismi, Catholici*, fol. A*4r.

[89]   Gerhard J. Bellinger has demonstrated that between 1566 and 1587, the year of Eder's death, there were 54 editions of the Roman catechism: Bellinger, Gerhard J. (1983), *Bibliographie des Catechismus Romanus Ex Decreto Concilii Tridentini ad Parochos 1566–1978*, Baden-Baden.

[90]   It is interesting to note in this context that the first catechism classes were run by laypeople. See O'Malley, *The First Jesuits*, p. 116.

the papal praise of Eder was bestowed on the one work for which he was entirely responsible, the *Oeconomia Bibliorum* of 1568.[91] Eder's other works were equally well received. The Dominican prior Dietrich von Herzogenbusch described the *Partitiones* as a pearl of incomparable price, while the 'Agenda Coloniensis ecclesiae' of 1614 recommended the use of Eder's *Compendium Catechismi Catholici* along with the Canisius catechism, more than four decades after its first publication.[92] Of particular value to Eder would have been the approval of Canisius, and this he had: in a letter of 1 December 1569 to Otto Truchsess von Waldburg, Canisius described how Eder had abridged the Roman catechism, in order that the book might better serve the schools.[93]

The two works from 1568, the *Oeconomia Bibliorum* and the *Partitiones* also clearly found a market: the volumes' original printers, Gervinus Calenius and Johanne Quentel of Cologne, published a new edition of both in 1571 that included the papal approval, and reissued the same version in 1582. A further new edition was even printed outside the German-speaking lands, in Venice by Dominicus Nicolinus in 1572. An important part of this readership appears to have been in the Jesuit colleges. Of the numerous copies consulted while researching this book, for example, almost all those with visible provenances came from Jesuit libraries.[94]

Eder's pedagogical writings were, furthermore, not only well received but apparently influential in their own right. The cathedral preacher of Speyer, Heinrich Fabricius, used Eder's *Compendium Catechismi Catholici* as the basis for a German version of the same, while Eder's *Partitiones* were later employed by a leading Jesuit, Antonio Possevino.[95] Possevino (1533–1611) acted as Papal legate and nuncio in Scandinavia and eastern

---

[91]   All three subsequent editions of the *Oeconomia Bibliorum* open with a letter of approval from Pius V to his 'beloved son, Georg Eder', dated 2 January 1569.

[92]   Cited in Paulus, N. (1895), 'Hofrath Dr Georg Eder. Ein katholischer Rechtsgelehrter des 16. Jahrhunderts', *Historisch-politische Blätter für das katholische Deutschland*, 115, 13–28, 81–94, 240, 26. Bahlmann, Paul (1894), *Deutschlands Katholische Katechismen bis zum Ende des sechzehnten Jahrhunderts*, Münster: Regensbergsche Buchhandlung, p. 56.

[93]   Braunsberger, Otto (ed.), *Beati Petri Canisii, Societatis Iesu, Epistulae et Acta*, Freiburg im Briesgau: Herder, vol. 6, p. 377.

[94]   Of the three copies of the *Oeconomia Bibliorum* and *Partitiones, Catechismi, Catholici* found at the Munich Staatsbibliothek, two had been in Jesuit ownership (classmarks 2 Exeg 187 and Exeg 190), while the third (Exeg 189) had belonged to a Franciscan foundation. A copy of the *Compendium Catechismi Catholici* also came from Jesuit possession: Catech 280.

[95]   Possevino, Antonio (1570), *Kurtzer Catholischer Catechismus Wie sich desselben die Heilig Ro. und Apostolisch Kyrch, von anfang biß dahero jeder zeit recht gebraucht. Auß dem grossen Catechismo so hie beuor vermug des Algemeynen Tridentischen Concilii Beschluß außgage, Der Catholische Jugend zu guten newlich mit fleiß gezogen, und jetzo in hoch teutsch ubergesetzt*, Cologne: Gervinus Calenius and Johanne Quentel. This work is almost identical to Eder's, even down to the use and positioning of the illustrations.

Europe between 1577 and 1587, and later rose to the order's hierarchy: that such a man saw fit to draw heavily on the writings of Eder says much about the quality and nature of Eder's service to the Church.[96]

---

[96]   Possevino, Antonio (1586), *Theologi Societatis Iesu, de Sectariorum nostri temporis Atheismis liber. Confutatio, item, duorum pestilentißimorum librorum, à Ministris Transsyluanie editorum, ac theseun Francisci Dauidis aduersus Sanctißimam Trinitatem. Praeterea, Antithesis haereticae perfidiae contra singulos articulos Orthodoxae fidei*, Cologne: Birckmann. In a section headed 'De Atheismis haereticorum', Possevino refers to Georg Eder as his source, pp. 83r–96v.

CHAPTER 4

1573: Imperial Condemnation

The year 1573 was a watershed in Georg Eder's career.[1] Until then, his service to the Catholic Church had not clashed with his imperial service. Indeed, the two had frequently complemented each other. In Eder, the Habsburg rulers had a competent functionary who helped bolster their authority and support the confessional peace, regardless of his personal views. From the Habsburgs, Eder received tacit support for his work for Catholic reform, even finding a place in imperial bodies such as the Klosterrat to pursue his Jesuit-inspired agenda. As late as September 1572 Eder had reaffirmed his relationship with the dynasty by speaking in public praise of the Emperor Maximilian II's son Rudolf, on the occasion of his coronation as King of Hungary.[2]

Such a background makes what happened in October 1573 all the more striking. It seems that the events took even the main protagonists themselves by surprise. At the end of September 1573 the latest in Eder's growing canon of Catholic pedagogical works was published. The *Evangelische Inquisition* was like those that had preceded it, in that its 227 pages were devoted to the laying out of correct Catholic doctrine in an orderly and accessible form. It differed, however, in that it was entirely Eder's own composition, was more polemical in tone, and was also his first work in German.

It is possible that Eder sensed some trouble brewing. Unlike his earlier works, this one was published in Dillingen, at the press of Sebald Meyer. It was also dedicated not to the emperor but to his two younger brothers, Ferdinand and Charles.[3] The work was published, furthermore, only months after Eder had written to the Jesuits concerning his increasing alienation at court over the fervour of his faith.[4] In this letter of 1 April 1573 to Magius, Eder had also expressed alarm at the confessional politics of the Habsburg court, and at the imperial handling of the situation:

---

[1]   When Eder is mentioned at all in histories of the period, it tends to be for his role in the *Evangelische Inquisition* crisis. For two recent accounts, see Louthan, Howard (1997), *The Quest For Compromise: Peacemakers in Counter-Reformation Vienna*, Cambridge: Cambridge University Press, pp. 127–29 and Sutter Fichtner, Paula (2001), *Emperor Maximilian II*, New Haven, CT: Yale University Press, pp. 195–6.

[2]   Eder, Georg (1573), *Orationes II. Gratulatoriae, Ad Rudolphum Sereniss*, Vienna: Stephan Creutzer.

[3]   Eder, Georg (1573), *Evangelische Inquisition Wahrer und falscher Religion*, Dillingen: Sebald Mayer, fol. * iir.

[4]   See pp. 70–71.

Therefore you must not cease, by God, from your daily prayers for the city of
Vienna, for the emperor, and for the archdukes, his sons. For truly we are able
to say, "Save us, Lord, we perish!" I myself know the ways and characters of
men, even of those who hold government. I know their counsels, and they are
all carried by deception ... I see nothing of hope, unless Caesar immediately
rushes against these evils.[5]

Such factors may however be coincidental. And even if Eder was feeling less
secure of his position by 1573, he clearly did not expect the *Evangelische
Inquisition* to precipitate the crisis that it did. Eder blithely remained at his
posts in Vienna immediately after the work's publication, and even gave
copies to the emperor's two eldest sons and to the emperor himself, via
Adam von Dietrichstein.[6]

What followed was dramatic. On 2 October 1573 Maximilian II issued
a decree against his Reichshofrat, with crushing terms.[7] Georg Eder was
never to write on the subject of religion again.[8] Every single copy of the
work, bound and unbound, was to be submitted to the Lower Austrian
government: none were to be retained. Full details of the numbers of
copies printed, and their places of destination, were to be sent without
delay to the Hofkanzlei. All copies already distributed in Vienna were to
be submitted immediately to the Lower Austrian government. The names
of those members of the theology faculty who had approved the work
were to be listed and given to the emperor. The printer's name was also to
be surrendered. Should any of these steps not be taken, Eder would lose his
post at court and suffer further, worryingly unspecified punishment.[9]

This was no empty threat. It was evidently composed with some passion
by the emperor who even had the decree read back to him before it was
formally issued.[10] He supplemented its terms with a missive sent the very
next day to Johann Egolf, the Bishop of Augsburg. The offending work

---

[5]   Extracts from this letter are printed in Socher, Antonius, S.J. (1740), *Historia
Provinciae Austriae Societatis Jesu Pars Prima*, Vienna: Kurtzböck, pp. 360–61.

[6]   Rudolf and Ernst had been back in Vienna since 1571 after their seven-year stay in
Spain. Dietrichstein, a Catholic, had been responsible for the boys' welfare while abroad. See
pp. 35–6.

[7]   Karl Schrauf notes that the decree against Eder was one of the sharpest ever issued
by Maximilian II. Schrauf, Karl (ed.) (1904), *Der Reichshofrath Dr Georg Eder. Eine
Briefsammlung. Als Beitrag zur Geschichte der Gegenreformation in Niederösterreich*,
Vienna: Adolf Holzhausen, p. xiii. Copies of imperial decree are also in Schrauf, pp. 1–4, and
in Raupach, Bernard (1736), *Evangelisches Osterreich, das ist, Historische Nachricht von den
vornehmsten Schicksalen der Evangelisch Lutherischen Kirchen in dem Ertz-Hertzogthum
Oesterreich*, Hamburg: Felginer, pp. 147–9 (in German), pp. 31–3 (in Latin).

[8]   Schrauf (ed.), *Der Reichshofrath Dr Georg Eder. Eine Briefsammlung*, pp. 3–4.

[9]   Ibid., pp. 3–4.

[10]   This detail comes from a letter by Ludwig Haberstock dated 8 October 1573, in
which he related Eder's plight to Duke Albrecht of Bavaria, ibid., p. 19.

had been published within the territory for which Egolf was responsible, and the emperor wished him to ensure that such an incident would never occur again. Egolf was not only to track down every copy of the *Evangelische Inquisition*, but also to personally examine all future works published in his episcopal territory.[11] The process of halting the spread of such writing in general, and Eder's book in particular, started much closer to home, however. The emperor saw to it that the two copies Eder had sent to his sons as gifts were removed from their possession.[12] In addition, the imperial decree in condemnation of Eder was posted in a variety of locations local to Eder: wine houses, bookshops and homes. Most crushing of all, it was read aloud at a meeting of the Privy Council at the court of which Eder was part.[13]

Eder's immediate response to his predicament was to write to the Emperor Maximilian, doing so in a letter in which his panic is palpable in almost every line.[14] Composed just four days after the issue of the imperial decree, Eder's written plea is an uncharacteristically haphazard jumble of points through which he attempts to regain favour. That this incident was a personal catastrophe for Eder is something he makes clear from the very first lines, where he describes his 'fall into disgrace' as something 'sudden and painful'.[15]

Eder appeals first to what he portrayed as the shared Catholicity of the emperor and the book he has just banned. The *Evangelische Inquisition* Eder reminds Maximilian, is simply a work designed to guide the 'poor, simple people' through the spiritual confusions of the day.[16] This is all he has ever sought to promote in his pedagogical writing, and indeed, Eder reminds Maximilian, one of his most successful works had been dedicated to the emperor himself.[17]

Eder's second point, however, was much less likely to endear him to Maximilian. Referring to a work by Johann Friedrich Coelestinus, a Lutheran, Eder points out that in spite of its defamation of the entire Catholic clergy, the book was still published.[18] The implication,

---

[11] Maximilian II to Johann Egolf, 3 October 1573, ibid., pp. 4–6.

[12] Chudoba, Bohdan (1952), *Spain and the Empire 1519–1643*, Chicago, IL: University of Chicago Press, p. 151.

[13] Eder later outlined these events in a letter to Eisengrein dated 20 October: Schrauf (ed.), *Der Reichshofrath Dr Georg Eder. Eine Briefsammlung*, pp. 23–6.

[14] Eder to Maximilian II, 6 October 1573, ibid., pp. 6–17.

[15] Ibid., pp. 6–7.

[16] Ibid., pp. 7–8. In his choice of phrase Eder is here echoing the exact wording of the text of the *Evangelische Inquisition* itself.

[17] Ibid., pp. 7–8. The work to which Eder was referring was his 1568 *Oeconomia Bibliorum*, Cologne: Gervinus Calenius and Johanne Quentel. As he indicates himself, by 1573 this tome had been reprinted twice.

[18] Schrauf (ed.), *Der Reichshofrath Dr Georg Eder. Eine Briefsammlung*, p. 8. The book to which he is referring would appear to be either *Christliche, summarische Antwort D.*

that Maximilian II's rule favoured the dissemination of inflammatory heresy over Catholic orthodoxy, is something that Eder wisely does not press, but rather he makes several more repetitive appeals to the purely pedagogical intention of his own book before getting to the essence of his defence.[19] The *Evangelische Inquisition* was not in opposition to the Augsburg Confession, Eder claims, but rather, it was an attempt to reveal the false teaching that conceals itself under its name.[20] As a result, Eder pronounced himself deeply pained by the emperor's charge that he had acted in opposition to the imperial authority.[21] Eder went on to add that it was not he who implied that the work had been printed with 'Röm. Kay. May. freyheit', the term that had so embarrassed Maximilian. Rather, asserted Eder, this was entirely the doing of the printer, Meyer, to whom the privilege had been granted in the first place.[22]

Any possibility of the emperor revoking his decision to halt the circulation of the *Evangelische Inquisition* was however greatly reduced by Eder's next step: clearly petrified by the terms of the decree, Eder submitted details of the whereabouts of every copy of the book, thereby making the emperor's suppression of the work all the easier. In view of its author's connections, the locations of the missing copies are hardly surprising: aside from those that Eder had presented to the emperor's two eldest sons and to the emperor himself, a handful of copies had been sent to individuals in Graz, Olmütz, Innsbruck and Munich.[23] That the latter three in particular were significant Jesuit bases explains the journey of the books there; that Eder had also received some help from his old friend Eisengrein (who he unhesitatingly implicated in his 'crime') also accounts for the transit of some books to Bavaria, where

---

J. F. Celestini auff etliche Gottslesterische Bepstische Bücher, zum theil wider jn, zum theil in Gemein, wider alle Euangelische Kirchen und Lerer, newlich ausgangen, published in 1571, or perhaps more likely *Pantheum, sive Anatomia et symphonia papatus, et praecipuarum haeresum veterum & praesentium. Das ist, gründliche und unwidersprechliche beweysung, aus Gottes Wort, Kirchen Historien, und der Papisten, Ketzer und Secten selbst eignen gewirdigten Büchern. Das der Babst der warhafftige offenbahret Antichrist sey, etc …,* published in 1568.

[19]   Eder to Maximilian II, 6 October 1573, Schrauf (ed.), *Der Reichshofrath Dr Georg Eder. Eine Briefsammlung*, p. 9.

[20]   Ibid., p. 11.

[21]   Ibid., p. 9.

[22]   Ibid, pp. 10–11. On this, Eder is correct. According to Karl Schrauf, Meyer had been issued with the imperial privilege on 20 September 1569, to remain valid for ten years. Meyer was therefore within his rights. Schrauf (ed.), *Der Reichshofrath Dr Georg Eder. Eine Briefsammlung*, p. xxi. Eder claims that his decision to have the work printed by Meyer in Dillingen rather than by a printer in Vienna was taken for purely financial reasons: the printers in Vienna had insisted that Eder pay for a number of the copies himself. Ibid., p. 12.

[23]   Ibid., p. 14

Eisengrein was by then based.[24] Eder confesses too that the printer may well have sent many copies on to Frankfurt, a centre of the book trade in the German lands, but adds that he himself only had one copy in his possession.[25] After promising to co-operate on another term of the imperial decree – the naming of those who had given theological approval to the work – Eder then offers, again unprompted, the name of the publisher in charge of distribution, a Georg Willer of Augsburg.[26] Having done as much damage as possible to the future circulation of his own book as he possibly could, Eder concludes by casting himself once more on the mercy of his 'Catholic emperor, my most gracious and beloved lord'.[27]

His plea fell on deaf ears. Indeed, Maximilian's only response was to use the information Eder had supplied to halt the book's spread. 19 October saw the issue of a further decree that demanded the submission to the Lower Austrian government of all copies of the *Evangelische Inquisition* within three days; having had Willer identified as the book's publisher, on 10 December the emperor supplemented his earlier mandates with a decree to Willer's home-city of Augsburg, demanding details of exactly how many copies Willer might have received from the printer at Dillingen.[28] 24 December saw the publication of a further decree on the subject, this time announcing an impending visitation of all Viennese bookshops, and in the meantime the emperor concluded weeks of correspondence with Johann Egolf, the Bishop of Augsburg, by requesting that he ensure the removal of Meyer's printing privilege.[29]

What had provoked such a response? In his discussion of this crisis in Eder's career, Howard Louthan emphasises a particular feature of the *Evangelische Inquisition*: its disparaging discussion of the 'Hofchristen'.[30] These Hofchristen or 'court Christians' were those characterised by Eder as full of learning and knowledge of this world, who dissembled and equivocated over their true religious beliefs to gain personal advancement.[31]

---

[24] Ibid., p. 14. It would soon become apparent that it was the Duke of Bavaria's approval of the book which helped save Eder's career as a writer of Catholic pedagogy. Copies would also have been sent to Innsbruck and Graz as the bases of the courts of Maximilian's brothers, the Archdukes Ferdinand and Charles, to whom the work had been dedicated.

[25] Ibid., pp. 12–13

[26] As well as those named in the *Evangelische Inquisition* as having offered approval, Eder adds that he sent the work to the rector of the college at Dillingen and to the theology faculty of Ingolstadt: ibid., pp. 12–13.

[27] Ibid., p. 16.

[28] Ibid., pp. 22–3 and pp. 56–7.

[29] Ibid., pp. 69–70, p. 70. Maximilian II to Egolf, Vienna, 15 November 1573, ibid., pp. 43–4, p. 43.

[30] Louthan, *Quest for Compromise*, p. 128.

[31] *Evangelische Inquisition*, pp. 165v–p. 166r.

Eder elaborated on this problem in some of the most vivid passages of the entire work. Some he described as half Lutheran and half Catholic, who moved whichever way the wind blows, 'like weathervanes: with the Catholics, they are Catholic; with the Lutherans, they are Lutheran.'[32] Another variety of Hofchristen Eder described as being neither Catholic nor Lutheran, as they had submerged their own views in the interests of peace.[33] Eder, however, advocated a different, higher goal: that of Catholic orthodoxy and religious purity. For Eder, wavering, equivocal confessional stances could lead only to soul-damning confusion. Referring to Paul's comments on those who were always learning, but never able to come to a knowledge of the truth, Eder stated that such people have turned the beautiful unity of the Catholic Church into a 'Babylonische Confusion' in which no one could distinguish any longer between white and black, or right and wrong.[34] As a result, commented Eder, 'the moderates do more damage to the Church than the heretics themselves'.[35]

It is possible that such passages were perceived by certain sections of the court as a personal attack. The characterisation of learned figures who put temporal affairs above spiritual conviction does seem to hint not so much at those within the emperor's own multi-confessional Hofakademie, but rather those Catholics at the court who tolerated the promotion of such persons and their views, without making any attempt to defend the truth. This was clearly a group particularly offended by Eder's writings: of the five who Eder himself later identified as having expressly supported his condemnation, at least two were Catholics and two others may have been.[36] Karl Schrauf has added that the main villain of the piece was in fact the Reichsvizekanzler Weber, the epitome of the Hofchristen who appeared devoid of any religious scruples at all.[37] Eder himself seemed to believe that Weber was responsible for the decrees: in

---

[32]   Ibid., p. 166r.

[33]   Ibid., p. 166v.

[34]   Ibid., p. 168r, citing II Timothy 3:7.

[35]   Ibid., p. 72v.

[36]   The five expressly named by Eder were Crato, the emperor's Protestant physician, Johann Freiherr von Heissenstein, Reichshofrat Christoph Zott, and two Catholic Reichshofräte, Wolfgang Unversagt and Johann Hegenmüller. That Heissenstein and Zott are not named specifically as Protestants in any primary or secondary material may imply that they were Catholics; that they remain unnoted for their confession may also suggest why they were so offended by Eder's words: they were exactly the sort of compromising, time-serving 'Hofchristen' that he wished to criticise. Eder mentioned the first three retrospectively in a letter to Duke Albrecht of Bavaria dated 11 December 1573. Hegenmüller had also sent a report to the Duke of Bavaria, his own ex-employer, on the situation, dated 7 November 1573. In this he expressed unease at the harshness of Eder's words in the *Evangelische Inquisition*. Schrauf (ed.), *Der Reichshofrath Dr Georg Eder. Eine Briefsammlung*, p. 59 and p. 40, respectively.

[37]   On Weber see pp. 27–8 and pp. 120–21. Ibid., pp. xvi–xix.

the same letter to Albrecht of Bavaria in which he named the three he regarded as having supported his condemnation, he stated that it was Weber who had caused all that had befallen him.[38]

Any upset within the court community, however, is unlikely to have been the sole reason behind the imperial decree against Eder. His opinions would have been well known long before the publication of the *Evangelische Inquisition*, through the years of practical work he had done in the name of Catholic reform. Any court member who felt personal affront at Eder's passion for the revitalisation of Catholic orthodoxy would have had ample opportunity to launch an attack on his progress. Eder was however protected first by Ferdinand I and then by Maximilian II who, despite their concern for confessional peace, remained fundamentally Catholic rulers who would permit and even support such efforts to minister to an ailing Church. For Eder to have received such a sharp condemnation, he must have caused greatest offence to the emperor himself. This Eder did in spectacular style. The content of the *Evangelische Inquisition* appears to mock every aspect of Maximilian II's life: his personal piety, his religious policy, and, worst of all, the very authority of which he was so protective.

The passages quoted above on Hofchristen may have caused offence to members of the Habsburg court in Vienna, but the one member who would have felt the greatest sting from Eder's words was the Emperor Maximilian II himself. He was as famous for his passion for learning as any other member of his court, but was also known for his apparent inability to commit personally to any one confession.[39] Chapter 1 has already demonstrated that Maximilian II was, in spite of a seemingly contradictory religious policy, an emperor who wished to promote Catholic reform as long as the religious peace and the imperial authority remained intact. In his own day, however, he was better known for an erratic pattern of personal devotion that left even his closest family members uncertain as to whether he was a Catholic or a Protestant.

As a young man Maximilian had consistently demanded the right to receive communion in both kinds, and in 1557 informed his father Ferdinand I that his conscience would not permit him to participate in Ascension Day processions in Vienna and Pressburg. He quarrelled violently with his father over his employment of the Lutheran court preacher, Sebastian Pfauser, and when Ferdinand insisted on Pfauser's dismissal, Maximilian begged asylum from a Protestant prince, Elector Frederick of the Palatinate. Relations with his cousins in Spain were also frequently tense over the question of Maximilian II's personal religion, particularly after Maximilian condemned Catholic celebrations of the St

---

38 Ibid., p. 59.
39 See p. 33.

Bartholomew's Day massacres of 1572, and the ferocity of inquisitorial methods in the Netherlands.[40] The mystery even prompted an alarmed Pope Pius IV to demand a written guarantee of Maximilian's personal orthodoxy, a document he received in 1563. Even when he died, however, three years after the *Evangelische Inquisition* crisis, the Emperor Maximilian II's personal confession remained unclear: on his deathbed, he refused the last sacrament in any form.[41]

The *Evangelische Inquisition* did not only appear to criticise the emperor for his personal worship: it was also an attack on his peace-seeking religious policy. The work contained specific statements about, for example, the 'false unity between the Roman Church and the Augsburg confession', but was in itself a challenge to such peace by highlighting the differences between the two confessions and the heresy of Protestantism.[42] Karl Schrauf has noted that even Eder's use of the word 'inquisition' in the title would have been provocative for non-Catholic readers.[43] The preamble to the terms of the emperor's condemnation of Eder reflect his anger at such potential damage to the peace for which he had worked so long.[44]

The greatest offence to the Emperor Maximilian appears, however, to have been caused on the very first page of the *Evangelische Inquisition*. Maximilian II was furious that the title page bore the phrase 'Mit Röm. Kay. May. Freyheit' or 'with imperial permission', which not only implied that he personally approved of the contents, but suggested that his authority was open to abuse and mockery.[45] Eder's crime was therefore to have besmirched the very authority on which Maximilian II's control relied, on which the peace rested, and for which he himself had once acted as supporter. Indeed, there is an apparently personal side to the emperor's condemnation of Eder: one of Maximilian II's first remarks in the decree refers to the fact that Eder's service at the court had been 'so long'.[46]

Analysis only of the imperial decree against Eder does not, however, entirely explain why his condemnation carried the much wider significance

---

[40]   Philip II was said to have described hearing news of the massacre of Huguenots as the happiest day of his life, while the pope had ordered celebratory medals to be cast.

[41]   Howard Louthan suggests that for Maximilian to have received communion in both kinds would have offended his family, while to have taken only the bread would have offended his own conscience. Louthan, *Quest for Compromise*, p. 87.

[42]   Eder, *Evangelische Inquisition*, p. 24r. This was in contrast to Eder's previous pedagogical works, which dealt only with Catholic doctrine.

[43]   Schrauf (ed.), *Der Reichshofrath Dr Georg Eder. Eine Briefsammlung*, p. xi.

[44]   Ibid., pp. 1–2.

[45]   See frontispiece for the title page from the 1573 edition of the *Evangelische Inquisition*. The claim of imperial permission that so infuriated the emperor is clearly visible at the bottom of the title page. This was also evident from the opening lines of the decree itself: Schrauf (ed.), *Der Reichshofrath Dr Georg Eder. Eine Briefsammlung*, p. 2.

[46]   Ibid., p. 2.

that it did. For this it is fruitful to return to the source of the problem: the *Evangelische Inquisition* itself. This was no ordinary book, written by no ordinary man. To the international Catholic community, Georg Eder was nothing less than a doctor of the Church, a now-established Catholic author whose writing had long been approved by its own leaders, including the pope himself. Eder was, it could easily be argued, only continuing his work for the salvation of souls by attempting to educate laity and clergy alike in correct Catholic doctrine.

Eder's defence of his own book was, for one thing, watertight in its justification of the teaching contained therein. Eder rested his authority to write about such matters on a number of points, the first being that the teaching role of the laity was one ordained by God: 'God has not only installed bishops and priests in the Church, but also ordained some to be doctors and teachers'. Such persons have, suggested Eder, served the Church well throughout history in the fight against heresy.[47]

Eder's second line of defence was temporal in origin: he reminded his readers that he was the holder of two doctorates, one in law and the other in theology.[48] It was however his third point of justification that would have provided a source of much contemporary rancour. Eder, as with all his previous works, had had the *Evangelische Inquisition* approved by high-ranking Catholic clerics and theologians. That these three were Dr Maximilian Brixien of the theology faculty of Vienna University, Dr Hieronymus Torren of the Ingolstadt theology faculty, and the Jesuit Theodoricus Canisius, none other than the half-brother of Peter, meant that the imperial condemnation of Eder's work had much broader repercussions than a decree against one man.[49]

Despite its infamous passages on the 'Hofchristen', the *Evangelische Inquisition* was, furthermore, overwhelmingly a work intended to instruct rather than inflame. It had long been Eder's wish to produce an instructional work for Catholics in the vernacular: his reluctantly abandoned plan to translate the Roman catechism into German a few years earlier bears testament to this.[50] The desire to educate is evident throughout the *Evangelische Inquisition*. The notion that Eder wants to help the 'poor, simple Christian people ... who don't know any more how or what to believe' is echoed many times throughout the work, both in language and sentiment.[51] In the *Evangelische Inquisition* Eder had

---

[47]   Eder, *Evangelische Inquisition*, fols **ii r–v. Eder added that there were examples from the present as well as the past.

[48]   Ibid., fols ** ii r–v.

[49]   Ibid., fols +++ iv verso. Eder had also sent two copies of the published version of the work to the 'fathers of the Society of Jesus' before the issue of the imperial decree. See Schrauf (ed.), *Der Reichshofrath Dr Georg Eder. Eine Briefsammlung*, p. xii.

[50]   Eder returns to this point in the *Evangelische Inquisition*, fol. ** v.

[51]   Ibid., p. 2v.

aimed specifically to counteract the damage done by false teaching and also a lack of competent Catholic teaching in which, Eder complained, the Catholics have themselves had begun to defend the very heretics they should be condemning.[52] Eder uses a common image of the time to portray his hope in writing the *Evangelische Inquisition*: that it might act as a spiritual 'cure' in the same way that a doctor would treat an ill patient.[53] The consequences of failure were also portrayed in vivid if hyperbolic language: 'today they are Lutheran, tomorrow Calvinist; the day after that Schwenkfeldian, soon Anabaptist, and finally Muslim'.[54]

Such a sensationalist style reflected Eder's intention to use the *Evangelische Inquisition* as a reader-friendly manual of Catholic orthodoxy to be believed and heresies to be shunned. Eder's writing style in the *Evangelische Inquisition* was always colourful, with a tone that on occasion sounded sermon-like: for example, on the Hofchristen again, Eder commented they 'are now white, then black; today cold, tomorrow warm; they say yes for a time, then no … they are weathervanes, blown to and fro in the wind'.[55] The book was, furthermore, effectively organised, with its question-and-answer format regarding what is heretical and what is Catholic truth providing a simple aid to the reader. Though there were no pictures, the main headings and key points were laid out in bold type. The text itself remained uncluttered by detailed theological notes, but there were extensive marginalia in which Eder revealed the orthodoxy of his sources. Not surprisingly, the bulk of these were either Biblical in origin or derived from the Council of Trent. As far as Eder was concerned, in the *Evangelische Inquisition* he was merely continuing the service to the Catholic Church that he had been performing since the 1550s. That the emperor condemned such a man for the publication of such a work caused a sensation in the Catholic Europe of the 1570s, with implications that were far-reaching for all concerned. In the world of late sixteenth-century confessional politics, Eder's situation had done nothing less than present the leaders of Catholic Europe with the perfect opportunity to launch a fresh attack on what they saw as the insufficiently clear religious stance of the Vienna court.

The *Evangelische Inquisition* and the furore that surrounded its publication cast a fresh spotlight on Maximilian II's confessional policies, and did so right across Europe. The terms of the imperial decree against Eder were relayed swiftly throughout the major Catholic courts

---

52   Ibid, fol. + verso; fols ++ iii r–v.
53   Ibid., fol. +++ verso.
54   Ibid., pp. 7r–v.
55   Ibid., p. 8r.

of Europe, propelling the affair into one of international political and religious import. The latter half of the sixteenth century was an age of increasing news-gathering and news-sharing between courts, and the tale of Maximilian's condemnation of his Reichshofrat was one that travelled far and wide, retold in terms not always favourable to the Habsburg emperor.

One such court was that of Madrid. As the base of the Spanish Habsburgs, there were already multiple links between the two courts, and by the second half of the sixteenth century there ran a steady stream of correspondence, both diplomatic and familial, between Vienna and Madrid. By October 1573 the leading Spanish diplomat in Vienna was Don Francisco Hurtado de Mendoza, Count of Monteagudo. Eder's case apparently made an impression on him: a later inventory of his library indicates that the only work in German out of more than three hundred volumes was the *Evangelische Inquisition*.[56]

It is, however, the language in which Monteagudo reported the case to Philip II that is particularly telling. His initial summary of the events was dated 18 October 1573, and in it he depicted the affair as being a clash between one of Vienna's most upstanding, outstanding Catholics and an emperor apparently more concerned for the protection of the Confession of Augsburg.[57] Along with a copy of the decree itself, Monteagudo even added a chilling observation from Adam von Dietrichstein, a man well-known and respected in Madrid.[58] According to Dietrichstein, wrote Monteagudo, in Vienna 'the Catholics held fewer freedoms than the heretics'.[59] Philip II's personal response to his cousin's behaviour is not known, but news of the imperial decree did spark off a strong reaction against Maximilian II in the broader hierarchy of Catholic Europe of which Philip was an important part.[60]

---

[56]   Item 37 was 'a book in German and Latin entitled "Inquisition"', Bouza, Fernando (1999), 'Docto y devoto. La biblioteca del Marqués de Almazán y Conde de Monteagudo (Madrid, 1591)', in Edelmayer, Friedrich (ed.), *Hispania-Austria II: Die Epoche Philipps II (1556–1598)*, Vienna: Verlag für Geschichte und Politik, pp. 247–310, p. 282. The *Evangelische Inquisition* was predominantly in German though it did have some Latin glosses.

[57]   'Doctor Hedero' attested Monteagudo, was a 'very honourable man' whose ability as a theologian had been approved by Vienna University. By contrast, the Emperor Maximilian had responded to his work with 'a decree in favour of the Confession of Augsburg', Fernandez de Navarrete, Martin (ed.) (1842), *Por el Marquís de la Fuensanta del Valle (Colección de documentos inéditos para la historia de Espanya)*, vol. 111, Madrid: Impenta de la Viuda de Calero, pp. 332–9.

[58]   On Dietrichstein's career in Madrid, see pp. 35–6.

[59]   Navarrete (ed.), *Por el Marquís de la Fuensanta del Valle*, p. 335.

[60]   It is unusual that of all moments in Eder's life, this is the one for which very little evidence of Jesuit support exists. Eder does mention the decree in a letter to Mercurian dated 28 October 1573, but this document is concerned mainly with the move of Eder's son to

This reaction took various forms, but the one that must have been of greatest relief to Eder was his receipt of a letter of personal consolation from none other than Cardinal Stanislaus Hosius in Rome.[61] Written on 21 November, Hosius is unequivocal in his support for Eder, even suggesting that the emperor's behaviour has rendered him a martyr for the faith:

> You whose former life will be able to be thought something of a death, this life is now of such a sort that nothing hoped for may seem to have been greater than it ... The crown of justice has been set in store for you, which the Lord will grant you on that day as a just judge, since you will have suffered persecutions for His name's sake ... .[62]

Hosius also promised practical aid:

> Yet I do not hope that in this vale of tears anything will be lacking to you. Whatever I might contribute for your help and honour I will gladly grant to the best of my ability, nor shall I permit any part of the duty of your best friend to be lacking in me. I have not yet seen your son, but as soon as I do, I will embrace him with whatever services of kindness I am capable... .[63]

The response to Eder's fate went higher, however, than to the rank of Cardinal. It is unclear precisely how and when Pope Gregory XIII came to learn of the emperor's action against Eder: the papal nuncio in Vienna, Giovanni Dolfin, had been based there since 1571, and certainly outlined the situation in a report of 10 October.[64] Like Monteagudo, Dolfin too presented the case as the work of a 'pious, sincere and ardent Catholic' being crushed by 'such a severe decree' of an emperor.[65] It is also unclear

---

the German College in Rome. ARSI, Epistolae Germaniae 153, fols 293r–294r. A possible explanation is that this matter went further into the realm of politics than the Society of Jesus felt comfortable with; it may also be, simply, that the letters have not survived.

[61]   Schrauf (ed.), *Der Reichshofrath Dr Georg Eder. Eine Briefsammlung*, pp. 44–5. Also in Hosius, Stanislaus (1584), *Opera Omnia, Tom. II.*, Cologne: M. Cholin, pp. 368–9. Eder's work clearly made a genuine impression on Hosius; five years later he recommended the *Evangelische Inquisition* to Duke Wilhelm of Jülich as a 'goldenes Buch': Hosius, *Opera*, p. 438, translation in Paulus, N. (1895), 'Hofrath Dr Georg Eder. Ein katholischer Rechtsgelehrter des 16. Jahrhunderts', *Historisch-politische Blätter für das katholische Deutschland*, 115, 13–28, 81–94, 240, especially 84.

[62]   Schrauf (ed.), *Der Reichshofrath Dr Georg Eder. Eine Briefsammlung*, pp. 44–5.

[63]   Ibid., p. 45.

[64]   Giovanni Dolfin, Bishop of Torcello, served as nuncio in Vienna from July 1571 until April 1578, and wrote approximately four to ten letters per month back to Rome where they were dealt with in the first instance by Cardinal Tolomeo Gallio of Como. On this process of information-sharing and processing, see Bues, Almut (ed.) (1990), *Nuntiaturberichte aus Deutschland 1572–1585*, part 3 vol. 7, Tübingen: Niemayer, pp. xii–xxiv.

[65]   Ibid., pp. 196–7.

exactly how the pope responded to the situation, as no documentation survives. What can be ascertained, however, is that he wrote a personal missive about the matter to the emperor himself on 21 November, and his comments may be inferred from Maximilian II's reply, which does remain extant.

In essence, it seems that the pope's main problem with the imperial decree against Eder's book was that the emperor had acted in a way which not only damaged Catholicism, but cast doubts on his personal orthodoxy. These at least are the two charges against which Maximilian seemed most at pains to defend himself in his reply.[66] He opened with the traditional Habsburg appeal – to illustrious forebears – as one point in favour of his adherence to Catholicism:

> I am in turn able to confirm the trust of your Holiness that he ought to expect from me, no less than from my forebears, in whose steps I have decided to follow, all those things which are able to be constantly displayed as by an obedient son, as a nourisher and defender of Catholic religion.[67]

Indeed, Maximilian went so far as to suggest that in his judgement, Georg Eder was a substandard defender of the Catholic faith: according to Maximilian, such writers should have the ability to deliver 'either a knock-out blow, or inflict the lightest wounds'.[68]

In contrast to the image he created of himself as a pious Catholic ruler, Maximilian II thus attempted to portray Eder as the criminal, who broke not only the terms of the peace, but also his employer's trust. In so doing, Maximilian also gave the pope a tacit reminder that his inheritance was not that of a heresy-free Spain, but rather that of a confessionally mixed central Europe:

> It is impossible for anyone who knows the German language to deny that in the book ... many things were written with injurious words ... According to the conditions of the peace, which were not my own novelties, but were determined by my sainted father ... and had often been repeated and confirmed by myself, it was most severely forbidden ... and this interdict should have been violated much less by [Eder] himself, acting beyond the limits of the province entrusted to him, than by just anyone.[69]

To resolve any lingering uncertainty about what should happen next over this matter, Maximilian finally dispensed with all niceties. After noting that he could not believe that the pope had been persuaded that Eder had been harshly treated, the emperor concluded curtly:

[66] Maximilian II to Gregory XIII, 24 December 1573, in Theiner, Augustin (ed.) (1856), *Annales Ecclesiastici*, vol. 1, Rome, pp. 126–7.
[67] Ibid., p. 126.
[68] Ibid., p. 127.
[69] Ibid, p. 127.

Since Your Highness in this difficult business offers himself to me and mine so promptly and well-disposed, I offer the thanks which are due with all reverence, not doubting that Your Holiness would not interrupt anything, either in this matter or any other ... .[70]

For Maximilian II, Eder's case and, by implication, the confessional politics of his lands, were a matter for his judgement and his jurisdiction alone.

What can be pieced together of this exchange between the pope and the emperor reveals much of the state of papal-imperial relations in 1573. For Maximilian II, the role of Holy Roman Emperor had of necessity evolved into one where the priority was the maintenance of control over a confessionally diverse range of peoples. Catholicism, although still the preferred confession, could not be promoted at the expense of peace and, with it, the fragile imperial authority. What had not changed for Maximilian, however, was a belief in the centuries-old freedom of the Holy Roman Emperor to legislate as he saw fit; to compound his beliefs in this particular case must have been the fact that Eder was not only a resident of the Habsburg lands themselves, but the emperor's very own court.

For Pope Gregory XIII, the revelation of Eder's case had accentuated a position on the part of the emperor that was untenable in both spiritual and practical terms. The emperor's own employee Eder might have been, but the decree against him had been issued in the imperial name. For the papacy, the very man appointed by God to act as a secular defender of the faith was now himself acting as a persecutor of that faith for the sake of political expediency. The emperor was, furthermore, misusing his power in realms that conflicted with ecclesiastical jurisdiction; once again, Eder's case had raised the age-old clash between secular and ecclesiastical authority.

In response there followed a curious episode which not only typifies the increasingly farcical turn Eder's life was taking, but has echoes of the ongoing struggle between emperor and pope over jurisdiction.[71] Aided by the conveniently timed deaths both of Eder's second wife and Bishop

---

[70]   Ibid., p. 127.

[71]   See pp. 31–2 for the tussles over the establishment of the Klosterrat. There is also a limited amount of evidence to suggest that the papacy sponsored translations of the *Evangelische Inquisition* in another move that would have conflicted directly with the imperial authority without actually breaking the terms of the decree. According to a letter sent from Gallio in Rome to Kaspar Gropper, dated 23 October 1574, the pope was anxious to receive a copy of the Latin translation of Eder's book: Schwarz, W.E. (ed.) (1898), *Die Nuntiatur-Korrespondenz Kaspar Groppers (1573–1576)*, Paderborn: Ferdinand Schöningh, p. 200. It is not impossible that this happened, but no copies of any such work survive. Even if such a translation had been published, it may be surmised it had a limited print-run and in any case would not have made as forceful a point to the emperor as the attempt to have Eder made Bishop of Gurk.

Urban of Gurk, the decision was taken in Rome to make the freshly-widowed Georg Eder of Vienna the new Bishop of Gurk.[72] As such, the papacy would make its allegiance in the 'Eder case' more than clear; Eder's episcopacy would act as a continued embarrassment to the emperor who had banned his book; Rome would have displayed its authority, and Eder himself would be safely ensconced in a remote, neglected see from whence he could cause few further diplomatic ripples.[73] This is not to say that the attempted bestowal of the Bishopric of Gurk on Eder was solely for cynical reasons.[74] In one of the earlier letters on the subject, the papal nuncio Dolfin referred to Georg Eder as one of the most sincere and zealous Catholics in the region; according to Cardinal Gallio, Eder was both Catholic and learned.[75] None the less, the attempted appointment still made waves.

The subject of Eder and his elevation to the rank of bishop occupied a considerable amount of the correspondence between Rome and Vienna between October 1573 when the idea was first mooted, and the closing months of 1574 when Eder's rejection of the plan became known. To transform a twice-married layman into a bishop of the Catholic Church was not something easily done. The Council of Trent had decreed only ten years earlier that certain minor functions could, in the absence of unmarried clerics, 'be supplied by married clerics of approved life, provided they have not married a second time'.[76] Not only did Eder fall into the twice-married category, but the post of bishop could hardly be described as minor. A special dispensation had to be produced, along with the consent of the Archbishop of Salzburg who held the right of nomination to the see for that election.[77] The latter proved to be slow to

---

[72]   Rosina Eder had died on 18 June 1573; according to Eder's own testimony, Bishop Urban of Gurk passed away on 13 October of the same year. See Eder's letter to Eisengrein, 20 October 1573, *Der Reichshofrath Dr Georg Eder. Eine Briefsammlung*, p. 26.

[73]   Eder's perception of the practical restrictions he would face in such a role appear to have been a key factor in his refusal to accept the bishopric when it was offered to him. As such, this episode is an important indicator of Eder's view of service to the church, and will be re-explored from that angle, as opposed to its political significance, in Chapter 6, pp. 133–4.

[74]   This complex incident is recounted in Schellhass, Karl (ed.) (1896), *Nuntiaturberichte aus Deutschland 1572–1585*, part 3, vol. 3, Berlin: A. Bath, pp. LXXIX–LXXXV, and Pastor, Ludwig von (1930), *The History of the Popes From the Close of the Middle Ages*, vol. 20, ed. Ralph Francis Kerr, London: Kegan Paul, Trench, Trubner & Co, pp. 83–4.

[75]   Dolfin to Gallio, 10 October 1573, and Gallio to Bartolomeo Portia, 15 November 1573, both cited in Schellhass (ed.), *Nuntiaturberichte aus Deutschland*, p. LXXIX·

[76]   Schroeder, Rev. H.J. (ed.) (1978), *The Canons and Decrees of the Council of Trent*, Rockford, IL: Tan Books, p. 175. Exactly why having been married twice should have posed a problem that having been married once did not, is unclear from the content of the decree itself·

[77]   The bishoprics of Freising, Passau, Vienna, Wiener-Neustadt and Gurk all lay within the Kirchenprovinz of Salzburg.

gain, and the Archbishop of Salzburg refused to grant his approval unless the appointment was supported in writing by the Dukes of Bavaria, the Archduke of the Tyrol, and the emperor himself. How Maximilian II responded when pressed for such a request unfortunately is not known, but by September 1574 reports were beginning to circulate that Eder was planning a third, earthly marriage rather than one to the Church. As Gallio succinctly informed Dolfin, 'Dr Eder is more suited to matrimony than priesthood'.[78] Soon after, on 22 October 1574, the Dean of Brixen, Christoph Andreas von Spaur, became the new Bishop of Gurk.

Eder seems to have suffered no recriminations for his decision to withdraw. Indeed, as a further outward symbol of his protection of Eder, by the end of 1574 the pope had awarded him with a papal medal, a personal letter, and a sum of money.[79] Despite its anti-climactic ending, the attempt to make Eder the Bishop of Gurk had still provided a focal point for the pro-Rome forces to rally around Eder and register their disapproval of Maximilian II's behaviour. The process had seen Eder's appointment and all that it stood for gain even the support of Maximilian II's own brothers, the Archdukes Ferdinand and Charles. Support for Eder also came, however, from the Wittelsbach Dukes of Bavaria, and in them – first Albrecht and then Wilhelm – Eder found new patrons who would support his work in a way that the Habsburgs would not and could not.

---

[78]   Gallio to Dolfin, Rome, 4 September 1574, in Bues (ed.), *Nuntiaturberichte aus Deutschland 1572–1585* part 3, vol. 7, p. 622.

[79]   Dolfin to Gallio, Vienna, 20 December 1574, in Bues (ed.), *Nuntiaturberichte aus Deutschland 1572–1585* part 3, vol. 7, p. 717.

CHAPTER 5

Wittelsbach Patronage, 1573–87

In 1574, just one year after the *Evangelische Inquisition* crisis, Georg Eder sat as the subject of a copper engraving.[1] The result is in itself a succinct summary of the aftermath of the imperial condemnation that rocked his career: though Eder's apparently ravaged physical features suggest a man under great stress, his title of imperial counsellor is still very much part of the picture. This is an expression in miniature of the results of the decree of 1573. In Vienna, the affair appears to have had no lasting impact on Eder's court career; beyond the city, however, Eder's case had become the focus of attention at the courts of Madrid, Rome and most of all, in Munich. As early as the end of 1573, Eder was aware that his future service to the Church rested under the alternative patronage of the Dukes of Bavaria.

It was the very public nature of Maximilian's response to Eder's work that had, in fact, enabled the emperor to permit Eder to retain his posts in Vienna. By proclaiming Eder's offence against the imperial name, by demonstrating his ability throughout the land to hunt down copies of a forbidden book, and by affirming his determination to uphold the religious peace, the Emperor Maximilian had reasserted the very authority that he felt Eder had shaken. To punish Eder further would have damaged the emperor's image as a protector of both confessions; to accept Eder back into the upper echelons of the court, however, meant that Maximilian II could appear magnanimous, could retain the services of a competent functionary, and, importantly, could keep Eder where he could see him. Thus, Eder returned to work as Reichshofrat within a fortnight of the decree's issue on 2 October 1573. The Reichshofrat Protokolle indicate that Eder was certainly present at their sitting on 14 October, while the records of the Hofkammerarchiv suggest that Eder was back in his post there by 4 January 1574 at the latest.[2] Eder remained in the Hofkammer until September 1586, a mere eight months before his death, while his career as Reichshofrat continued for a full decade after the publication of

---

[1]   See Figure 5.1. This is the second and final surviving portrait of Eder and was, according to Karl Schrauf, done by Martino Rota of Sebenico, a copper engraver at the courts of Maximilian II and Rudolf II: Schrauf, Karl (ed.) (1904), *Der Reichshofrath Dr Georg Eder. Eine Briefsammlung. Als Beitrag zur Geschichte der Gegenreformation in Niederösterreich*, Vienna: Adolf Holzhausen, p. vii.

[2]   HHStA, RHR Protocolla rerum resolutarium XVI 37, fol. 176r; HKA, Expedit. Regist. nö 103, fol. 8r.

5.1   1574 copper engraving of Eder. By permission of the British Library
       (shelfmark 010920.m.28)

the *Evangelische Inquisition*, until September 1583.[3] Eder also retained
his standing within Vienna University: as well as acting twice more as the
dean of the law faculty in the 1580s, he was elected as university rector
for the summer semester of 1580, the winter semester of 1581–82, and
the summer semesters of 1582 and 1584.[4] 1581 even saw the publication

---

[3]   HKA, Expedit. Regist. nö 145; 24 September 1583, HHStA, RHR Protocolla rerum
resolutarium XVI 24, fol. 217 v.
[4]   Eder was dean of the law faculty for the winter semesters of 1580–81 and 1582–
83.

of another of the speeches Eder had made at so many doctoral promotions before, while his standing had apparently survived sufficiently for his daughter Regina to make an advantageous match in the same year with Geheimer Rat Leonhard Dilherr.[5] Judging from the content of the ceremony, also commemorated in published form, the event was a high-profile occasion in which the likes of the poet laureate Elias Corvinus participated.[6]

Eder's name did not disappear as an author of Catholic works either. The terms of the emperor's condemnation did not preclude the reprinting of writings by Eder that had already entered the public domain. Perhaps due to the quality of his work, but more likely a ploy by printers to cash in on his new-found notoriety, Georg Eder's religious writings from the late 1560s and early 1570s experienced something of a revival in the years post-1573. Eder's first theological works and arguably his most successful, the *Oeconomia Bibliorum* and the *Partitiones, Catechismi, Catholici* had already each been reprinted twice in new editions, one from Cologne in 1571 and one from Venice in 1572. What must have been an already flooded market was, however, supplemented by yet another reprint in 1582 of each work, again from Cologne.[7]

Other works by Eder were reissued in slightly different forms. For example, the press of Joannes Parant in Lyon issued a work bearing Eder's name with the title *Methodus Catechisimi Catholici* in 1579. On closer inspection, this was nothing more than an almost verbatim copy of Eder's work from 1569, the *Catechismus Catholicus*.[8] The same printer reprinted another of Eder's works two years later: 1581 saw the publication of the second part of 1570's *Compendium Catechismi Catholici*, this time alone and under the title of *Confessio Catholica S.S. Concilii Tridentini*.[9]

---

[5]   Eder, Georg (1581), *Quaerela Iustitiae, Lites nunc fieri omnio fere Immortales. In Coronatione Magnifici Nobilis & Clarissimi Viri, Domini Alexii Strauss, V.I. Doctoris Academiae Viennensis pro tempore Rectoris. Per D. Georg Ederum*, Vienna: Stephan Creuzer.

[6]   *Epithalamia. In nuptias nobilis et Praestantis viri D Leonardi Dilheri S.Rom.Caes. Mtis Aulae familiaris etc Sponsi ac Nobilis...Reginae filiae Magnifici...Doctoris Domini Georgii Ederi...Sponsae. a clariss. et honestiss. viris tum prosa tum metrica oratione... conscripta. Anno MDLXXXI*. The 26 page document was published in Vienna in 1581.

[7]   Eder, Georg (1582 reprint), *Oeconomia Bibliorum Sive Partitionum Theologicarum Libri Quinque...*, Cologne: Gervinus Calenius and Johanne Quentel ; Eder, Georg (1582 reprint), *Partitiones, Catechismi, Catholici, Eius Nimirum Qui Ex Decreto Concilii Tridentini ...* , Cologne: Gervinus Calenius and Johanne Quentel.

[8]   Eder, Georg (1579), *Methodus Catechisimi Catholici Antea docte ex Decreto. S. Concilii Tridentini S.D.N. Pii V. Pont. Max. Iussu scripti, Ad Parochos Nunc vero pio Ecclesiae iuuandae studio Hoc ordine ita accommodati, ut ne Dum Parochis utilis: at publice etiam Pueris in scolis proponi queat. D. Geor. Ederi. S.C.M. Consiliarii cura ac labore*, Lyon: Joannes Parant.

[9]   Eder, Georg (1581), *Confessio Catholica S.S. Concilii Tridentini Paulo III Iulio III Pio IIII & V Pont. Opt. Max De praecipuis Christianae Religionis Articulis, hoc potissimum*

Prague was the origin of a final reprint: 1585 saw the publication there of *Symbolum der Evangelischen Predicanten*, an 18-page exposition in German of the main points of the Creed, and apparently lifted from a combination of Eder's earlier religious writings.[10]

There was, however, one reprint that did explicitly break the terms of the imperial decree against Eder. Just one year after the issue of the condemnation, a new edition of Eder's *Evangelische Inquisition* appeared, like the first edition but missing the 'Mit Röm. Kay. May. Freyheit' that had caused such a furore. It remains impossible to tell by whom and where this illicit version was printed, but it does seem that Eder himself had no direct hand in the publication of the new edition. In a letter to Duke Albrecht dated 28 August 1574, Eder comments that he had been informed that 1000 copies of the *Evangelische Inquisition* had been reprinted in German.[11] That Eder was, at this stage, still nervous about any such obvious flouting of the imperial decree may be seen from a subsequent comment. The Cologne printer, Cholin, had also expressed an interest in publication of a Latin version of the banned work; Eder remarked, however, that he was afraid to act on such interest lest he fall into even deeper disgrace.[12] None the less, with or without Eder's say-so the *Evangelische Inquisition* was reprinted once more in his lifetime, in 1580 at the Ingolstadt press of David Sartorius.[13]

Eder's continued – and understandable – nervousness over any reprints of the *Evangelische Inquisition* show why, for him, it could never again be truly business as usual at the Habsburg court of Vienna. He had kept his posts, he even appears to have maintained his status, but the emperor's response to the *Evangelische Inquisition* had told Eder in no uncertain terms that he would have to be extremely circumspect in

---

seculo controuersis. D. Georg Edero I.C. Necnon. S. Caes. M. Consiliario Collectore, Lyon: Joannes Parant. Interesting in terms of the Jesuit influence on Eder is that the one surviving copy of this version is bound with several other works including the *Imitatio Christi* (MüSB Res Conc 235). As recent doctoral work by Max von Habsburg demonstrates, this was a key devotional text not only beloved of Catholic Europe, but held in particular esteem within the Society of Jesus. Habsburg, Maximilian von (2001), 'Thomas a Kempis's "Imitation of Christ": Devotional Literature in an Age of Confessional Polarity', unpublished Ph.D. dissertation, University of St Andrews.

[10]   Eder, Georg (1585), *Symbolum der Evangelischen Predicanten Darauss klärlich erscheinet, dass sie nit einen einigen Articul unsers heiligen, alleinseligmachenden, den sie nichte eintweders verspottet, oder verfalschet, oder gar verworssen hetten. Menigklich zur Warnung Auss Evangelischer Inquisition D Georgii Ederi. Cum Consensu Reuerendissi DD Martini Archiepiscopi Pragensis*, Prague: printer unknown. Only one copy of this work survives, and that is in an extremely fragile condition: MüSB Polem. 835. There is no evidence to suggest that Eder had any personal input into the issue of this work.

[11]   Schrauf (ed.), *Der Reichshofrath Dr Georg Eder. Eine Briefsammlung*, pp. 86–9, p. 89.

[12]   Ibid., p. 89.

[13]   This version was also missing the reference to imperial permission.

the future in how he went about disseminating Catholic teaching. Eder had fallen foul of the first rule of aulic Catholicism – due reverence for Habsburg authority – in quite spectacular fashion. The fall had, however, awakened him to the need to find a new secular patron who would be less concerned with the maintenance of confessional peace and parity, and more able to support a thoroughgoing vision of Catholic reform. The events of autumn and winter 1573 suggested to Eder that Albrecht of Bavaria might be just such a figure.

Duke Albrecht of Bavaria reacted to the *Evangelische Inquisition* crisis in a manner that reflected his own complex relationship with the Habsburg emperor. This was one of multiple layers – dynastic, political, confessional – every one of which fed the growing rivalry between the two powers.[14] The Duchy of Bavaria shared a substantial border with Upper Austria; it was one of the Habsburg lands' closest neighbours and as such was, even by virtue of its size and geographical cohesion, ever a simmering threat. The Wittelsbachs were certainly linked to the Habsburgs by important family ties: in the decades under consideration here, the Duke of Bavaria, Albrecht V (who ruled the territory 1550–79) was married to Anna of Austria, Maximilian II's sister. 28 August 1571 saw the wedding in Vienna of Albrecht V's eldest daughter Maria to Maximilian II's youngest brother, Archduke Charles of Inner Austria.[15] There survive some cases of cosy co-operation between the two families: according to Paula Sutter Fichtner's recent biography of Maximilian II, the Habsburg emperor and the Wittelsbach duke shared a love of the work of the Netherlandish musician Orlando di Lasso. The brothers-in-law would exchange his musical compositions, while it seems they also indulged each other's taste for Hungarian wine. In addition, Sutter Fichtner notes, 'a variety of fish and game – live, dead and in varying stages of decomposition – travelled from Munich to Vienna or the other way around'.[16]

In early-modern Europe, it was not, however, unusual to have Habsburg in-laws: in this period, the Habsburgs had married into every royal and

---

[14]　Though there is some quality historiography on Bavaria in the sixteenth century, there is very little that deals specifically with Wittelsbach-Habsburg relations in the same period. On the confessional situation in early-modern Bavaria see in particular Kraus, Andreas (ed.) (1988), *Handbuch der Bayerischen Geschichte*, Munich: C.H. Beck; Myers, W. David (1996), 'Die Jesuiten, die häufige Beichte, und die katholische Reform in Bayern', *Beiträge zur Altbayerischen Kirchengeschichte*, 42, 45–58, and Brandmüller, Walter (ed.) (1993) *Handbuch der Bayerischen Kirchengeschichte*, vol. 2, St Ottilien: EOS Verlag Erzabtei.

[15]　Albrecht was succeeded by his eldest son, Wilhelm V, who ruled from his father's death in 1579 until 1598. Duke Wilhelm died in 1626 at the age of 78.

[16]　Sutter Fichtner, Paula (2001), *Emperor Maximilian II*, New Haven, CT: Yale University Press, p. 33.

major noble family on the continent, with the sole exception of Scotland. Nor could such pleasantries conceal the growing tensions between the two dynasties. There were, firstly, the political tensions that had marked their recent pasts and threatened the peace of their immediate future. The border between Wittelsbach and Habsburg territories was, for example, under constant dispute: as late as the 1620s Duke Maximilian of Bavaria occupied parts of Upper Austria for a time. The spectacular growth of the Wittelsbach university at Ingolstadt was a constant source of Habsburg jealousy in the light of Vienna University's ailing fortunes.[17] What might have been a relatively innocuous dispute over the right of jurisdiction over the bishopric of Passau became yet another power struggle, while the Wittelsbach-dominated Landsberg League, in existence since 1556 for the defence of Catholicism in the empire, was an additional source of tension between the two powers.[18]

Indeed, it was over the question of confessional politics that the greatest source of antagonism between the Habsburgs and Wittelsbachs lay. It is not simply that the Dukes of Bavaria demonstrated themselves to be much more unequivocally in favour of Catholic reform than their Habsburg counterparts. It is true that as individuals the Wittelsbachs were able to demonstrate their Catholic orthodoxy in more visible forms than the Austrian dynasty. From Albrecht V onwards, the senior Wittelsbach sons were educated at Jesuit-dominated Ingolstadt University, and the family themselves played an active role in the sponsorship of Jesuit work in their territories. Albrecht V saw to it that the new Jesuit colleges at Ingolstadt and Munich each received 4000 gulden per year from his personal coffers, while junior male family members were pushed into episcopal sees that might otherwise have fallen into the wrong hands.[19] The more notorious examples are those of the elevations of Albrecht's two youngest sons to the bishopric: in 1564 Ernst was made Bishop of Freising at the age of eleven, while 1567 saw his younger brother Philip become Bishop of Regensburg at three years of age.[20] Such placements

[17]   Mühlberger, Kurt (1991), 'Zu den Krisen der Universität Wien im Zeitalter der konfessionellen Auseinandersetzungen', *Bericht über den achtzehnten österreichischen Historikertag in Linz veranstaltet vom Verband Österreichischer Geschichtsvereine in der Zeit vom 24. bis 29. September 1990*, Veröffentlichungen des Verbandes Österreichischer Geschichtsvereine 27, pp. 269–77, especially p. 271.

[18]   Johnston, Rona Gordon (1996), 'The Bishopric of Passau and the Counter–Reformation in Lower Austria, 1580–1636', unpublished D. Phil. dissertation, University of Oxford, pp. 27–30. This climaxed in the 1590s, but had been grumbling for decades as both dynasties sought control over the largest diocese in the Holy Roman Empire. The League of Landsberg was only disbanded in 1598.

[19]   Schwarz, W.E. (ed.) (1898), *Die Nuntiatur–Korrespondenz Kaspar Groppers (1573–1576)*, Paderborn: Ferdinand Schöningh, pp. ix–x.

[20]   On this see Soergel, Philip (1993), *Wondrous In His Saints: Counter-Reformation Propaganda in Bavaria*, Berkeley, CA: University of California Press, especially pp. 78–9.

could however play an important role in defending against heresy whilst enhancing Wittelsbach authority: in 1583, after the departure of Gebhard Truchsess von Waldburg, Ernst was made Archbishop of Cologne with the collaboration of the Spanish regime in Brussels. Cologne thus became a Bavarian secundogeniture outside the Wittelsbachs' own territory.

It was this very ability to make political capital out of Catholic devotion that rendered the Wittelsbachs such a serious threat to their Habsburg neighbours. As has been seen throughout this study, the confessionally and physically disparate nature of the Austrian Habsburg inheritance meant that it was the power of the imperial name itself on which unity, peace and above all authority rested. The Wittelsbachs did not have the imperial title – in itself undoubtedly a sore point – but they were in a position to exert their authority in their own territory by doing exactly what the Austrian Habsburgs dared not: eradicating Protestantism by force.

What is striking about the Wittelsbachs' drive to purge Protestantism from their lands is the speed with which the policy was formulated and implemented. In 1558, Albrecht V appointed the uncompromising Simon Eck as his chancellor, and together they produced ordinance after ordinance that directly attacked those who persisted in participating in evangelical worship. The property of any ducal subject who remained Protestant was to be seized; anyone who crossed borders to attend Protestant services was to be fined between 50 and 100 florins; and in 1568, all such legislation fell under the control of a Geistliche Rat, composed of secular as well as ecclesiastical officials, and established to supervise levels of orthodoxy within the Bavarian territory.[21] By 1570, all Bavarian Protestants were required to either renounce their beliefs or emigrate, and one year later Duke Albrecht overturned all the concessions made in 1556 that had once granted communion in both kinds and the toleration of clerical marriage. The force of such steps was, however, largely possible through Duke Albrecht's uncompromising stance taken against the Protestant Bavarian nobles at the Ingolstadt diet of 1563. Not only did the duke dismiss the assembly when the Lutheran contingent requested further religious concessions, but the very next year he took what was the illegal step of seizing the Count of Ortenburg, the ruler of a small territory who had recently initiated pro-Lutheran reforms. A series of trials followed in which Ortenburg and other Lutheran noble associates were deprived of their lands, and through which the Wittelsbach Duke imposed his authority afresh over his territory.

Ernst would also become Bishop of Hildesheim, Liège, Halberstadt and Münster.

[21]   Ibid., p. 77. The Geistliche Rat was responsible for the promotion of correct Catholic belief within the duchy's schools, universities, and in broader public life.

For the Dukes of Bavaria, Catholicism thus became the tool with which they imposed unity on and asserted control over their own lands. It was also a way, however, in which they could demonstrate their own particularist tendencies within the Holy Roman Empire of which they were part. Just as the Protestant nobles used their territorial confession to express their own separate identity within the empire, so the Wittelsbachs used Catholicism to the same end. It was, however, in many ways more threatening to the Habsburg emperor. By enforcing Catholicism in his own lands in a way that the Austrian Habsburgs could not, Duke Albrecht was in effect beating the emperor at his own game. By fulfilling the role of secular defender of the faith far more effectively than circumstances had permitted either Ferdinand I or Maximilian II to do, by the 1570s it was the Duke of Bavaria who was the de facto secular champion of Catholicism in the empire.

In such a context, the case of Eder and the imperial decree against him provided the Wittelsbachs with a further cache of confessional ammunition with which to challenge their Habsburg rivals. Although Eder was himself a Bavarian, there is no evidence to suggest that Duke Albrecht V had ever heard of him before 1573.[22] It does seem that Albrecht had, however, finished reading a copy of the *Evangelische Inquisition* before news of its condemnation had filtered through to his court. On 9 October 1573 Albrecht V composed a personal letter of congratulation to Eder. He had, wrote Albrecht, been given the book by his chancellor, Eck, and had been particularly impressed by the clarity with which Eder had outlined correct Catholic belief.[23] Such a feat would, Albrecht assured Eder, result in no small rewards in terms of the revival of the Catholic Church.[24]

The warmth of Albrecht's tone to Eder suggests that the duke was personally pleased to see his beleaguered confession receive the support of a competent writer. There was also a political aspect to such praise: for Albrecht V, the content of Eder's *Evangelische Inquisition* was in itself a support to his religious policy of promoting Catholic orthodoxy as an expression of ducal authority. What happened next, however, gave the Wittelsbach duke even more opportunity to assert his position within Catholic Europe as a whole. Albrecht heard of Eder's fate from no less than four sources. The first to write was Ludwig Haberstock, a Bavarian representative based in Vienna. In a letter dated 8 October, Haberstock told the duke that the decree against Eder was the sharpest

---

[22]   This view is supported by the fact that in a letter dated 21 January 1574, and therefore relatively early in their relationship, Eder felt it appropriate and necessary to fill Albrecht V in on the details of his career to that point. Schrauf (ed.), *Der Reichshofrath Dr Georg Eder. Eine Briefsammlung*, pp. 71–9, especially p. 78.

[23]   Ibid., pp. 20–21.

[24]   Ibid., pp. 20–21.

issued in living memory, and that its terms had given the opponents of Catholicism much cause to celebrate.[25] Next to report on the matter was Johann Egolf, Bishop of Augsburg, who wrote to Albrecht from Dillingen on 16 October.[26] Despite having co-operated with the emperor in tracing all copies of the work, Egolf made his personal sympathies known to Duke Albrecht in his description of the 'good, pious Dr Eder'.[27] A third, more critical reporter was Johann Hegenmüller. A Reichshofrat like Eder, Hegenmüller had previously served as a counsellor in the Wittelsbach court and on 7 November expressed some reservations to his ex-employers about the ferocity of Eder's language within the pages of the *Evangelische Inquisition*.[28]

In agreement with Haberstock and Egolf, however, was the fourth person to inform Albrecht of what had happened: Martin Eisengrein. Eder had written to his friend and accomplice Eisengrein twice within three days, outlining his situation.[29] Since his departure from Vienna in 1562, Eisengrein had become a powerful figure within the political and ecclesiastical hierarchy of Bavaria. Of him, Philip Soergel has commented that his 'career exemplifies the blurring that occurred between state and clerical functions as the Wittelsbachs worked to establish their hegemony over religion'.[30] As such, Eisengrein participated in the Wittelsbach Geistliche Rat as an examiner of clerical standards, while it was also he who played a leading role in the procurement of the Freising bishopric for Albrecht's young son Ernst. As a result, Eisengrein had been suitably rewarded by the duke in whose territory he served: amongst other positions, he was made provost of collegiate churches in Passau, Moosburg and Altötting, while in 1570 he was elected superintendent of Ingolstadt University. Eder could therefore hardly have explained his predicament to a more influential friend. On 30 November Eisengrein finally took action on his Viennese colleague's behalf, and composed a

---

[25]   Ibid., pp. 19–20.

[26]   Ibid., pp. 21–2. BHStA, Kurbayern Äußeres Archiv, Status Ecclesiasticus-Religionsacta des Erzhauses Österreich, Tom. X fol. 23r–v.

[27]   Ibid., p. 22.

[28]   Ibid., pp. 39–42. Full version in BHStA, Kurbayern Äußeres Archiv, Status Ecclesiasticus-Religionsacta des Erzhauses Österreich, Tom. X fol. 70r–72v. For more on Hegenmüller's confessional stance, see p. 35.

[29]   Eder's first letter to Eisengrein was dated 20 October 1573. In it, he detailed all the terms of the decree against him and his 'unhappy book'. On 23 October, Eder wrote again of his persecution and expressed his deep appreciation of Duke Albrecht's earlier letter of praise for his now-condemned book. It may well have been that Eder was aware of Eisengrein's favoured position at the Wittelsbach court and was angling for Albrecht's further intervention. Schrauf (ed.), *Der Reichshofrath Dr Georg Eder. Eine Briefsammlung*, pp. 23–6 and pp. 36–8, respectively.

[30]   Soergel, *Wondrous in His Saints*, p. 106.

long letter to the Wittelsbach duke in which he described the religious and political implications of Maximilian II's decree.[31]

Eisengrein's opinion would have carried much weight, not only for the esteem in which he was held at the Wittelsbach court, but also because he had substantial personal experience of the situation in Vienna.[32] Forceful too were the arguments he placed before Duke Albrecht in favour of intervention on Eder's behalf. His chief tactic was to argue that Maximilian II had behaved in a way that was theologically and politically reprehensible. Citing the gospel of Matthew on the necessity of making a true confession of one's faith, Eisengrein suggested to Albrecht that there were numerous examples from history of spiritual dissimulation amongst rulers.[33] Clearly implying that Maximilian II's actions had rendered him another such guilty party, he added that Christ himself had expressly forbidden such behaviour.[34] Eisengrein's argument also had, however, a contemporary flavour: he outlined the results of such misrule on the city of Vienna itself, where heretical preaching was rife and causing severe damage to the cause of Rome.[35] Eisengrein's portrayal of his intended recipient as a blessed defender of the faith, Duke Albrecht, was in flattering contrast.[36]

It is doubtful whether Albrecht V actually needed Eisengrein to provide him with such justifications for intervention in Eder's fate. Albrecht's response to Eder's plight was swift, unequivocal, and seemingly tailor-made for the duke's procurement of optimum political capital. In the issue of Eder's possible elevation to the rank of bishop, Duke Albrecht took the pro-papal side. His own immediate response was, however, to help Eder's cause by directly flouting the terms of the imperial decree against him. In a letter dated 19 December 1573, the Wittelsbach duke wrote to Eder telling him that he would buy all remaining copies of the *Evangelische Inquisition* from Willer in Augsburg: evidently they had been neither seized nor submitted by this point.[37] He was, furthermore, successful in this. In a letter of 21 January 1574 Eder thanked him for rescuing the bulk of the copies, while the legacy of Albrecht's intervention

---

[31]   Ibid., pp. 45–53, especially p. 46.

[32]   Not only had Eisengrein lived in Vienna between 1553 and 1562, but he had also spent two years there in the late 1560s. While in Vienna in 1569 he had become personally involved in a dispute over the non-participation of university members in the annual Corpus Christi procession through the streets of the city. On that occasion, Eisengrein persuaded the emperor to demand their participation, regardless of personal confessional scruples.

[33]   Matthew 10:32–3: 'Whoever acknowledges me before men, I will also acknowledge him before my Father in heaven. But whoever disowns me before men, I will disown him before my Father in heaven' (NIV version).

[34]   Schrauf (ed.), *Der Reichshofrath Dr Georg Eder. Eine Briefsammlung*, p. 47.

[35]   Ibid., pp. 49–50.

[36]   Ibid., p. 53.

[37]   Ibid., pp. 68–9.

can still be seen even today in the survival of at least four copies of a work that Maximilian II had wished to see wholly eradicated. How many more copies were actually in circulation in the sixteenth century can only be imagined, but it has been estimated that from a probable initial print-run of 1500, Willer would have had approximately 1400 copies in his possession.[38]

Wittelsbach employment of Eder's case as a vehicle with which to challenge the authority of the Austrian Habsburgs did not stop, however, in 1574. The growing Bavarian bureaucracy had, by the 1570s, become increasingly partial to the gathering of news and information from across Europe as a means of enhancing its own security and position.[39] Based on the premise that knowledge is power, as the sixteenth century progressed the Munich court became a growing repository for thousands of reports from regions that were particularly combustible: France, the Spanish Netherlands, Bohemia and Hungary.[40] As such, and for the reasons already discussed, Vienna was thus of special interest to the Wittelsbachs. Although in geographical terms their courts were relatively close, as the sixteenth century went on increasing numbers of Bavarian 'Agenten' bolstered the formal correspondence between Vienna and Munich with their own news, insights and gossip.[41] The Haberstock and Hegenmüller

---

[38]   Ibid., pp. 71–9, especially p. 72. Four copies of the 1573 edition of the *Evangelische Inquisition* were examined in the researching of this book: one in the British Library (3908.ccc.77.), two in the Österreichische Nationalbibliothek (252.036–B.Fid (=21–150); 77.Dd.16), and one in the Bayerisches Staatsbibliothek (4 Polem. 1004a). Examination of further library catalogues suggest that at least a further four copies are in existence: at the Herzog August Bibliothek, Wolfenbüttel; St John's University, Collegeville, MN; Eastern Mennonite College, Harrisonburg, VA, and the University of Michigan, Ann Arbor, MI. On the numbers of copies of the *Evangelische Inquisition*, see Schrauf (ed.), *Der Reichshofrath Dr Georg Eder. Eine Briefsammlung*, pp. xxiii–xxiv.

[39]   For the only monograph on this subject, see the aged but magnificent work by Leist, Friedrich (1889), *Zur Geschichte der auswärtigen Vertretung Bayerns im XVI. Jahrhundert*, Bamberg: Buchner. For an edited collection of such materials, see Goetz, Walter (ed.) (1898), *Briefe und Akten zur Geschichte des sechzehnten Jahrhunderts mit besonderer Rücksicht auf Baierns Fürstenhaus*, vol. 5, *Beiträge zur Geschichte Herzog Albrechts V und des Landsberger Bundes 1556–1598*, Munich.

[40]   BHStA, Kurbayern Äußeres Archiv, Korrespondenzakten-Auswärtige Residenten, signatures 4365 4372, 4385–94, 4428–37 and 4441–52 respectively.

[41]   Leist notes this use of the term 'Agenten' to describe such correspondents, but such a term is not intended to be suggestive of sinister infiltration or espionnage: *Zur Geschichte der auswärtigen Vertretung Bayerns*, p. 2. Exactly who was in regular touch with the Munich court would have been no secret in Vienna, though some of the material contained in their reports was certainly highly sensitive. For the apparent increase in their numbers in Vienna throughout the sixteenth century, ibid., pp. 4–6. The formal diplomatic correspondence from the period between Wittelsbach and Habsburg family members is located in BHStA, Kurbayern Äußeres Archiv, Korrespondenzakten-Österreichisches Korrespondenz, signatures 4456–66 inclusive. The subjects covered in this material include matters of state, foreign travels, dynastic marriages and recent deaths.

who first reported Eder's fate to Duke Albrecht were two such figures, as were Reichshofrat Timotheus Jung, Reichshofrat and Reichsvizekanzler Siegmund Viehauser, and court counsellors Georg Ehrenpreis and Andreas Erstenberger.[42]

By the late 1570s, however, for various reasons these reporters were unable to offer news from Vienna to the extent to which Duke Albrecht would have wished: such a communications problem must have been all the more frustrating as the year 1578 marked an apparent renewal of Habsburg efforts to limit the exercise of Protestantism, with all the subsequent agitation that such efforts brought.[43] The solution was clear: Georg Eder would be the new Viennese correspondent, in a choice that benefited both Munich and their new appointment. For the Wittelsbachs, Eder's reports would not only keep them informed of what was happening at the rival court, but alert them to any further instances when Bavarian intervention might be politically and religiously expedient. In addition, their open patronage and employment of Eder – still an internationally known confessional cause célèbre – would act as a constant undermining of the Habsburg religious policy that had once seen Eder's writings condemned. From Eder's perspective, the arrangement brought him the chance to bind himself closer still to the new patron whose protection promised much that the Habsburgs could never provide. By 15 March 1577 at the latest, Eder had started writing the first of at least 123 detailed reports to the Wittelsbach Dukes of Bavaria, thus beginning a process that would endure throughout the final decade of his life in Vienna.[44]

It is difficult to ascertain the extent to which Eder's reports to Bavaria were composed of what the Wittelsbachs wanted to hear, what Eder wanted them to hear, and what the real situation actually was in Vienna. Eder's Bavarian correspondence certainly bore all the hallmarks of one purporting to fulfil the requirements of the early-modern 'Nachrichtendienst', or news-service. For one thing, Eder wrote to the Wittelsbachs not only with frequency, but with the regularity that they

---

[42]   BHStA, Kurbayern Äußeres Archiv, Korrespondenzakten-Auswärtige Residenten, signatures 4291–349 inclusive.

[43]   None of these figures appear to have sent many bulletins at all between 1577 and 1587, the period in which Eder was most active in the role. In the case of Jung, it seems that matters of state took him away from Vienna and his reports were not only increasingly erratically timed, but from a series of non-Viennese locations: Augsburg, Prague and Cologne (signature: 4312 XX/2 1568–77). Hegenmüller too appears to have been away from Vienna for significant periods for the 1570s: between 1577 and 1579 he was in a position to send only eight missives from Vienna, in comparison to the 53 sent by Eder over the same eventful period (signature: 4316).

[44]   Schrauf (ed.), *Der Reichshofrath Dr Georg Eder. Eine Briefsammlung*, pp. 96–7. Eder may have started sending his communiqués before 1577. However, it was around this time that Jung and Hegenmüller were less able to correspond regularly from Vienna, so Eder may well have been asked to step in at that point.

apparently demanded. The role of the correspondent, at least as far as the Wittelsbachs were concerned, was to write regularly, regardless of whether or not there was much to report. According to Leist, it was common for sixteenth-century Bavarian correspondents to write back to Munich with the remark that they were doing so in spite of a lack of anything that constituted actual news.[45] Evidence internal to the reports indicates that Eder himself clearly fitted into this pattern. In a particularly short missive from 1577, Eder remarked that it was so quiet in Vienna at that point, the duke would have more news of his own in one day than he had for an entire week.[46] In another letter, dated 4 October 1578, Eder explicitly assured Duke Albrecht that he would write, if not weekly, then fortnightly.[47] This was evidently a promise Eder tried hard to keep. From what survives, it seems that Eder averaged approximately one letter per fortnight, though at one point, between April and July 1578, he was writing almost one report per week to the Munich court.[48] That there are several surprising gaps in the pattern of report-writing may be explained by the fact that some batches of Eder's correspondence are simply no longer extant.[49]

The other key function of the Nachrichtendienst was, as its title suggests, to communicate news from other courts. Again, Leist's survey of such correspondence is instructive as he observes that Bavarian reports often included such suggestions that the information included was

---

[45] Leist notes the frequency of such phrases as: 'everything at the court is quiet in terms of news', 'there is hardly any news at this time' and 'unfortunately this last week has brought up nothing worthy of mention', Leist, *Zur Geschichte der auswärtigen Vertretung Bayerns*, p. 18.

[46] Eder to Albrecht, 30 November 1577, Schrauf (ed.), *Der Reichshofrath Dr Georg Eder. Eine Briefsammlung*, pp. 125–8, especially p. 126.

[47] Perhaps as a way of 'covering' for any possible lapses in his report-sending, on one occasion Eder even used the age-old line that the post was unreliable, ibid., pp. 232–5, especially p. 232.

[48] What can be reconstructed of Eder's report-writing suggests that the rate fluctuated somewhat: between 20 December 1578 and 30 May 1579 he sent 12 reports, an average of one every two weeks. Much the same rate was achieved between 13 July 1579 and 1 December 1579, and between 25 March 1581 and 1 August 1581 when Eder posted 11 missives and nine missives respectively. The period from January until 30 July 1580 saw Eder write 17 such letters, at an average of three per month. According to Leist, mail was carried between courts on average only once or twice a week: Leist, *Zur Geschichte der auswärtigen Vertretung Bayerns*, p. 19.

[49] No letters survive for the periods between the end of July and 4 October 1578; 27 October 1580 and 9 January 1581; 26 January to 6 May 1584, and between 25 August 1585 and 2 November 1586. In some instances Eder may have been away from Vienna on court business: a letter of 4 October 1578 suggests as much. Schrauf (ed.), *Der Reichshofrath Dr Georg Eder. Eine Briefsammlung*, p. 232. That not all of Eder's letters have been preserved is suggested by the existence in the Bayerisches Hauptstaatsarchiv of short summaries of two of Eder's letters that had apparently been dated 31 October 1581 and 19 April 1582, but which can no longer be found: BHStA, Staatsverwaltung, Auswärtige Staaten und bayerische Beziehungen zu denselben, signature 1931 fol. 20r–v

accurate and the result of determined enquiry. That the correspondents wished to cover their own reputations should a piece of information later be found to be incorrect can be seen from the regular peppering of their reports with such phrases as 'it is said', 'it is reliably reported', 'I gather from a reliable noble' and 'as far as I can gather'.[50]

Eder too appears to have made an effort to fulfil this important function. In one letter, he explains apologetically that his lack of news on the Viennese court was due to his having been confined to the house for 12 days due to illness.[51] In another, dated 5 October 1577, Eder was able to unveil, however, something of a scoop over the sudden disappearance in the night of the Archduke Matthias from Vienna to Brussels.[52] Matthias' mission to become Governor-General of the Spanish Netherlands was one that had been shrouded in secrecy. The major fear was, quite rightly, the opposition of Philip II, who regarded the presence of the young Austrian archduke as a threat to Spanish authority in that notoriously troubled region.[53] Such an episode would have been of much interest to the Wittelsbachs. Aside from the basic political value of having such knowledge as soon as possible, Matthias' move heralded the possible widening of the division between the two branches of the rival Habsburg dynasty, as well as the exacerbation of the confessional strife in the Spanish Netherlands: both were scenarios that offered the Bavarians the chance to further strengthen their own position within Catholic Europe. Eder was not only the one who sent them this gem of information, but he made sure the Wittelsbachs realised the difficulties he had faced in uncovering such material.[54]

---

[50]   Leist, *Zur Geschichte der auswärtigen Vertretung Bayerns*, p. 27. Despite his efforts, Eder did not always get his facts straight. In a letter to Duke Albrecht dated July 1578, Eder refers to Graf Nikolaus von Salm as Bishop of Passau. Schrauf (ed.), *Der Reichshofrath Dr Georg Eder. Eine Briefsammlung*, pp. 228–31, especially p. 230. As Schrauf points out, the Bishop of Passau from the von Salm family was Wolfgang, not Nikolaus, a fact that Eder should have known well: see p. 43.

[51]   19 January 1578, ibid., p. 144.

[52]   Ibid., pp. 119–20, especially p. 120. Although Matthias left Vienna at the beginning of October 1577, he only made his official entry into Brussels on 18 January 1578. Eder's report was therefore the unearthing for the Wittelsbachs of a highly sensitive piece of information that would not become public knowledge for another three-and-a-half months.

[53]   On Matthias' moonlight flit to Brussels, the political tensions surrounding his move, and his disastrous tenure there, see Louthan, Howard (1997), *The Quest for Compromise: Peacemakers in Counter-Reformation Vienna*, Cambridge: Cambridge University Press, pp. 143–54.

[54]   '... matters concerning the Archduke Matthias are here kept so secret and quiet, that I was not able to find out any details before'. Eder to Duke Albrecht, 30 November 1577, Schrauf (ed.), *Der Reichshofrath Dr Georg Eder. Eine Briefsammlung*, pp. 125–6, especially p. 126.

There is however an important sense in which Eder's reports departed from their formal function and were in fact more reflective of Eder's own agenda, in which he hoped to persuade the Wittelsbach duke to intervene to an even greater extent in the revival of Catholicism.[55] The typical Bavarian report covered a broad range of topics, from events at court and affairs of state to more mundane matters including, on one occasion, the death of a dog.[56] In this, Eder's reports differed from the usual correspondence flowing back to Munich. He rarely wrote of any external political events; instead, Eder's comments in virtually every report were focused on two topics and two topics alone: the desperate state of Catholicism in Vienna and its environs; and the cause of this problem, namely, Habsburg misrule.[57]

There are several possibilities as to why Eder alone focused almost entirely on confessional news. There had been a precedent for a Bavarian 'religious' correspondent set by none other than Martin Eisengrein who had exchanged more than 45 letters with Duke Albrecht in the space of only two years while he was based at the Vienna court in the late 1560s.[58] It may also be that such was the extent of the problems faced by Catholicism in the Vienna of the 1570s, the Bavarian duke wished to have one informant dedicated to that topic. However, Eder must have been aware that his portrayal of the entire situation as one of desperate gravity, with the Habsburg emperor as the villain of the piece, would not displease his Bavarian patron and protector, since it was still over confessional matters that the greatest source of tension and rivalry between Habsburg and Wittelsbach lay.

It was thus under the guise of the Nachrichtendienst that Eder created a portrait of religious life in Vienna part-based in fact and part-based on

---

[55]   As Chapter 6 will reveal, Eder also used his reports as a means of persuading Duke Albrecht to help reignite his stalled career as a Catholic writer. In this context, it is worth noting that Eder's letters tend to be substantially longer than those of the other Bavarian correspondents writing from Vienna at the time. For example, those sent by Hegenmüller between 1572 and 1575 rarely covered more than two folio sides; Eder's were rarely less than that: BHStA, Kurbayern Äußeres Archiv, Korrespondenzakten–Auswärtige Residenten, signature 4315. The extra length of Eder's letters may be accounted for by his regular pleading of his particular circumstances and also the personal fervour with which the perilous confessional state of Vienna drove him to write.

[56]   Leist, *Zur Geschichte der auswärtigen Vertretung Bayerns*, pp. 27–31.

[57]   Only once does Eder mention what would have been a regular occurrence: the arrival of ambassadors at the Viennese court. In a letter dated 9 February 1578 he wrote of the arrival of the ambassadors from Moscow and Portugal, but said little more about their visit: Schrauf (ed.), *Der Reichshofrath Dr Georg Eder. Eine Briefsammlung*, pp. 144–6, especially p. 146. Similarly, references to the crucial subject of the Ottoman threat and to Hungary barely make it into double figures throughout the hundreds of pages of commentary sent back to Munich by Eder.

[58]   Soergel, *Wondrous in his Saints*, p. 122.

the image he wished to create. Two of the most striking passages from the entire body of his Bavarian correspondence were devoted to descriptions of the moral and physical bankruptcy of the Catholic Church in Lower Austria. From the first of these, dated 29 December 1577, Eder's skill as an orator can also be imagined: 'everything is in confusion, with neither song books nor prayer books ... neither chalice nor altar, neither candle nor candlestick ... almost all is destroyed and deserted'.[59] In the same letter, Eder raised what he evidently regarded as an even more serious problem: the lack of clerics who could teach correct doctrine with consistency and uniformity: 'there are hardly any ordained priests ... each has his own way ... '.[60] This is a subject to which he returned with some passion ten months later: 'I don't believe that there are two prelates in the whole land who have remained true to their faith ... they almost all have wives ... quite a few no longer know how to perform the Mass ... they are worse than the laity'.[61]

Eder's reference to the laity at the end is telling. Not only does it echo his own belief in the potential of the laity to live lives as pleasing to God as those of the clergy, but the entire passage expressed his concern that the clergy still had a responsibility to act as moral and spiritual examples for the laity to emulate, not outclass. The consequences of such immorality for the future of the Catholic Church in Lower Austria as presented by Eder, are dire. In one passage, Eder reported how in St Michael's parish, a sexual scandal amongst the clergy there was capitalised on to such effect by the Lutheran preachers, that 3000 more people attended the Protestant services than had previously been the case.[62] Even more gloomy was Eder's long-term prognosis of the situation. On 12 January 1577 he reported to the Bavarian duke that in an entire month, not two children had been brought to Stephansdom for baptism: as a result, 'the church will soon become a desert'.[63]

If Eder's presentation of the state of the Catholic Church was bleak, it was not the Church itself that Eder portrayed as being solely at fault. He

---

[59]   Eder to Duke Albrecht, Schrauf (ed.), *Der Reichshofrath Dr Georg Eder. Eine Briefsammlung*, pp. 130–34, p. 132. That Eder's tone in his letters occasionally falls into such memorable polemic, and that, on occasion, he echoes phrases found in his published works, may also suggest that Eder uses his reports not merely as a means of forwarding information but of making his case in favour of Catholic reform.

[60]   Ibid., p. 132.

[61]   Eder to Duke Albrecht, 4 October 1578, ibid., pp. 232–5, especially p. 232.

[62]   Eder to Duke Wilhelm V of Bavaria, 7 September 1584, Bibl, Victor (ed.) (1909), 'Die Berichte des Reichshofrates Dr Georg Eder an die Herzoge Albrecht und Wilhelm von Bayern über die Religionskrise in Niederösterreich (1579–1587)', *Jb.f.Lk.v.NÖ*, Neue Folge 8, 67–154, especially 136–7. Duke Albrecht V of Bavaria died on 24 October 1579; as a result, all of Eder's subsequent reports were addressed to his son and successor, Wilhelm.

[63]   Schrauf (ed.), *Der Reichshofrath Dr Georg Eder. Eine Briefsammlung*, pp. 93–5, p. 95.

could not avoid, however, placing at least some of the blame at their door. In a vivid image that he also employed in the *Evangelische Inquisition*, Eder describes how the shepherds have run away and left their flock to the mercy of the wolves.[64] What dominates his representation of the situation in Vienna to his Bavarian recipients is, though, rather the role of the secular powers in allowing such spiritual predators to thrive: the local nobility, the court hierarchy, and the very point from which protection should have come: the emperor himself.

The theme that is most heavily prevalent in Eder's presentation of the confessional situation in which he has to operate is that of the behaviour of the local nobility. In every way he portrayed them as a virtually impassable hindrance to all efforts to restore the Catholic Church: politically, religiously and personally. However suspect its value as an objective commentary, Eder's Bavarian correspondence provides several fascinating snapshots of how the seemingly innocuous rites of passage such as a wedding, baptism, or funeral could inflame a volatile religious situation and act as a barometer of the dominant confessional climate.

Of these types of ceremony, it is that of marriage on which Eder had most to say, perhaps because of the public and symbolic nature of the unions celebrated.[65] This was certainly the case in the marriage in 1580 of the son of the late Catholic Geheimer Rat and Hofkriegsratpresident Georg Teufel, and the daughter of Lutheran Freiherr Oswald von Eitzing. To Eder's outrage, though the Archduke Ernst denied his blessing, von Eitzing none the less insisted that the ceremony was conducted according to Lutheran rites. The marriage thus went ahead at the wish of the bridegroom and though it had to take place outside Vienna, 21 carriages

---

[64]   Eder to Duke Wilhelm, 29 April 1580, Bibl, ed., 'Die Berichte ... ', 108–11, especially 111. Full version in BHStA, Kurbayern Äußeres Archiv, Status Ecclesiasticus-Religionsacta des Erzhauses Österreich, Tom. XI fols 68r–74v. In the *Evangelische Inquisition*, Eder likewise decribes the Lutheran preachers as 'wolves who hide their sharp teeth with sweet words and their rough wolves' hair with sheeps' skin', p. 13r. This may well have been a common image in the circles within which Eder moved. As well as having a biblical origin, the phrase had also been used by Ignatius of Loyola who opined that it was better for the flock to have no shepherd than to have a wolf for a shepherd. Cited in Donnelly, John Patrick (1994), 'Some Jesuit Counter-Reformation Strategies in East-Central Europe, 1550–1585', in Thorp, M.R. and Slavin, A.J. (eds), *Politics, Religion and Diplomacy in Early Modern Europe: essays in honor of De Lamar Jensen*, Kirksville, MO: Sixteenth Century Journal Publishers Incorporated, pp. 83–94, p. 84

[65]   There was however one marriage ceremony which Eder reported primarily on account of a startling incident that occurred at the wedding feast. In a letter dated 5 October 1581, Eder describes how at a wedding celebrated at the castle of Richard Strein, a past member of Maximilian II's Hofkammer, the overburdened floor had collapsed, leaving at least three guests dead. Eder to Wilhelm V, Bibl (ed.), 'Die Berichte ... ', 123. BHStA, Kurbayern Äußeres Archiv, Status Ecclesiasticus-Religionsacta des Erzhauses Österreich, Tom. XII fols 74–77r. Charitably, Eder refrained from writing what he must have thought: Strein was a Protestant, and the tragedy thus a reflection of God's anger.

and 100 horses carried the guests to see the union sanctified by a Lutheran preacher in yet another symbolic attack on Habsburg authority.[66]

The nature of high-profile burials and baptisms were further subjects on which Eder lingered in some detail, again in part because they could be counted as 'news' but also because they revealed much of the confessional situation in Vienna. In a letter dated 20 December 1578, Eder describes the funeral rites of the aforementioned Georg Teufel, in which the origins of his son's later willingness to acquiesce over a Lutheran wedding ceremony may be identified. According to Eder, Teufel was buried against his own wishes for a Catholic funeral, 'without the cross, without light, without anything … '.[67]

Eder's concern for the younger generation also applied to members of the nobility. As well as the lack of confessional awareness on the part of the likes of Teufel's son, Eder saw infant baptism being used as a political and even dynastic weapon. In a report dated 13 May 1580, Eder describes how the young Herr von Schönkirchen, a convert to Catholicism against the will of his Lutheran father, had himself become a father. The young man had wished his child to be baptised as a Catholic, but his father, Ludwig von Schönkirchen, himself took the child outside Vienna to be baptised as a Lutheran.[68]

Such dramatic events were less regular, however, in occurrence and less regularly reported by Eder than the weekly Auslaufen to exactly the sort of location as that at which the Schönkirchen baby had been baptised or the von Eitzing marriage had been solemnised. As Eder himself noted on several occasions, the Auslaufen involved the movement of literally thousands of people to Lutheran services beyond Vienna's walls on a weekly basis. At one point, Eder wrote excitedly that a ban on the regular Lutheran exodus might work: on 17 February 1579 he remarked that not the sixth, seventh or eighth of people had left the city as had done so in previous weeks.[69] Two years later, however, he dolefully commented that the Auslaufen over the Wienerberg towards Inzersdorf showed no sign of ending.[70] By 1585, Eder had to concede that despite the many

---

[66]   Eder reports on this telling episode at length over two reports: one dated 29 April 1580 and the other dated 13 May from the same year, Bibl (ed.), 'Die Berichte … ', 109 and 112, respectively.

[67]   Schrauf (ed.), *Der Reichshofrath Dr Georg Eder. Eine Briefsammlung*, pp. 245–55, especially pp. 247–8.

[68]   Bibl (ed.), 'Die Berichte … ', 112–13, especially 112. Full version in BHStA, Kurbayern Äußeres Archiv, Status Ecclesiasticus-Religionsacta des Erzhauses Österreich, Tom. XI fols 220–222r.

[69]   Bibl (ed.), 'Die Berichte … ', 72–3, especially 72. Full version in BHStA, Kurbayern Äußeres Archiv, Status Ecclesiasticus-Religionsacta des Erzhauses Österreich, Tom. XI fols 71r–75v.

[70]   Eder to Duke Wilhelm, 28 September 1581, ibid., 122. Full version in BHStA, Kurbayern Äußeres Archiv, Status Ecclesiasticus-Religionsacta des Erzhauses Österreich,

punishments that were being meted out on a daily basis, around 3000 people had still left the city on the Sunday previous.[71]

In his descriptions of such a situation, Eder revealed to his Bavarian recipient the effect of the Lutheran tendencies of certain members of the nobility on the worship patterns of the entire population. By taking the terms of Maximilian II's Religions-Konzession of 1568 at its most literal, they had used their private residences as a base for the provision of a Lutheran ministry.[72] Eder suggests, however, that the agenda of certain members of the Lutheran nobility was more proactive even than that. The Oswald von Eitzing named above as having insisted on a Lutheran marriage ceremony for his daughter was also singled out by Eder along with two other members of the nobility for having their own preachers to whom crowds would flock every week.[73] Six years later, Eder reported how Herr Albrecht von Pücheim zu Horn gave shelter to five preachers from foreign parts; that only a few months earlier Eder had complained of the presence in Vienna of Protestant preachers from Bohemia, Hungary and Moravia makes the implication clear.[74]

Eder presents such attacks on the authority and wishes of the Habsburg dynasty as the height of disloyalty: were it not for the emperor, he wrote angrily just before the Landtag of 1580, these nobles would not have so much as a bowl of soup to eat.[75] Yet another feature of his reports is the level and extent of political protest with which the Habsburgs had to deal in Vienna, with the Lutheran nobility either as participants or sponsors. This Eder portrays as constant, dramatic and potentially explosive.

The most significant such protest, and the one which Eder took greatest pains to describe in detail, was the so-called Sturmpetition of 19

Tom. XII fols 68r–71v.

[71]   Eder to Duke Wilhelm, 19 March 1585, ibid., 144–6, especially 144. Full version in BHStA, Kurbayern Äußeres Archiv, Status Ecclesiasticus-Religionsacta des Erzhauses Österreich, Tom. XII fols 212–213v.

[72]   See p. 24 for the exact terms.

[73]   The other two named by Eder in this context were Freiherr Johann Wilhelm von Roggendorf, Landmarschall of Lower Austria 1566–92, and Niclas III Graf zu Salm, a relative of the von Salm family who had earlier acted as Eder's patrons: Eder to Duke Albrecht, 21 January 1574, Schrauf (ed.), *Der Reichshofrath Dr Georg Eder. Eine Briefsammlung*, pp. 71–9, especially p. 76.

[74]   Eder to Duke Wilhelm, 21 March 1580, Bibl (ed.), 'Die Berichte ... ', 104–106, especially 104. Full version in BHStA, Kurbayern Äußeres Archiv, Status Ecclesiasticus-Religionsacta des Erzhauses Österreich, Tom. XI fols 198–201r. Eder to Duke Wilhelm, 20 September 1579, Bibl (ed.), 'Die Berichte ... ', 97. Full version in BHStA, Kurbayern Äußeres Archiv, Status Ecclesiasticus-Religionsacta des Erzhauses Österreich, Tom. XI fols 159–162r.

[75]   Eder to Duke Wilhelm, 21 March 1580, Bibl (ed.), 'Die Berichte ... ', 104–106, especially 105. Full version in BHStA, Kurbayern Äußeres Archiv, Status Ecclesiasticus-Religionsacta des Erzhauses Österreich, Tom. XI fols 203–204v.

July 1579.[76] The period May–June 1578 had seen attempts on the part of the new emperor, Rudolf II, to limit the impact of his father's Religions-Konzession.[77] As a result, the Lutheran church, book shop and school in Vienna were forcibly closed, Lutheran preachers expelled, and efforts made to halt the process of Auslaufen: indeed, it is of such an effort that Eder had written so hopefully in the letter dated 17 February 1579, discussed above. Aside from their disregard for such laws as evidenced by their continued protection of Lutheran preachers and facilitation of Lutheran worship, the Lower Austrian nobles voiced their anger in political terms that drew in the physical support of the pro-Lutheran elements of the populace. Eder's ducal recipient must easily have been able to imagine the alarming scene that met the young Archduke Ernst on 19 July 1579: '... when the archduke went to the window to see the people, 6000 people fell to their knees and cried with loud voices to grant them the word of God ... '.[78]

Nor was this the only such protest that Eder describes in his Bavarian reports. There had been similar occasions before the Sturmpetition, and similar ones afterward, but more frightening still was the release of Lutheran frustrations into outbreaks or potential outbreaks of religious violence.[79] As early as 1577, Eder reported a particularly offensive outrage against the Jesuit church in Vienna: 'ten days ago a large crucifix was torn down from the front of the Jesuit church, one arm nailed to the church door and the image of Christ thrown in the mud'. He went on to describe how the 'enemies of the cross of Christ' continued to abuse the damaged icons for a further three hours.[80] In a much later report, Eder also describes how the Lutheran traders in Vienna used even the conflict over the calendar reform as a means of bullying some Catholic nuns.[81]

---

[76]   See p. 34.

[77]   The terms were announced on 6 May, and made law on 21 June 1578.

[78]   Eder to Duke Albrecht, 10 August 1579, Bibl (ed.), 'Die Berichte ... ', 90–93, especially 90. Full version in BHStA, Kurbayern Äußeres Archiv, Status Ecclesiasticus-Religionsacta des Erzhauses Österreich, Tom. VII, fols 156r–161r.

[79]   For example, in a report dated 27 April 1578, before the stricter laws were even announced, Eder described the sort of intimidation faced by the ruling dynasty in Vienna, when a crowd of 200 gathered in front of the Habsburg court, Schrauf (ed.), *Der Reichshofrath Dr Georg Eder. Eine Briefsammlung*, pp. 160–61. Similarly, there was another protest in the name of the Gospel reported by Eder in a report of 17 February 1579: Bibl (ed.), 'Die Berichte ... ', 72–3, especially 72. Full version in BHStA, Kurbayern Äußeres Archiv, Status Ecclesiasticus-Religionsacta des Erzhauses Österreich, Tom. XI, fols 71r–75v.

[80]   Eder to Duke Albrecht, 30 November 1577, Schrauf (ed.), *Der Reichshofrath Dr Georg Eder. Eine Briefsammlung*, pp. 125–8, especially pp. 126–7.

[81]   On the Gregorian calendar reform of 1582, see p. 31. In a report dated 26 January 1584, Eder described to Duke Wilhelm how the Lutheran traders held 'their' Christmas after the New Year and fired guns throughout the whole night, shooting at the 'poor nuns' in the St Lorenz Church. Bibl (ed.), 'Die Berichte ... ', 135–6, especially 136. Eder had anticipated such confessional strife over the reform. On 6 October 1582, he had remarked dryly: 'the new calendar has not been published here yet; that will lead to major confusion', ibid., 129–

Such was the atmosphere of fear and intimidation in the city, the Corpus Christi procession of May 1578 erupted into chaos in Vienna's so-called Milchkrieg or 'milk war'.[82] As the procession passed by the traders at the Kohlmarkt, en route to Stephansdom, some onlookers pressed forward to see the emperor, who was participating in the city's celebration for the first time in 15 years. As the milk-stalls began to topple over, in the subsequent confusion a rumour circulated that the Protestants were about to massacre the Catholics in an alternative, Viennese version of St Bartholomew's Day. Such was the pre-existing atmosphere in the city, the suggestion was apparently considered not beyond belief, and the entire procession descended into an unseemly, panic-ridden struggle in which the participants in the procession fled into the cathedral and safety. This too is an event which Eder portrays in great detail to the Bavarian duke, lingering in particular on the subsequent confusion of the incident in which no one knew who was friend or enemy.[83]

This representation of Vienna as a place of simmering religious tensions is one which Eder also applied to the Viennese court. In his reports to the Bavarian dukes, Catholics in the Habsburg court were mentioned either for the unusual strength of their devotion or for their rarity, both features that in themselves denote their increasing status in Eder's eyes as an endangered minority. For example, of the imperial counsellor, Helfreich Guet, Eder wrote that he was alone as a Catholic amongst others 'without number'.[84] Likewise, Eder's description of Jakob Kurtz von Seftenau, a man who would later become Reichsvizekanler, is striking on account of its inclusion of the terms pious, learned and Catholic all within the same sentence in the context of the Viennese court.[85] The Catholic ally within the court of whom Eder wrote most was, however, none other than the

---

30, especially 130. Full version in BHStA, Kurbayern Äußeres Archiv, Status Ecclesiasticus-Religionsacta des Erzhauses Österreich, Tom. XI, fols 145–148r.

[82]   For a summary of this incident, see Louthan, *The Quest for Compromise*, pp. 155–6.

[83]   Eder to Duke Albrecht, 30 May 1578: Schrauf (ed.), *Der Reichshofrath Dr Georg Eder. Eine Briefsammlung*, pp. 202–205.

[84]   Eder to Duke Albrecht, end July 1578, Schrauf (ed.), *Der Reichshofrath Dr Georg Eder. Eine Briefsammlung*, pp. 228–31, especially p. 230. In a later letter to Duke Wilhelm, dated 31 December 1584, Eder refers to the same man in glowing terms he otherwise rarely employed: 'Herr Guet is a pious, upright ... man', Bibl (ed.), 'Die Berichte ... ', 140–42, especially 140. Full version in BHStA, Kurbayern Äußeres Archiv, Status Ecclesiasticus-Religionsacta des Erzhauses Österreich, Tom. XI, fols 189–191r.

[85]   Eder to Duke Wilhelm, 6 May 1584, ' ... a fine, pious, learned and Catholic man ... ' Bibl (ed.), 'Die Berichte ... ', 136; Stieve, Felix (ed.) (1885), 'Briefe des Reichshofrathes Dr G. Eder zur Geschichte Rudolfs II und der Gegenreformation in Österreich unter der Enns', *MIÖG*, 6, 440–49, especially 448.

Empress María herself. He describes her as 'a trusted helper', 'the pious empress', and a known source of Catholic patronage and protection in an otherwise hostile environment.[86]

The impact of such a numerically small Catholic presence in the higher echelons of the court is one which Eder depicts as having serious consequences for the religious composition of the court as a whole. A particularly poignant description is that of 29 December 1577, in which Eder writes of his excitement and emotion over the fact that several Catholics had been elected to important posts, and that the subsequent Christmas had seen an attendant rise in those publicly participating in Catholic communion rites: 'his majesty has at the end of 78 appointed a Catholic Burgermeister, Catholic judge and two Catholic counsellors ... there have not been so many at our Christmas service in the last ten years, with a remarkable number going openly to the altar: this was such a comfort to see, that my heart was lifted and eyes overflowed'.[87] Eder's tearful joy was, however, short-lived: in reports from 1578 and 1579, he again returned to his main theme of the distinctly non-Catholic ethos and make-up of the Habsburg court in Vienna.[88]

Another feature of Eder's representation of the court in his letters to Munich was an echo of one of the themes of his *Evangelische Inquisition*: the presence of those who call themselves Catholics but were in fact motivated solely by personal and political gain. Even the terms Eder uses to describe such figures were reminiscent of the vivid language of the controversial published work: 'one is frigid, the other tepid and another hot'.[89] Describing the son of Johann Baptist Weber, Eder's terminology was similar: 'neither cold nor hot, and neither fish not flesh'.[90] His bitter conclusion also echoed

---

[86]   On the Empress María, see p. 34. Eder to Albrecht, 4 May 1578, Schrauf (ed.), *Der Reichshofrath Dr Georg Eder. Eine Briefsammlung*, pp. 162–4, p. 163. Writing to Albrecht shortly after his condemnation by the emperor, Eder reveals his suspicion that his arch-enemy, Johann Baptist Weber, prevented him from being warned in advance about his impending fall, lest he turn to the empress or the Spanish ambassador for help: 11 December 1573, ibid., pp. 57–63, p. 59. In another missive dated 27 April 1578, Eder again identifies the empress as a potential source of aid: ibid., p. 158.

[87]   Eder to Albrecht, ibid., pp. 130–34, p. 132. MacHardy, Karin J. (2003), *War, Religion and Court Patronage in Habsburg Austria. The Social and Cultural Dimensions of Political Interaction, 1521–1622*, Basingstoke: Palgrave Macmillan, p. 63.

[88]   In a letter to Duke Albrecht dated 9 February 1578, Eder wrote that although there are some Catholics at the court, there remain many more opponents, Schrauf (ed.), *Der Reichshofrath Dr Georg Eder. Eine Briefsammlung*, pp. 144–6, p. 146. In another letter to Albrecht, dated 2 September 1579, Eder complained that all offices, high and low, had become dominated by non-Catholics; indeed, in the whole Kriegsrat he remarked that there were no Catholics to be found at all, Bibl (ed.), Die Berichte ... ', 93–7, especially 95.

[89]   Eder to Bavarian Chancellor Christoph Elsenheimer, February 1578, in Stieve (ed.), 'Briefe des Reichshofrathes Dr G. Eder ... ', 440–42, especially 441.

[90]   Eder to Wilhelm, 8 January 1587, Bibl (ed.), 'Die Berichte ... ', 152.

that of the *Evangelische Inquisition*: such 'Hofchristen' do more damage to the Church than the heretics themselves.[91]

In such portrayals of the confessional situation in the Vienna of the 1570s and 1580s, ulterior motives and personal vengeance on Eder's part are not hard to identify. The Lutheran nobles and their patronage of anti-Catholic preaching and protest acted as a serious frustration to Eder's cherished hopes for Catholic revival and reform. Eder's remarks on the confessional equivocation of certain members can easily be linked to personal grudges on Eder's part, especially in the wake of the *Evangelische Inquisition* crisis.[92] There may also be a sense in which such a negative representation of what was happening on the Habsburgs' own doorstep was intended as an ego boost to his new Wittelsbach patrons, in which they could feel themselves superior to their Austrian rivals. It is worth remembering at this point, however, that this was the same environment in which Eder had thrived for many years, and a court from which pro-Catholic religious policies were still emanating, however feeble their impact on the ground. What is therefore most significant about the tone of Eder's reports of Vienna is the massive change in his world-view that it represents: an explicit and implicit complete volte-face on the part of one of the Habsburg dynasty's most faithful supporters with regards to the role of the secular authority in the defence of Catholicism. Up to 1573, Eder had worked within the constraints of Habsburg religious policy to achieve Catholic reform; they had been not only his employers, but the local and imperial temporal rulers to whom he had been content to entrust the fate of the Church. The events of 1573 had, however, forced the Austrian Habsburgs to show their true colours, not only to Eder but to the world: in a choice between defence of Catholicism and defence of their own authority, it was the latter that the emperor chose to protect, even at the expense of the former. For Eder, his condemnation and the subsequent reaction to it across Europe opened his eyes to the necessity of and possibilities for a new political landscape, in which loyalty should be placed along the confessional boundaries rather than historical and geographical ones.

---

[91]   Eder to Wilhelm, 6 October 1582, ibid., 129–30, especially 130. Full version in BHStA, Kurbayern Äußeres Archiv, Status Ecclesiasticus-Religionsacta des Erzhauses Österreich, Tom. XII, fols 145–148r.

[92]   Eder regarded Reichsvizekanzler Weber the elder as the main source of his woes: see pp. 88–9. Thus Weber and his son feature regularly as examples of exactly the type of courtier who were infecting the court with their confessional tepidity. In a particularly cutting comment to Duke Wilhelm, dated 6 May 1584, Eder could not help attacking Weber the elder even after he had died: 'no-one asks after Weber any more, although at a time it appeared as if the country could not be ruled without him', Bibl (ed.), 'Die Berichte ... ', 136.

Eder's subsequent portrayal of the Habsburg emperor himself thus reflects this disillusionment: his difficulty appears to be not with the office of the emperor, or with the Habsburg dynasty per se, but the fact that the convergence of the two has spelled such catastrophe for Catholicism. The bulk of Eder's reports to Munich were written when Rudolf II was Holy Roman Emperor and his younger brother Archduke Ernst was based in Vienna as regent.[93] Eder's comments on Ernst were generally favourable: on at least three occasions he remarks that the archduke was trying his best, but receiving no support.[94]

It is thus the emperor himself who Eder portrays as being the ultimate source of all the confessional problems in Lower Austria.[95] Not only was his support of Ernst portrayed as inadequate, but his rule denounced as one in which his responsibilities as the apex of the temporal and spiritual hierarchy remained woefully unfulfilled. It was not just that the emperor had passed religious concessions in effect favourable to Protestants, but his lack of resolve had apparently led to the decimation of Catholic piety.[96] Under such circumstances, Eder therefore had little choice but to take the step of turning to a rival temporal authority, the Bavarian Wittelsbachs, for the enforcement of Catholic reform. In his own words, part flattery and part fact: 'I know of no Catholic prince in the world who I would rather have as a patron and protector ... '.[97] Eder's enthusiastic compilation of such a vast body of reports for the Munich court provides evidence of this striking shift in allegiance; it also offers evidence of a telling change in tactic, in which Eder used the vehicle of court correspondence as a means of impressing on his new patron the political and confessional virtue of his cause.

---

[93] See p. 22.

[94] In letters to Duke Wilhelm dated 26 January 1584, 23 January 1584, and 19 March 1585, Eder made virtually the same comment. Bibl (ed.), 'Die Berichte ... ', 135, 144–5, and 145, respectively.

[95] Interestingly, one of Eder's reports may point to Rudolf II's increasingly noticeable mental instability. In a letter to Wilhelm of Bavaria dated 9 November 1582, Eder notes that the emperor was always melancholy and preferred to be alone, ibid., 130. Full version in BHStA, Kurbayern Äußeres Archiv, Status Ecclesiasticus-Religionsacta des Erzhauses Österreich, Tom. XII, fols 155–157v.

[96] Eder to Wilhelm, January 1580, ibid., 99–100, especially 100. Full version in BHStA, Kurbayern Äußeres Archiv, Status Ecclesiasticus-Religionsacta des Erzhauses Österreich, Tom. XI, fol. 12–17v. On the subject of the religious concession sanctioned by the Habsburg emperor, Eder commented that 'no Catholic reformation can suffer this concession', Eder to Albrecht, 2 September 1579, Bibl (ed.), 'Die Berichte ... ', 93–7, especially 95. In the light of existing historiographical debate over the use of the term 'Catholic Reformation', Eder's employment of the term is in itself interesting.

[97] Eder to Albrecht, 17 July 1577, Schrauf (ed.), *Der Reichshofrath Dr Georg Eder. Eine Briefsammlung*, pp. 102–104, p. 103.

CHAPTER 6

'Whoever is not like a Jesuit, is not a Catholic'

In January 1585, in a letter composed towards the end of his life, Georg Eder went back to one of his favourite subjects: the dangers of lukewarm Catholicism, as embodied by the Hofchristen of the Viennese court. According to Eder, such persons would say that they were Catholic, but 'not Jesuit Catholic'.[1] Eder's response was simple, unequivocal, and a fitting epitaph to his entire life: 'I reply, also openly, whoever is not like a Jesuit, is not a Catholic'.[2] Eder's final years in Vienna, after the *Evangelische Inquisition* crisis of 1573 and before his death on 19 May 1587, were ones in which he was able to recover a great deal of his capacity for service to the Catholic Church both in word and in deed.[3] His inspiration for this came almost entirely from his lifelong mentors and supporters: the Society of Jesus. Eder had new secular patrons in the form of the Wittelsbach dynasty, and as the previous chapter demonstrates, he went to great lengths to court that patronage. The older

---

[1]   Eder to Duke Wilhelm, 23 January 1585, Bibl, Victor (ed.) (1909), 'Die Berichte des Reichshofrates Dr Georg Eder an die Herzoge Albrecht und Wilhelm von Bayern über die Religionskrise in Niederösterreich (1579–1587)', *Jb.f.Lk.v.NÖ*, Neue Folge 8, 67–154, especially 142–4.

[2]   Ibid., 142–4.

[3]   Uncertainty appears to have surrounded the date of Eder's death. Aschbach and more recently Robert Evans are just two of several who identify 1586 as the year of Eder's death: Aschbach, Joseph Ritter von (1888), *Geschichte der Wiener Universität. Die Wiener Universität und Ihre Gelehrten, 1520 bis 1565*, Vienna: Adolph Holzhausen, p. 174, and Evans, Robert J.W. (1979), *The Making of the Habsburg Monarchy 1550–1700*, Oxford: Clarendon Press, p. 42. The same error appears in Locher, D. Joanne Joseph (1773), *Speculum Academicum Viennense, sen magistratus antiquissimae et celeberrime Universitatis Viennensis, a primo eiusdem auspicio ad nostra tempora chronologice, historice, et lemmatice, exhibitus a D. Joanne Josepho Locher J.U.D.*, vol. 1, Vienna: Kaliwoda, p. 169, and Sorbait, Paul de (1669), *Catalogus Rectorum et illustrium virorum archigymnasii Viennensis 1237–1669*, Vienna: Matthaeus Cosmerov, p. 126. The mistake appears to stem from the 1645 version of the *Catalogus Rectorum* compiled by Jonas Litters. In it, Eder is described as having 'departed to heaven' on 19 May 1586, p. 86. However, that Eder authored at least seven letters in the first four months of 1587 indicates that this cannot be correct. It seems most likely that Eder died on 19 May 1587. See Duhr, Bernhard (1907), *Geschichte der Jesuiten in den Ländern deutscher Zunge*, vol. 1, *Geschichte der Jesuiten in den Ländern deutscher Zunge im XVI. Jahrhundert*, Freiburg im Briesgau: Herder, p. 145, for a citation from the Viennese Jesuits' Hauschronik for 19 May 1587 as referring to the loss of Eder on that date.

Eder was, though, a more circumspect man. He had learned the hard way that secular rulers were just that – secular – and did not always represent the option that was best for the revival of the Catholic Church. Thus the years 1573–87 were ones in which Eder used the support of the Wittelsbachs all he could, but refused to compromise where their wishes seemed to contradict what was best for the faith.

The evidence of this change in Eder's mind may be seen in one of his later published writings: the *Christliche Gutherzige und Notwendige Warnungschrifft* of 1580. A much shorter work than was usual for Eder, at only 34 pages in length, it had a short-term, and local, political aim rather than a long-term pedagogical one.[4] Rhetorically addressed to the members of the fourth estate of Upper and Lower Austria, the book attempted to demonstrate their fate if the current situation was allowed to continue. After recounting the recent history of heretical teaching in the region, Eder chillingly foretold the future as one of 'disobedience, rebellion, war, murder, fire, bloodletting and eternal destruction'.[5] It is at this point that Eder introduced the mantra: 'One must be more obedient to God than man in matters of religion and belief', suggesting that should the authority of the secular powers ever conflict with the law of God, then it is always the latter that should be obeyed.[6]

That Eder demonstrated such a belief in his dealings with the Habsburgs after 1573 is not altogether surprising in view of their treatment of him, though in the context of his history of service it does mark a striking departure. For example, in the closing months of 1584 he rejected an offer to head the imperial Klosterrat. His official reason was that he was too old; in private, he told Duke Wilhelm of Bavaria that he found its operation disorderly.[7]

More striking still, however, is Eder's willingness to say no to his new Wittelsbach patrons when, on occasion, they too seemed to be acting

---

[4]   Eder, Georg (1580), *Ein Christliche Gutherzige und Notwendige Warnungschrifft An Den Vierten Stand der löblichen Statt und Märckt, ainer Ersamen Landschafft in Oesterreich under und ob der Enns: Daß man Gott in Religion und Glaubenssachen mehr gehorsamen solle, als den Menschen Und Was Innhalt diß Spruchs von dem Gehorsam der Augspurgerischen Confession zuhalten sene. Durch H. Georgen Eder D*, Ingolstadt: David Sartorius.

[5]   Eder offers a list of men who have polluted the local religious purity of the area with their false teaching, including Michael Stifel. ibid., fols A iii r–v. Ibid., fol. Bi r.

[6]   Eder went on to elaborate by commenting that the Christian Church does have two heads, but that the spiritual authorities alone have power over Church affairs: ibid., fol. Bi v.

[7]   On Eder and his rejection of the Klosterrat presidency, see Sattek, Johann (1949), 'Der niederösterreich Klosterrat', unpublished dissertation, University of Vienna, p. 123. Eder to Wilhelm, 31 December 1584, Bibl (ed.), 'Die Berichte ... ', 140–42, especially 141. Full version in BHStA, Kurbayern Äußeres Archiv, Status Ecclesiasticus-Religionsacta des Erzhauses Österreich, Tom. XII, fol. 189r–191r.

against God's laws and the best interest of the Church. 1580 saw a considerable clash between the papacy and Duke Wilhelm of Bavaria.[8] The trouble had started in the reign of Albrecht, when the foundation of such bodies as the Bavarian Geistliche Rat of 1568 was regarded by Rome as an excessively invasive secular intrusion into ecclesiastical matters. Despite Wilhelm's assurances to Gregory XIII on his accession to the dukedom in 1579 that he would not interfere in any ecclesiastical matters that did not pertain to him, the duke and the pope clearly retained different conceptions of what Wilhelm's jurisdictional boundaries actually were. When the papal representative in Munich, Ninguardia, was compelled to report to Rome that the old interferences were still continuing, it was to Eder that Wilhelm turned for advice.

Such a request was loaded with significance for the relationship between Eder and the patrons who had done so much to help him in the past, and who could still do so much for him in the future. Despite his formal role as Reichshofrat, Wilhelm could reasonably have expected Eder to fight his corner no matter what the legal technicalities decreed the outcome should be. Eder, however, did no such thing, but rather took the side of Rome; in a declaration dated 26 October 1580, he concluded that custom could never justify an abuse of power, and as such advised Duke Wilhelm to return to the pope to negotiate their differences. Tail between legs, Wilhelm reluctantly did so, and in the spring of 1581 sent his own court preacher, Martin Dum, to the pope to ask for absolution for what had been done in the past, as well as for the papal confirmation of the claims now put forward for the future.[9]

This 'new' Eder was not, however, above using the help of the secular powers to reignite his career as a writer of Catholic pedagogy, and this he persuaded the Wittelsbachs to do in two ways: by offering him financial support to aid his material survival, and by persuading the emperor to overturn the ban on his writing on religious matters. Like

---

[8]   It is worth reflecting that when a similar legal confrontation occurred between Ferdinand I and Paul IV in 1558, Eder had been quick to take the emperor's side of the dispute. Indeed, it was Eder's action at this point that contributed to his rise at the Habsburg court: see pp. 45–6.

[9]   On this episode see Pastor, Ludwig von (1930), *The History of the Popes From the Close of the Middle Ages*, vol. 20, ed. Ralph Francis Kerr, London: Kegan Paul, Trench, Trubner & Co, p. 159ff, and Aretin, Carl Albert von (1842), *Geschichte des bayerischen Herzogs und Kurfürsten Maximilian des Ersten*, vol. 1, Passau: Carl Pleuger, pp. 292–6. The text of Eder's judgment still exists, though not written in his hand and wholly illegible: BHStA, Jesuitica (signature 960), fols 1–4. That both Wittelsbach dukes maintained their patronage of Eder, despite his rejection of the Gurk bishopric in 1574 (which they had also advocated) and his pro-papal stance in 1580, may suggest the genuine respect in which Eder was held in Munich. Or, it could simply be that their patronage of him was such an embarrassment to the Habsburgs that they were willing to endure some insubordination to keep him on side.

most Habsburg employees, the payment of Eder's wages was irregular to say the least. In the four Hofstaatsverzeichnisse in which Eder's prescribed wages are listed – those of 1563, 1567, 1574 and 1576 – the monthly rate designated for him appears to have remained static, at 50 gulden.[10] The amount prescribed was not, however, the amount Eder claims to have received. In the letter to Duke Albrecht cited above, dated 28 August 1574, Eder complains that he had received no payment of any type for five years.[11] In a letter to Adam von Dietrichstein dated 12 January 1577, Eder states that he was owed six years' salary.[12] A few months later, it was again to the Wittelsbachs that he turned. In a letter to Duke Albrecht, dated 24 May 1577, he wrote that he had received no salary for seven years and as a result one son was in the care of the pope, and the other living under the provision of the Society of Jesus at Olmütz.[13]

Judging from the apparent faultiness of Eder's memory of when he was last paid – according to these reports it could have been in 1569, 1570, or 1571 – he was as inconsistent over financial details as his Habsburg employers. Whatever the case, it does appear that Eder was struggling. It has already been noted that he was not from a wealthy background.[14] It was also concern for his family's financial well-being that was one of the reasons Eder had given for rejecting the bishopric of Gurk in favour of a third marriage. In a letter to Duke Albrecht of Bavaria dated 28 August 1574 and in the middle of the Gurk negotiations, Eder informed his new patron that his five children were a central feature of his thoughts, and that as a result he was considering marriage to the widow of the recently-

---

[10]   1563: HHStA, Hofarchiv: Hofstaatsverzeichniss O Me A /SR 183 (1563–1600) Nr. 45a, fol. 1v. 1567: Fellner, Thomas and Kretschmayr, Heinrich (eds) (1907), *Die Österreichische Zentralverwaltung I Abteilung Von Maximilian I. bis zur vereinigung der Österreichischen und Böhmischen Hofkanzlei (1749)*, vol. 2, *Aktenstücke 1491–1681*, Vienna: Veröffentlichungen der Kommission für neuere Geschichte Österreichs, p. 188 and ÖNB Bibl. Pal. Vind. Cod. 14458, fol. 5v. 1574: Hofstaatsverzeichniss O Me A /SR 183 (1563–1600) Nr. 50, fol. 6r. 1576: ibid., Nr. 55, fol. 8r and Fellner and Kretschmayr, *Die Österreichische Zentralverwaltung*, p. 193. By comparison, some of his colleagues were earning more, in theory at least. For example, the list of 1576 is the final one in which Eder is mentioned as Reichshofrat and in which some monetary recognition of his first 13 years of service might be expected. Yet only one member has a lower wage than Eder, while four others, the aforementioned Gail, Jung, Hegenmüller as well as Johann Tonner von Truppach were to receive substantially more. See Fellner and Kretschmayr, *Die Österreichische Zentralverwaltung*, pp. 192–3.

[11]   Schrauf, Karl (ed.) (1904), *Der Reichshofrath Dr Georg Eder. Eine Briefsammlung. Als Beitrag zur Geschichte der Gegenreformation in Niederösterreich*, Vienna: Adolf Holzhausen, pp. 86–9, especially p. 88.

[12]   Ibid., pp. 93–4, p. 95.

[13]   Ibid., pp. 98–100, especially p. 100. On these two sons, see p. 64.

[14]   For more on Eder's finances, see pp. 43, 62–4, 67.

deceased Burgermeister of Vienna, Georg Prantstetter.[15] These wedding plans never came to fruition, but the fact that such a possibility was even mooted does suggest anxiety over his family's temporal security.

According to Leist's study of the Bavarian correspondence of the sixteenth century, the Wittelsbachs usually supplied some form of reimbursement for their agents' efforts.[16] This did not necessarily have to be monetary: in a report of 1567, Johann Hegenmüller requested 'winter clothes for his children'.[17] Payment in cash was, however, also provided. In a report of 15 March 1570, the Prague-based Peter Obernburger wrote of his wish to thank the duke for the 100 cronen he had been sent.[18] The Dukes of Bavaria evidently came to Eder's rescue in the same way: income or not, he did not starve, and in a letter dated 31 December 1584 Eder specifically credited Duke Wilhelm of Bavaria as having saved him from terrible poverty.[19]

More problematic, though, was the resumption of a writing career. As has already been demonstrated, the writing of Catholic pedagogical works was a central aspect of Eder's ministry; in addition, he was deeply affected by the fact that he, a Catholic, had had his writing banned by a supposedly Catholic emperor. Eder was frank about his concern over this aspect of the decree right from the start of his Bavarian correspondence. In one of his first letters to Duke Albrecht, dated 11 December 1573, Eder states that the prohibition on his future writing was the worst aspect of the imperial condemnation.[20] As a result, Eder's reports from Vienna were also littered with references to his attempts to publish again as a Catholic writer, and it was to the Wittelsbachs that he looked for support. Some of this requested backing reflects the age-old problems faced by any writer trying to finish a lengthy work. In a letter dated 15 March 1577, Eder promises that his new work and the sequel to the *Evangelische Inquisition, Das guldene Flüß*, would be ready in a month.[21] A few months later, Eder wrote that the extent of his responsibilities

---

[15]   Schrauf (ed.), *Der Reichshofrath Dr Georg Eder. Eine Briefsammlung*, pp. 86–9, especially p. 87. Georg Prantstetter had died on 6 May 1574.

[16]   Leist, Friedrich (1889), *Zur Geschichte der auswärtigen Vertretung Bayerns im XVI. Jahrhundert*, Bamberg: Buchner, pp. 10–11.

[17]   Ibid., p. 10.

[18]   Cited ibid., p. 11.

[19]   Bibl (ed.), 'Die Berichte ... ', 140–42, especially 141. Full version in BHStA, Kurbayern Äußeres Archiv, Status Ecclesiasticus-Religionsacta des Erzhauses Österreich, Tom. XII, fols 189–191r.

[20]   Ibid., 57–63, especially 62.

[21]   Ibid., 96–7, especially 96. Eder, Georg (1579; 1580 reprint), *Das guldene Flüß Christlicher Gemain Und Gesellschaft, das ist, ain allgemaine richtige Form der ersten, uralten, Prophetischen und Apostolischen Kirchen gleich als ain Kurtze Historia Von der hailigen Statt Gottes ...* , Ingolstadt: David Sartorius.

as Reichshofrat were preventing him from working on a desired third volume.[22]

The most serious difficulty was, however, one exclusive to Eder. His Bavarian correspondence in the months leading up to the eventual 1579 publication of *Das guldene Flüß* reveals his concern that the new work should somehow circumnavigate the terms of the 1573 decree that banned him from ever writing on religious matters again. It was thus to the Wittelsbachs that he looked for assistance, by ensuring that they themselves saw and approved the work prior to publication. Such a tactic was not only a means of eliminating any error or confessional faux pas from the new work's pages, but also of ensuring the continued political support of the Wittelsbachs should the new Emperor Rudolf II decide to continue the enforcement of his father's ban on Eder's writing.[23]

Once again, Eder's new patrons came to the rescue. As early as 19 December 1573, in the immediate aftermath of the issue of the imperial decree of condemnation, Duke Albrecht of Bavaria pledged to help Eder over the term that banned his future writing on religious matters.[24] Five years later, as the completion of *Das guldene Flüß* drew nearer, Albrecht approached the new emperor, Rudolf II, directly.[25] Writing from Gengen on 25 May 1578, the Wittelsbach duke almost goaded his Habsburg rival into permitting the publication of Eder's new work.[26] His language in places betrays a striking similarity to that employed on occasion by Eder himself: for example, in portraying Eder as a voice of Catholic orthodoxy, he contrasts him with the 'hell hounds and savage wolves'

---

[22]   Eder to Duke Albrecht, 14 September 1577, Schrauf (ed.), *Der Reichshofrath Dr Georg Eder. Eine Briefsammlung*, pp. 114–15, especially p. 115.

[23]   In a letter to Albrecht dated 15 March 1577, Eder refers to this wish that the draft text be proofread, and adds that he has enclosed a copy, ibid., pp. 96–7, p. 96. It seems that such preventative measures were wise; on 29 December of the same year, Eder wrote to Duke Albrecht telling him that Hans von Trautson had told the Bishop of Neustadt that the language of Eder's new work was excessively 'sharp' in places, such as passages in which Lutheranism is described as having been founded by Satan. ibid., pp. 96–7, especially p. 96. On the Trautson dynasty, see p. 42. How Trautson the elder saw a draft of Eder's work, or whether he actually had seen such a draft, is unclear.

[24]   Schrauf (ed.), *Der Reichshofrath Dr Georg Eder. Eine Briefsammlung*, pp. 68–9, especially p. 68.

[25]   Eder had already written to Rudolf himself at great length on 19 May 1578, in a letter that pointed out the continued abuse of the terms of the Religions-Konzession of 1568. Ibid., pp. 169–80. It is interesting that Eder wrote after the initial steps had been taken by Rudolf II to eradicate Lutheran worship in Vienna through the closure of the Lutheran church, bookshop and school: see p. 118. It may be that Eder wanted to write as a means of strengthening the emperor's resolve, or as a signal of his continued loyalty to the dynasty.

[26]   Schrauf (ed.), *Der Reichshofrath Dr Georg Eder. Eine Briefsammlung*, pp. 182–202.

of heresy.[27] It was, however, the emperor's responsibilities as temporal defender of Catholicism on which Albrecht laid greatest emphasis, the very responsibilities which Rudolf's father appeared to have so dramatically forsaken in 1573. Albrecht presents Eder's work as needful for the defence of Catholicism, and the emperor as the man whose duty it was to protect the passage of such a work. [28]

Rudolf II did not, it seems, interfere in the publication of Eder's *Das guldene Flüß* in the following year. Why he ignored the terms of his father's legislation is not known: Rudolf may merely have wanted to emphasise his own identity as emperor; he may have accepted the advice of an older ruler who was, after all, also his uncle, or, as his efforts at otherwise stemming the Lutheran tide through legislation suggest, he was simply less open to confessional compromise than his father.[29] There may also have been a sense in which Rudolf II had begun to recognise, albeit dimly, that it was Catholicism that gave the Habsburg dynasty the very authority which it was struggling to maintain in the Austrian lands.[30]

Whatever the case, what is more significant is that the resulting work had the patronage of Bavaria stamped all over it, literally and figuratively. Dedicated to Duke Albrecht himself, *Das guldene Flüß* was published within the Bavarian sphere of influence at the press of David Sartorius in Ingolstadt.[31] As such, the publication of *Das guldene Flüß* and Eder's long-awaited return to the world of Catholic writing was a further outward sign of the Wittelsbach patronage of Eder and, by implication, their zeal for Catholicism. There still survives what appears to have been the very copy of the work presented to Duke Albrecht by Eder himself, but it is worth remembering at this stage that there was more to Eder's return to Catholic writing than political game-playing.[32] The Wittelsbachs may have used Eder to make a political statement, but he too had used them, the secular power, as a means of furthering his own ministry.

Just as Bavaria became a source of practical and political patronage for Georg Eder in the years after 1573, so too it increasingly became a place from whence spiritual direction emanated. The duchy was, as the

---

[27]   Ibid., p. 184. On the use of 'wolf' imagery in Eder's writing, see p. 115.

[28]   Schrauf (ed.), *Der Reichshofrath Dr Georg Eder. Eine Briefsammlung*, p. 201.

[29]   In this context it is worth remembering that Rudolf and his younger brother Ernst had spent their formative years at the ultra-Catholic court of their uncle Philip II in Spain, at the wishes of their Spanish mother and against the wishes of their father.

[30]   This was, however, a position which neither political circumstance nor Rudolf II's increasingly unstable mind permitted him to put into consistent practice. On Rudolf II's reign, see Evans, Robert J.W. (1973), *Rudolf II and his World: A Study in Intellectual History 1576–1612*, Oxford: Oxford University Press.

[31]   Eder, *Das guldene Flüß*, fol.)(ii r.

[32]   The copy in question is physically impressive, not only ornately bound but with gilt edges to the pages, MüSB Res/4 Polem 1001. Duke Albrecht had founded his library in 1558.

sixteenth century wore on, an increasingly potent stronghold of the Jesuits and their supporters. It was none other than Canisius himself, Eder's friend since adolescence, who had in 1555 personally agreed with Duke Albrecht the terms for the establishment one year later of a Jesuit college in Ingolstadt. The university itself soon became dominated by members of the Society of Jesus and their influential adherents. It has already been noted that Eder's other faithful associate, Martin Eisengrein, not only rose to prominence within the Wittelsbach administrative hierarchy, but also held high office at Ingolstadt University.[33] Though never a Jesuit himself, his attitudes and values rendered him almost indistinguishable from those who were.

Another Ingolstadt figure closely linked to the Society of Jesus was Albrecht Hunger.[34] Hunger had studied for three years in Rome at the German College, and became a doctor of theology in 1571 after he had been teaching at Ingolstadt University for four years. His domination of high office at the university was such that he was elected to the office of university rector no less than seven times between 1568 and 1595, but it was for the strength of his zeal for Catholic reform that he was particularly valued by the Wittelsbachs. When Eisengrein died prematurely in 1578, it was Hunger who effectively became his successor, with roles in the Wittelsbach Geistliche Rat as a member of the Visitations Commission and as General Inspector for a planned Bavarian seminary.

Eder's attraction to Bavaria did not just lie, therefore, in the potential for Wittelsbach patronage, attractive a prospect though that was. Ingolstadt in particular was a geographically close, politically powerful, and spiritually vigorous source of support for Eder's beleaguered piety, and the final 14 years of his life were ones in which the Catholicism of the Society of Jesus continued to act as Georg Eder's ultimate guide. This guidance was, however, one that could easily work in tandem with Wittelsbach patronage. When Eder sent his work to Duke Albrecht for approval, both he and the duke knew that it would be primarily the Jesuits at Ingolstadt who would peruse the contents. In two of his letters on the subject of the intended publication of *Das guldene Flüß*, Eder was quite specific about his wish to have the text examined not only by Jesuits, but by those competent in the German language. As a result, in the letter of 12 June 1577, Eder told Duke Albrecht that he had already sent a copy to the Jesuits in Vienna, but because they only had one German theologian

---

[33]   See pp. 70, 74, 86 and 107; also Freninger, Franz Xaver (1872), (ed.), *Das Matrikelbuch der Universität Ingolstadt-Landshut-Munich*, Munich: A. Eichleiter.

[34]   On Hunger (1545–1604), see Boehm, Laetitia; Müller, Winfried; Smolka, Wolfgang J. and Zedelmaier, Helmut (eds) (1998), *Biographisches Lexikon der Ludwig-Maximilians-Universität München*, vol. 1, *Ingolstadt-Landshut 1472–1826*, Berlin: Duncker & Humblot, p. 196. Hunger was rector in 1568, 1572, 1573, 1574, 1586, 1590 and 1595.

in their ranks, he also wanted to send a copy to Munich for forwarding to Ingolstadt.[35] Several months later, Eder even informed Albrecht that in addition to having Eisengrein read the draft text, he wanted Canisius to do the same.[36]

Such a concern on Eder's part reflects his wish for theological precision and the avoidance of any potential future recriminations on his initial return to writing on matters of religion. The forwarding of such drafts to others is something that Eder did on at least one other occasion: the title page of what would later be his 1580 publication, *Malleus Haereticorum*, was enclosed with a report to Duke Albrecht.[37] Perhaps more significant still, however, is the fact that within the Society of Jesus, it was compulsory for every Jesuit to place his writing before censors approved by the order's General or the local superior. A Jesuit Eder may not have been, but the way in which he deliberately courted the feedback of their theologians at Ingolstadt and beyond does suggest that he willingly operated according to their standards.[38]

The continued influence of the Jesuits on Eder's work may also be seen in the content of his religious writing in the post-1573 period. Of the four works written by Eder after the *Evangelische Inquisition*, the only one to fall outside the category of being specifically pedagogical in purpose was the *Christliche Warnungschrift*, discussed above. The others all bear remarkable similarities to each other and to those works of Eder's published between 1568 and 1570.[39] As before, Eder had substantial works published in consecutive years: *Das guldene Flüß* in 1579, *Malleus*

---

[35]   Schrauf (ed.), *Der Reichshofrath Dr Georg Eder. Eine Briefsammlung*, pp. 100–102, especially p. 102.

[36]   12 October 1577, ibid., pp. 122–23, especially p. 123.

[37]   Eder, Georg (1580), *Malleus Haereticorum, De Variis Falsorum Dogmatum ...* , Ingolstadt: David Sartorius. Eder to Duke Albrecht, 20 December 1578, BHStA, Kurbayern Äußeres Archiv: Status Ecclesiasticus-Religionsacta des Erzhauses Österreich, 4241 fol. 63r. It is worth noting that the text clearly changed between draft form and publication, as even the original title 'Furores Haereticorum' or 'The Madness of Heretics' became 'Malleus Haereticorum' or 'Hammer of the Heretics'. Whether the change was made for theological, political, or cosmetic reasons is not clear.

[38]   It is telling that this was also a two-way trade. When the Vienna-based Jesuit, Georg Scherer, began work in 1583 on his *Gründlicher Bericht ob es wahr sei, dass auf eine Zeit ein Pabst zu Rom schwanger gewesen und ein Kind gebohren habe*, published in Vienna by Nassinger in 1584, Georg Eder was one of those to whom he sent an early draft. Such an exchange may be nothing more than a reflection of the two men's friendship, noted below, but may well point to the high regard in which the Jesuits held Eder, regardless of his lay status. On this exchange, see Wiedemann, Theodor (1873), 'Die kirchliche Bücher-Censur in der Erzdiöcese Wien. Nach den Acten des Fürsterzbischöflichen Consistorial-Archives in Wien', *AÖG*, 1, 215–520, especially 279.

[39]   See pp. 76–81.

Haereticorum in 1580, and *Mataeologia Haereticorum* in 1581.[40] Every one was published at the press of Sartorius in Ingolstadt; every one bore the theological approval either of members of the Society of Jesus or Ingolstadt University, and every one was designed to inform and educate the reader in the ways of Catholic orthodoxy.

Das guldene Flüß has already been identified as a potentially controversial work that announced Eder's return to writing on religious affairs. Aside from the political significance of its publication, the work itself is nothing more than a continuation of the *Evangelische Inquisition*, this time Eder having apparently avoided passages of obvious offence to Protestants or Habsburg authority. Unlike its predecessor, which sought to set out the flaws in the evangelical position, *Das guldene Flüß* acted as a complementary volume that aimed rather to set out the truth of Catholicism. Bearing the official approval of the Vienna-based Jesuit and doctor of theology, Peter Busaeus, and Albert Hunger of Ingolstadt University, the format was also as user-friendly as that of the *Evangelische Inquisition*.[41] With points explained in question- and-answer style, the book as a whole was divided into four sections, including one offering a short history of the Catholic Church and another providing a summary of Christian belief in 11 chapters.[42] That the work was intended primarily for a non-clerical or at least less-educated audience is suggested by its composition in the vernacular as well as its format, though lengthy Latin quotations in the margins suggest that *Das guldene Flüß* may also have been of some value to the more advanced reader.[43]

---

[40]   Eder, Georg (1581), *Mataeologia Haereticorum Sive Summa Haereticarum Fabularum* ... , Ingolstadt: David Sartorius.

[41]   Eder, *Das guldene Flüß*, fols A1r–v.

[42]   It is in this context that the meaning of the book's title becomes clear: 'Das guldene Flüß' refers to the passage of Christian truth, ibid., p. 57.

[43]   It is also worth noting that it was the production of *Das guldene Flüß* that apparently provoked the only known published refutation of Eder and his arguments. 1581 saw the publication of the anonymously written and published *Lehr, Glaubens, and Lebens Jesa und der Jesuwider, das ist, Christi un Antichristi. Gegensatz, Antithesis und Vergleichung. Sonderlich wider die Evangelische Inquisitio und das Gulden Fluss ... G.Eders ...* . Its author was one Georg Nigrinus, a Lutheran minister based in Echzell, whose work was framed as a direct response to Eder's *Evangelische Inquisition* and *Das guldene Flüß*, fol. B8 v. A blow-by-blow contradiction of every major point raised by Eder in these works, Nigrinus also took the opportunity to deliver some personal insults to his 'blind and foolish' Catholic foe, fol. K vii v. It is telling that one of the counts on which he attacks Eder is for his dabbling in theological matters at all: 'It would have been better for him if he had remained in his own profession, rather than touching theology with unwashed hands', fol. C iii r. A second work by Ningrinus, published the year later and in a new edition in 1589, also mocked Eder's writing, even its title: *Papistische Inquisition und gulde Fliis der Römischen Kirchen ... sonderlich wider Doctor G. Eders Evangelische Inquisition und gulden Flüss zugericht, etc.* None of Nigrinus' works, however, appear to have been printed more than once, unlike those by the man whom he set out to challenge.

Eder's two other works from this period almost certainly had a different readership in mind, as they were both written entirely in Eder's more usual publishing language of Latin. The first, 1580's *Malleus Haereticorum*, had the same orthodox credentials as that published the year before. Approved on this occasion by Gregorius de Valentia, another Ingolstadt Jesuit, and dedicated to none other than Pope Gregory XIII, the *Malleus* was a 510-page thematically arranged summary of every type of heresy that had ever attacked the true faith, with the Catholic response to such heresies also supplied.[44] The 296-page *Mataeologia Haereticorum* of the following year was similar in content but different in arrangement: this time, the 'heresies' were listed in alphabetical order for ease of reference in the educational establishments for which they were intended.[45] Numerous footnotes were again employed to provide the more scholarly reader with further material, and it is noteworthy that Eder always fully referenced the Catholic response to each heresy, but not the source of the heresy itself, no doubt for fear of aiding the propagators of false teaching. Once again, this work had attained approval before its publication, and once again, this had been issued by Albert Hunger of Ingolstadt University.[46]

Eder's service to the Church in these final years, however, took the form of much more than words. Eder continued to work for Catholic reform as a layman, and did so with remarkable energy and efficacy. To return to the matter of Eder's rejection of the Gurk bishopric, it seems that through the welter of changing, sometimes contradictory excuses Eder made for his declining of the post, his main fear was that as bishop he would be unable to serve the Church as effectively as he could do in his existing state.

Eder's citing of his fears for his children's financial well-being have already been noted as one reason he gave for rejecting the see, even though the pope and the Olmütz Jesuits had already demonstrated themselves willing to pay for the education and welfare of two of his sons.[47] Another reason given by Eder for turning down the offer was his concern that the dispensation necessary for a twice-married layman to become

---

[44]   Eder, *Malleus Haereticorum*, back page. Dedication to Gregory XIII, ibid., fol. 2*r ff. The second edition, published in 1581, was slightly extended and came to 543 pages.

[45]   There survive two copies of the *Mataeologia Haereticorum* at the Munich Staatsbibliothek that were certainly used in Jesuit educational institutions. Signature 'Polem. 833' bears the provenance 'Collegii Societatis Jesu Monachii 1581' in the handwriting on the title page, while 'Polem. 834' is inscribed with 'Collegii Societatis Jesu Monachii ex hareditue D Adam Schiemot'.

[46]   Ibid., fol. T4v.

[47]   See p. 64.

a bishop would be the cause of public scandal.[48] In the same letter to
Duke Albrecht, dated 28 August 1574, Eder added that the Archbishop
of Salzburg and Archduke Charles of Inner Austria had both warned him
that the Emperor Maximilian did not want to see him in the bishopric.[49]
It might be commented that neither the displeasure of Maximilian II nor
the international scandal of the *Evangelische Inquisition* publication had
prevented Eder from functioning to such an extent that he was able to
negotiate the retrieval of most copies of the book as well as the survival of
his own career.[50]

It is, however, far more consistent with what else is known of Eder's life
and character to accept at face value what else Eder had to say about his
decision to reject the bishopric. In the letter of 28 August 1574, Eder wrote
that he would be able to serve the Church where he is, through writing and
other means, just as well in his capacity as a layman.[51] Eder concluded with
a vow that he would seek to fulfil throughout the remainder of his life: 'I
will in no way fail to serve the Church through writings and otherwise; I
still want to do as much as more, as if I were a priest'.[52] Realistically, to act
as Bishop of Gurk in a remote and neglected see would have most likely
curtailed Eder's work for Catholic reform. His plan to remain as he was,
where he was, acts as an unequivocal statement of the potential of the laity
to enact religious change in the latter half of the sixteenth century.

---

[48]   Eder to Albrecht, 28 August 1574, Schrauf (ed.), *Der Reichshofrath Dr Georg Eder.
Eine Briefsammlung*, pp. 86–9, especially p. 87.

[49]   Ibid., p. 87.

[50]   It could be added that high ecclesiastical posts had been offered to laymen before,
and rejected, with no obvious recriminations or career implications. Hans Khevenhüller, the
imperial ambassador in Madrid between 1563 and 1603, was at one point asked by Philip II
of Spain to stand for nomination as cardinal. According to Howard Louthan, 'Khevenhüller
refused and remained in Spain as Rudolf's representative. He was the emperor's primary
source of foreign news, and through his office the Austrian diplomat sustained a conservative
pressure on imperial policy'. It seems that Khevenhüller felt, like Eder, that he could play a
more significant part in the situation he was already in. Louthan, Howard (1997), *The Quest
For Compromise: Peacemakers in Counter-Reformation Vienna*, Cambridge: Cambridge
University Press, pp. 131–2. Georg Gienger of the Geheimer Rat had also been asked by
Ferdinand I to become Bishop of Vienna in 1562, after his wife Magdalena had died in the
previous year. He too refused and continued to serve at the Vienna court until his death in
1577. On Gienger, see pp. 44–5 and p. 55.

[51]   Schrauf (ed.), *Der Reichshofrath Dr Georg Eder. Eine Briefsammlung*, pp. 86–9,
p. 88. It is noteworthy, however, that Eder pledged to remain celibate. Perhaps, though
maintaining the legitimacy of the lay role in the church, Eder was also persuaded that family
life would hinder his efforts.

[52]   Ibid., p. 89.

It must be noted, however, that Eder's service to the Church in this period was more like that of a bishop than that of a priest.[53] Indeed, although a new bishop, Johann Kaspar Neuböck, had been successfully nominated to the see of Vienna in 1574, it would be another seven years before he actually based himself in the city. To compensate for his absence, Eder and another layman, Friedrich Hipp, were given the temporary administration of the Vienna diocese.[54] Perhaps as part of this function, Eder also appears to have resumed his earlier work of filling vacant ecclesiastical positions with suitable clerics. There survives a particularly well-documented example of this, from 1579, when Eder, Oedt and Hillinger went on Klosterrat business to fill the position of priest at the parish of St Michael, recently vacated by Martin Radwiger.[55] What is particularly interesting about the hunt for a new incumbent are the qualities that apparently most pleased Eder and his colleagues in the replacement they found, a 35-year-old priest by the name of Johann Harbort. In their report of 6 September 1579, Eder, Oedt and Hillinger drew the Archduke Ernst's attention to three facets of Harbort's abilities: the depth of his learning, his competence at preaching, and the upstanding nature of his personal life, all of which, they said, qualified him for the task.[56] That Eder and the Jesuits appear to have had particular input into this decision may not only be inferred from Harbort's possession of the very qualities most prized by the Society of Jesus, but from a more concrete piece of evidence. According to the report sent to Archduke Ernst, Harbort had also been educated at the Jesuit college in Vienna, and as a result his qualities were beyond question.[57]

Another career in which Eder was particularly instrumental was that of the young Melchior Khlesl, and in this instance the impact of Eder's patronage had a profound and long-term impact on Catholic reform in Vienna and further afield. It seems that Eder's initial patronage of Khlesl

---

[53] This echoes Eder's claim that while the bishopric of Vienna was vacant, he had done so much, it was as if a bishop were there: see p. 74.

[54] Neuböck was Bishop of Vienna 1574–94. Several items of correspondence survive between Neuböck and Eder, but most are in note form and are therefore very difficult to read. The fuller versions appear to be no longer extant. DAW, Bischofsakten Johann Kaspar Neuböck (1574–94), Kop. Reg. Nr 101–200 (1582–93), letters 133 and 138; DAW, Epistolare des Bischofs Neuböck (1578–82), Wiener Protokolle 9, Standort I B 1, 55 (69), 57 (71), 77 (93), 92 (113), 97 (119).

[55] Eder himself had selected Radwiger only seven years earlier. Whether Eder had made a bad choice, or whether he had chosen a man of such high quality that his ministry was demanded elsewhere, is not known.

[56] Wiedemann, Theodor (1880), *Geschichte der Reformation und Gegenreformation im Lande unter der Enns*, Prague: Tempsky, vol. 2, p. 179, citing the Consistorial-Acten. Harbort was subsequently made priest of the parish of St Michael on 12 September 1579.

[57] Ibid., p. 179.

may well have been merely out of duty to his Catholic associates in Ingolstadt and Passau. Khlesl himself had, like Harbort, been educated at the Jesuit college in Vienna, and as a result could not graduate from Vienna University. In 1579 the 27-year-old travelled to Ingolstadt to receive his degrees from the Faculties of Philosophy and Theology, and on his return to Vienna was ordained priest in the parish of St Peter. In the meantime, Eder himself had been contacted by his own Ingolstadt associate, Albert Hunger, as well as Bishop Urban of Passau, both of whom urged his support for the younger man.[58] Khlesl subsequently became Dompropst of Stephansdom and, as part of that title, Kanzler of Vienna University. One year later, in 1580, he became Passau Offizial, and in Khlesl's energetic hands all offices became tools of Vienna-based Catholic reform with long-term implications. Khlesl's hold on offices continued to expand in the years after Eder's death: in 1588 he became Bishop of Wiener-Neustadt, and in 1602 he was installed as Bishop of Vienna. It was, however, in his work as 'Generalreformator' that Khlesl played the most active role in the stimulation of Catholic reform, with his efforts, similar to those of Eder, to secure competent preachers for the area and to work towards the foundation of a Tridentine Seminary for priests in Vienna.

In all of this, it was the Jesuits who acted as Eder's greatest supporters and inspiration. It was they who had most influenced him as a young man at Cologne, it was they who provided the physical and metaphorical template for his pedagogical writing, and it was they who offered a model of Catholic ministry that eschewed traditional roles for a more dynamic force in society. As late as 1583, at the age of 60, Eder could still report excitedly how that one of the better-known Jesuits in Vienna, Georg Scherer, had performed a remarkable exorcism on a Viennese girl, allegedly possessed by 12 652 evil spirits. According to Eder, Scherer's banishment of the demons was so effective, that the girl, one Anna Schlutterpauerin, was well enough to visit a local shrine.[59] It is Scherer too who Eder credited with the winning of souls on a massive scale,

---

[58]   DAW, Bischofsakten Melchior Khlesl (1598–1630), Kop. Reg. Nr. 1–100 (1555–84), letter 33, recommendation for Khlesl from the Vice-Chancellor of the University of Ingolstadt, Dr Albert Hunger, to Eder, 20 June 1579; letter 34, letter of Bishop Urban of Passau, to Eder, concerning the same, 17 July 1579. In a letter to Duke Albrecht of Bavaria, dated 10 August 1579, Eder wrote of the petition from the Bishop of Passau: Bibl (ed.), 'Die Berichte … ', 90–93, especially 92. Full version in BHStA, Kurbayern Äußeres Archiv, Status Ecclesiasticus-Religionsacta des Erzhauses Österreich, Tom. VII, fol. 156r–161r.

[59]   Eder to Wilhelm, 9 September 1583, Bibl (ed.), 'Die Berichte … ', 132–3, especially 133. Full version in BHStA, Kurbayern Äußeres Archiv, Status Ecclesiasticus-Religionsacta des Erzhauses Österreich, Tom. XII fols 170r–172r.

reporting to Duke Wilhelm that the Jesuit had been responsible for the conversion of 200 people in a few days at nearby Waidhofen.[60]

The lifelong Jesuit impact on Georg Eder went, however, deeper than one-off events. Eder appears to have been genuinely and deeply inspired by the ethos of the Society of Jesus, as his unstinting praise from a letter of 7 September 1584 suggests:

> what one does for a Jesuit, one does for God Himself ... who has to deal with Jesuits finds in their speech, in their dealings ... in short in all things, that one is as the other, as if they are one person ... [and as if] they all have the single spirit of God ... with them lies the true religion ... .[61]

In a world of confessional politics, court intrigue and shifting definitions of what it meant to be a Catholic, it seems that for Georg Eder, it was the Society of Jesus that offered the best answers.

---

[60]   20 December 1586, Bibl (ed.), 'Die Berichte ... ', 151–2, especially 151. Full version in BHStA, Kurbayern Äußeres Archiv, Status Ecclesiasticus-Religionsacta des Erzhauses Österreich, Tom. XII fols 228r–v.

[61]   Eder to Duke Wilhelm, ibid., 136–9, especially 138–9. Full version in BHStA, Kurbayern Äußeres Archiv, Status Ecclesiasticus-Religionsacta des Erzhauses Österreich, Tom. XII fols 178–181r.

Conclusion

It is hard to quantify the legacy of Georg Eder's life and career. As the depressed tone of much of his private writing suggests, even Eder was not always entirely certain of the value of his contribution to Catholic reform. His religious writing was, as has already been noted, frequently derivative of the works of others and of his own, earlier efforts. Although some of his books were reprinted as many as four times, this may well have been a result of his increasing political notoriety. Nor was a single one of Eder's works reprinted after 1585. Aside from the public orations delivered in his memory by the Vienna-based Jesuits, after Eder's death in 1587, it was largely as if he had never existed.[1]

What then can the case of Georg Eder say to a book entitled 'Catholic Belief and Survival in Late Sixteenth-Century Vienna'? One of the benefits of having examined the realities of such a complex career, with all the contradictions and difficulties contained therein, is the potential to cast new light on the broader, equally complex environment in which that life was lived. For example, that Eder's promotion in this period was so heavily contingent on the display of an almost sacred regard for Habsburg authority, speaks volumes about the priorities and problems of Habsburg rule in a multi-confessional age. The speed with which Eder's star rose and later fell was in direct proportion to his reverence for the image of imperial authority, while his subsequent involvement with the Dukes of Bavaria highlights the necessity of secular support for Catholic reform, particularly in the absence of adequate sanction from the local authority. Even this, however, was not always what it could have been, and the extent of Eder's service to the Church, aided by this Bavarian backing but ultimately inspired, influenced and informed by the Jesuits, raises another key issue: the role of the laity at every stage in the process of the implementation of Catholic reform and revival.

Such conclusions also have some broader implications. Firstly, the vicissitudes of Eder's career illustrate that in the latter half of the sixteenth century, 'Catholic' meant different things to different people. Eder himself concluded, as we have seen, that 'whoever is not like a Jesuit, is not a Catholic', and ultimately decided that theirs was the truest path to Catholic reform.[2] Yet he had also had to deal for many years

---

[1]   See p. 65.

[2]   Eder to Duke Wilhelm, 23 January 1585, Bibl, Victor (ed.) (1909), 'Die Berichte des Reichshofrates Dr Georg Eder an die Herzoge Albrecht und Wilhelm von Bayern über

with two sets of rulers who considered themselves equally 'Catholic': for the Austrian Habsburgs, this was a Catholicism tailored to allow for much political manoeuvering in the name of peace and the maintenance of their power; for the Wittelsbachs, this was a Catholicism outwardly more obedient to Rome, but one that still placed dynastic interests above all else, to the extent of making a three-year-old boy Bishop of Regensburg.[3]

Eder's career reflects too the fact that the politics of Catholic leadership were still in a state of dramatic flux in the Europe of the latter half of the sixteenth century. The case of Eder draws attention to the three-way rivalry between pope, Holy Roman Emperor, and Duke of Bavaria, all of whose behaviour over Eder's fate reveals their own agendas. Eder's career illustrates vividly the political tightrope act that was survival in the Austrian Habsburg lands, for ruler and courtier alike. Eder's changing fortunes show the fragility of a Habsburg authority denuded of its spiritual force when confronted with a potentially explosive local and international confessional situation. Aulic Catholicism, of the variety necessarily practised in the reigns of Emperors Ferdinand I, Maximilian II and Rudolf II, proved a hard policy to maintain amidst the confessional extremes of Europe in the second half of the sixteenth century. Eder's situation highlights too the significance of the emerging threat of Bavaria as rivals for leadership of Catholic Europe, and it is telling that when the Austrian Habsburgs did finally regain control in their own lands as well as the empire, in the seventeenth century, it was a form of Catholic rule directly influenced by the Wittelsbachs themselves.

This key element in the revival of the Catholic Habsburg state – the restoration of an emperor with the will and ability to impose an unequivocally Catholic confession on his inheritance – was personally and politically modelled on that of Wittelsbach Bavaria. Once again the Habsburgs were ultimately saved by the twin dynastic policies that had made them in the first place: strategic marriage agreements and the ability to capitalise on premature deaths. In 1571 the devoutly Catholic Duchess Maria of Bavaria (1551–1608), daughter of Duke Albrecht and Maximilian II's sister Anna, was married to her uncle, Archduke Charles of Inner Austria.[4] After his death in 1590, it was Maria who not only acted as regent between 1590 and 1595, but was her eldest

---

die Religionskrise in Niederösterreich (1579–1587)', *Jb.f.Lk.v.NÖ*, Neue Folge 8, 67–154, especially 142–4.

3   See p. 104.

4   On the remarkable life of Maria of Bavaria, see Sánchez, Magdalena S. (2000), 'A Woman's Influence: Archduchess Maria of Bavaria and the Spanish Habsburgs', in Kent, Conrad, Wolber, Thomas and Hewitt, Cameron M.K. (eds), *The Lion and the Eagle: Interdisciplinary Essays on German-Spanish Relations over the Centuries*, New York and Oxford: Berghahn, pp. 91–197.

and succeeding son Ferdinand's unofficial counsellor right up to her own death in 1608. That she ensured that Ferdinand, like all her children, had exclusively Jesuit confessors and went to Jesuit colleges, resulted in the formation of a personally devout Catholic ruler who translated this into public policy not only as ruler of Styria but ultimately as Holy Roman Emperor.[5]

Georg Eder was not, however, in a position to foresee such a turn of events in the 1570s and 1580s, and his turn to the patronage of the Wittelsbachs was based simply on their ability to support his career as a servant of the Catholic Church in a way that the Habsburgs dared not. In similar vein, Eder's service to his faith reflects the importance of creative adaptation to circumstances as a means of ensuring the survival of Catholicism in the second half of the sixteenth century. This is not to say that Eder's Catholicism was merely reactive: his was a piety of initiative that had as its ultimate goal the reform of the Church.

Eder and his faith survived by taking opportunities as and when they arose. Eder laboured for the faith in his local area and, through his writing, for the Catholic community much further afield. He co-operated with what powers he could, when he could, and he sought to bring change in the short term through influencing clerical appointments and in the long term through education. The case of Eder puts, furthermore, the Council of Trent into its proper perspective. Its catechism and initiatives certainly appear to have moved Eder to action in the 1560s, but his devotion to Catholicism had been established long before. Eder's story also illustrates the fluidity of roles within Catholicism in the period during and immediately after Trent, where the boundary between lay and clerical, secular and spiritual were, as has been demonstrated throughout this book, far from rigidly defined.[6]

---

[5]   After the death of his two cousins, Emperor Rudolf II in 1612 and Emperor Matthias in 1619, neither of whom left any legitimate issue, Ferdinand became Emperor Ferdinand II and ruled as such until his death in 1637. As Regina Pörtner argues in her recent monograph, in his own territory the 'outcome of the confessional struggle was above all determined by Ferdinand II's energetic and ultimately successful attempt to realize the political potential of his constitutional position ... ', by preventing co-ordinated opposition: Pörtner, Regina (2001), *The Counter-Reformation in Central Europe: Styria 1580–1630*, Oxford: Oxford University Press, p. 2. See too Bireley, Robert (1994), 'Confessional Absolutism in the Habsburg lands in the Seventeenth Century', in Ingrao, Charles W. (ed.), *State and Society in Early Modern Austria*, West Lafayette, IN: Purdue University Press, pp. 36–53.

[6]   Analysis of the role of laymen in the work of Catholic reform may well be a fruitful area of further research. In the researching of this book, it was noticed that at least two other laymen served the Catholic Church in ways and situations strikingly similar to those of Eder in this period. Pörtner's study of Styria, cited above, makes mention of Wolfgang Schranz von Schranzenegg, a lawyer, counsellor and Vizekanzler at the court of Archduke Charles. Schranz acted as adviser to Maria of Bavaria and was also go-between for the courts of Munich and Graz from the 1570s. Like Eder, Schranz too had close Jesuit connections: Pörtner, *The Counter-Reformation in Central Europe*, pp. 209–11. A study by Maria Barbara Rößner (1991), *Konrad Braun (ca. 1495–1563) – ein katholischer Jurist,*

Eder's is also a story whose emotional verisimilitude adds the frailty of human nature to the broader processes and movements so beloved of historians. Georg Eder was a very human being, who had to square the demands of his faith and conscience with the need to eke out a career and living of his own. That his writings or name do not appear to have successfully survived the test of time suggests that Eder was above all a man of his own day. The problems faced by Eder were problems peculiar to a man living in his particular situation, Vienna, at a particular time, when the Catholic religious and political hierarchy itself was still coming to terms with the practicalities of confessional division.

This is not to say, however, that Eder only made an impact in his own lifetime. On the contrary, the fruits of Eder's work could be seen in the generations that followed him, both in Vienna and across Europe. Eder's self-proclaimed priority throughout his life was that of the welfare of the Catholic Church, and on this he had a significant impact, directly and indirectly.[7] His support of the young Melchior Khlesl, for example, ensured his legacy would continue into the next generation; that Khlesl himself did much to stimulate the revival of Catholicism in the city and university of Vienna may be seen as an echo of Eder's work, carried out under less constricted circumstances.[8] For Eder himself, the priority was the pedagogical writing that dominated so much of his career. As Eder characterised his own war on heresy, he was a 'Latin soldier', and his work helped lay the foundations for the re-education of the very generation of clergy who would lead the revival of Catholicism into the next century, and beyond.[9]

Politiker, Kontroverstheologe und Kirchenreformer im konfessionellen Zeitalter, Münster: Aschendorff, offers some parallels between the careers of Eder and Konrad Braun, another layman active in the Catholic Church in the same period.

[7]   This may be seen throughout Eder's career as discussed in the pages of this book. Eder himself summed up his own position very succinctly in a letter to Duke Albrecht of Bavaria, dated 30 May 1579: 'The welfare of the Catholic religion is of more importance to me than my own welfare', in Bibl (ed.), 'Die Berichte ... ', 80–87, especially 80.

[8]   Khlesl certainly did not have a blank cheque to institute reform, and the reign of the Emperor Matthias in particular led to some reverses. It was, however, under Khlesl's episcopacy that Ferdinand II's Pragmatic Sanction of 13 October 1623 saw the full incorporation of the local Jesuit college into Vienna University, with the Jesuits given substantial control. This had been an event long desired by Eder. In a letter to Duke Wilhelm of Bavaria dated 15 September 1584, Eder had commented that he would be pleased to see such a union, ibid., pp. 139–40, p. 140. Full version in BHStA, Kurbayern Äußeres Archiv, Status Ecclesiasticus-Religionsacta des Erzhauses Österreich, Tom. XII fols 182–184v.

[9]   The full, dryly humorous quotation, reflects Eder's emphasis on correct education over force and coercion: 'I am a Latin soldier; I have in my house nothing more than a few breadknives ... ', Eder to Duke Albrecht, 30 May 1579, Bibl (ed.), 'Die Berichte ... ', 80–87, especially 83.

Select Bibliography

Primary sources

Manuscripts

ARSI, Epistolae Germaniae 153, fols 56r–58v, 235r–v, 251r–v, 293r–294r.

BHStA, Jesuitica, signature 960, fols 1–4.

BHStA, Kurbayern Äußeres Archiv, Korrespondenzakten-Auswärtige Residenten, signatures 4291–4349.

BHStA, Kurbayern Äußeres Archiv, Korrespondenzakten-Österreichisches Korrespondenz, signatures 4456–4466.

BHStA, Kurbayern Äußeres Archiv, Status Ecclesiasticus-Religionsacta des Erzhauses Österreich, signatures 4231 (Tom. I)–4242 (Tom. XII).

BHStA, Kurbayern Äußeres Archiv, Status Ecclesiasticus-Religionsacta des Römischen Reichs, signature 4255.

BHStA, Staatsverwaltung, Auswärtige Staaten und bayerische Beziehungen zu denselben, signature 1931, fols 20r–v and signature 3609 fol. 093/92.

DAW, Bischofsakten Johann Kaspar Neuböck (1574–94), Kop. Reg. Nr 101–200 (1582–93), letters 133 and 138.

DAW, Bischofsakten Melchior Khlesl (1598–1630), Kop. Reg. Nr. 1–100 (1555–1584), letters 33 and 34.

DAW, Epistolare des Bischofs Neuböck (1578–82), Wiener Protokolle 9, Standort I B 1, 55 (69), 57 (71), 77 (93), 92 (113), 97 (119).

HHStA, Graf Chorinsky Quellensammlung, Die Relationen des nö Kammerprokurators Dr Georg Eder 1561 (2 vols).

HHStA, Hofarchiv, Hofstaatsverzeichniss O Me A /SR 183 (1563–1600), Nr 45a (1563), Nr 45 b (1563/4), Nr 50 (1574), Nr 55 (1576), Nr 56 (1576), Nr 64 (1588).

HHStA, Reichshofrat, RHR Protocollum rerum resolutarum XVI 26a (January 1565–April 1569), 36a (January 1572–December 1574), 37 (January–December 1573), 38 (January–December 1574), 39 (August 1574–December 1575), 41 (January 1575–December 1577), 42 (January–November 1577), 44 (August 1577–March 1578), 45 (December 1577–October 1579), 47 (January 1578–December 1580),

48A (October 1579–December 1582), 50 (January 1581–December 1584), 51 (June 1582–January 1583).

HHStA, Staatenabteilung Italien, Rom Varia 1551–59, Fasz. 2 (alt 1, 2), fol. 9r.

HKA, Expedit. Regist. nö 26 (1552), 30 (1554), 37 (1557), 41 (1558), 42 (1558), 45 (1559), 48 (1560), 50 (1561), 51 (1561), 52 (1561), 54 (1562), 56 (1562), 64 (1564), 68 (1565), 71 (1566), 72 (1567), 76 (1567), 80 (1568), 84 (1569), 85 (1570), 90 (1570), 95 (1571), 98 (1572), 100 (1573), 103 (1574), 107 (1575), 108 (1575), 132 (1582), 136 (1583), 145 (1586).

HKA, Reichsakten, Fasz. 150/A, fols 351 r–v, fols 353 r–v, fol. 355r.

ÖNB, Autographenkatalog, Alter Bestand, signature 36/48 –1.

ÖNB, Bibl. Pal. Vind. Cod. 8727.

ÖNB, Bibl. Pal. Vind. Cod. 11648, fols 92v–96r.

ÖNB, Bibl. Pal. Vind. Cod. 14458, Hofstaatsverzeichnis 1567, fol. 5v.

UAW, Fac. Jur. Matrikel 3, (1558–1606), microfilm 074.

UAW, Hauptmatrikel IV, M4 1518 II–1594 I, microfilm 017.

UAW, Phil. Akten, Ph9 (1497–1559), Ph10 (1559–1616), microfilm 066.

UAW, Schrauf, Karl, Konvolut, Altes Biographisches Material-Eder.

UAW, Theol. Akten, Th3 (1508–49) and Th4 (1567–1644), microfilm 075.

UAW, Th15 (1395–1549) and Th16 (1569–1666), microfilm 076.

Printed

Bezold, Friedrich von, ed. (1882), *Briefe des Pfalzgrafen Johann Casimir*, vol. 1, Munich: M. Rieger.

Bibl, Victor, ed. (1900), 'Briefe Melchior Klesls an Herzog Wilhelm V von Baiern', *MIÖG*, 21, 640–73.

Bibl, Victor, ed. (1900), *Klesl's Briefe an K. Rudolfs II. Obersthofmeister Adam Freiherrn von Dietrichstein (1583–1589)*, Vienna.

Bibl, Victor, ed. (1909), 'Die Berichte des Reichshofrates Dr Georg Eder an die Herzoge Albrecht und Wilhelm von Bayern über die Religionskrise in Niederösterreich (1579–1587)', *Jb.f.Lk.v.NÖ*, Neue Folge, 8, 67–154.

Bibl, Victor, ed. (1909), 'Eine Denkschrift Melchior Khlesls über die Gegenreformation in Niederösterreich (c. 1590)', *Jb.f.Lk.v.NÖ*, Neue Folge, 8, 155–71.

Boni, Rocco (1559), *Austriados Libri Quatuor ad invictissimum Ro. Imperatorem Ferdinandum primum, & Serenissimum Bohemiae Regem D. Maximilianum suae Maiest. Filium, carmine heroico descripti & approbati à Magnifico Viro D. Georgio Edero I.C. Caesareo Rectore dignissimo & Collegio Poëtico celeberrimi Archigymnasii Viennensis; Quod poema inscribitur Oraculum*, Vienna: Michael Zimmermann.

Braunsberger, Otto, ed. (1896–1923), *Beati Petri Canisii, Societatis Iesu, Epistulae et Acta*, 8 vols, Freiburg im Briesgau: Herder.

Bues, Almut, ed. (1990), *Nuntiaturberichte aus Deutschland 1572–1585*, part 3 vol. 7, Tübingen: Niemayer.

Camesina Ritter v. San Vittore, Albert, ed. (1881), *Urkundliche Beiträge zur Geschichte Wien's im XVI. Jahrhundert*, Vienna: Alfred Hölder.

Dengel, Ignaz Philipp, ed. (1939), *Nuntiaturberichte aus Deutschland 1560–1572*, part 2, vol. 6, Vienna: Adolf Holzhausen.

Eder, Georg (1551), *Georgii Eder De Illustriss. Principis et D.D. Nicolai Comitis a Salm & Neuburg ad Oenum, S. Ces & Reg. Ro. Mai. A Consiliis secretioribus, militiae & exercitus per Hungariam Ducis supremi & c. viri antiqua virtute & religione clarissimi, morte intempestiua & occasu lamentabili Oratio Funebris, ipso funere Viennae, in praesentia illustriss. Principum & Comitum a Salm, Ro. Reg. Mai. Regiminis, totius Cleri, Academiae, Senatusque Viennesis amplissmi, in aede sacra D. Dorotheae, in summa hominum prestantissimorum frequentia, ab Autore recitata*, Vienna: Egidius Aquila.

Eder, Georg (1557), *Ius Non Opinione Inductum, Sed Natura Constitutum Et Certa scientia conclusum esse ac ob id boni & aequi rationem adeoq. Iustitiam ipsam, sine Iurisperitorum interpraetione atq; consilio, inter homines haud quaq; conseruari, nec ullam Remp: recte gubernari posse, Oratio legalis. Per D. Georg Eder I.U.D. Re. Maiestatis à Consilijs & fisci austriaci aduocatû habita Viennae Austriae XIIII. Septembris, Anno LVII dum Petro Rotio Doctoream dignitatem in U. I. conferret. Item Petri Rotii I.U.D. De Iuris Et iniuriae Sacerdotis Oratio. Subiuncta Est Quaestio Iuris à Petro Rotio in dubium vocata, eiq. annexa est, Doctissima Clarissimi Viri M. Ioannis Rexij Facultatis Artium Decani ad eam Responsio*, Vienna: Raphael Hofhalter.

Eder, Georg (1558), *Laurea poetica, ex caesareo privilegio in celeberrimo archigymnasio Viennensi tribus nuper viris eruditiss: Eliae Corvino, Ioanni Lauterbachio, & Vito Iacobaeo, in maxima Reuerendissimorum Principum, Comitum, Baronum, Nobilium, ac doctissimorum hominum frequentia, summa cum gratulatione collata. A Paulo Fabricio, Caesaris et archiducum austriae mathematico, Medicinae Doctore, edita, in gratiam et honorem illustris ac generosi domini D: Sigismundi Liberi Baronis in Herberstein, Neiperg et Guetenhag, &c. Trium Imperatorum Consiliarii & Oratoris amplissimi, Viri plane Heroici, ac optime de bonarum literarum studiis meriti*, Vienna: Raphael Hofhalter.

Eder, Georg (1558), *Triumphus D. Ferdinando I. Ro. Imperator invictiss. P.P. Augustiss. Archigymnasii Viennensis nomine pro foelicibus Imperii auspiciis renunciatus. Per D. Georg Eder I.U.D. Caes: S. Maiestatis Consiliarium, & pro tempore Rectorem. Ad Eundem Panegyrica aliquot doctissimorum hominum carmina, eiusdem scholae nomine, pro communi congratulatione de Imperii fascibus tam foeliciter adeptis, conscripta. Quoru[m] autorum nomina sequens exhibet pagina*, Vienna: Raphael Hofhalter.

Eder, Georg (1559), *Catalogus Rectorum Et Illustrium Virorum Archigymnasii Viennensis: in quo praeter elegantissimam temporum seriem, summa queadam continentur quasi capita earum rerum, quae celeberrime huic Academiae sub cuiusq magistratu memoria contigerunt dignae. Ab anno M.CC. XXXVII usque ad annum M.D.LIX Cum Duabus Praefationibus ad celeberrimum I. C. Georgium Gienger Caesari Ferdinando a consiliis arcanis & praefectum Laureacensem: Virum eruditione & prudentia vere illustrem acomni virtutum genere absolutißimum, debonis literis & hac Academia praeclarißime, meritum. Per Georg: Eder. I.C. Caesareum Frisingensem eiusdem Academiae pro tempore Rectorem. Viennae Austriae*, Vienna: Raphael Hofhalter.

Eder, Georg (1559), *Georgii Ederii I.C. Caesa: Frisingen. Orationes sex In Celeberrimo Archigymnasio Viennen: derebus publicis, cum Academiae nomine coram Caesarea Maiestate, tum alias ex publicis concionibus, ad ipsam Academiam ab Authore, dum clarissimis viris doctoream dignitatem conferret, recitate, ac partim antea quoque, partim nunc de nouo aeditae*, Vienna: Raphael Hofhalter.

Eder, Georg (1559), *Luctus Archigymnasii Viennen: Pro Funere D. Caroli Quinti Ro. Imperatoris Augustisimi, Patriae Patris feliciss, Editus; In Honorem Augustiss. Familiae Principum Austriae primorum eiusdem Archigymnasii fundatorum. Per Georg. Eder I.U.D. Caesar. Consiliarum & pro tempore Rectorem*, Vienna: Raphael Hofhalter.

Eder, Georg (1568), *Oeconomia Bibliorum Sive Partitionum Theologicarum Libri Quinque: Quibus Sacrae Scripturae Disposito, Seu Artificium Et Vis atque ratio, in tabulis velut ad viuum exprimitur, & ita ob oculos ponitur, ut non modo absolutissimam complectantur uniuerse Theologie summan atque Methodum, sed Commentarii etiam vice haberi queant. Opus Magno Studio Et Labore Congestum, Et Ad Solidam Divinarum literarum cognitionem, artemq caelestis philosophiae recte per discendam accommodatißmum: Quod non iniuria quis uel aurea Catenam, uel Clauem dicat totius doctinae Christiane. Authore D. Georgio Edero I. C. Frising. Divorum Impp. Ferdinandi Augustissime memorie I. & nunc Cesaris Maximiliani II. Consiliario Aulico Imperiali. His Adiecimus Etiam, Cum Propter Argumenti Similitudinem, Tum ut studiosus Lector, quis sacrae scripturae sit usus, vivum habeat exemplar, Partitiones Catechismi Catholici Tridentini eodem D. Georgio Edero authore*, Cologne: Gervinus Calenius and Johanne Quentel.

Eder, Georg (1568), *Partitiones, Catechismi, Catholici, Eius Nimirum Qui Ex Decreto Concilii Tridentini, Pii V. Pont. Max. Iussu, ad parochos primum editus: Nunc Vero Facilioris Cognitionis Gratia in luculentam hanc Epitomen & commodas aliquot Tabulas, sic digestus atque distributus est, Ut Omni Hominum Et Aetati Et Conditioni magnopere usui esse poßit: Per D. Georgium Ederum Frising S. Caesareae Maiestatis Consiliarum &C. Paulus Ad Tit III. Haec sunt bona & utilia hominibus. Stultas autem questiones, & genealogias, & contentiones, & pugnas legis deuita: Sunt enim inutiles & vanae & c.*, Cologne: Gervinus Calenius and Johanne Quentel.

Eder, Georg (1569), *Catechismus Catholicus Qui Antea Quidem Ex Decreto Concilii Tridentini, Pij V. Pontificis Maximi iussu, ad Parochos praecipue scriptus nunc vero pio Ecclesiae iuuande studio, in compendium redactus, ad captninnentutis Christianae sic partitus est & accommodatus, ut in scholis etiam pueris utiliter proponi queat. Cum Praefatione Ad Illustrissimum Principem & D.D. Ernestum Comitem Palatinum Rheni, ac utrinsq. Bauariae Ducem &c. Ecclesiae Frisingensis Administratorem, pro Ecclesia Romana, aduersis eam calumnia, qua blaterant aliqui, in ea verum Catechisum hactenus aut non traditem, aut non recte propositum. Per D. Georg Eder Frisingensem, S. Caesar. Maiestat. Consiliarium*, Cologne: Gervinus Calenius and Johanne Quentel. .

Eder Georg (1570), *Ad Rubricam Codicis De Summa Trinitate, & C. Oratio Eximii atque Celeberrimi uiri, Domini Georgii Aederi Frisingensis, I. C. & c. Consiliarii Caesarei, & c. Pro Fide Catholica Habita Viennae Austriae XVI. Septembris Anno LXVIII. Dum Clarißimis uiris, D. Ioanni Schuartzentaler, ac D. Martino Puschman Neapolitanis &c. in V.I. Doctorea Conferret insignia*, Bautzen: Johannis Vuolrab.

Eder, Georg (1570), *Compendium Catechismi Catholici, Quo Ut Antea semper, ita etiamnum ex Decreto Concilii Tridentini pie recteq; S. Romana & apostolica utitur Ecclesia. Cui nunc primum accessit Confessio Catholica Universi Concilii Tride[n]tini, de praecipuis Doctrinae Christiane Articulis, hoc potißimum seculo controuersis. Per D. Georg. Eder. Iurecons. Frisingen. S. Cesar. Maiestat. Consiliar*, Cologne: Gervinus Calenius and Johanne Quentel.

Eder, Georg (1571; 1582 reprint), *Oeconomia Bibliorum Sive Partitionum Theologicarum Libri Quinque ...* , Cologne: Gervinus Calenius and Johanne Quentel.

Eder, Georg (1571; 1582 reprint), *Partitiones, Catechismi, Catholici, Eius Nimirum Qui Ex Decreto Concilii Tridentini ...* , Cologne: Gervinus Calenius and Johanne Quentel.

Eder, Georg (1572), *Oeconomia Bibliorum Sive Partitionum Theologicarum Libri Quinque ...* , new edition, Venice: Dominicus Nicolinus.

Eder, Georg (1572), *Partitiones, Catechismi, Catholici, Eius Nimirum Qui Ex Decreto Concilii Tridentini ...* , new edition, Venice: Dominicus Nicolinus.

Eder, Georg (1573), *Evangelische Inquisition Wahrer und falscher Religion Wider Das gemain unchristliche Claggeschray, Das schier niemand mehr wissen Künde, wie oder was er glauben solle: In forma aines Christlichen Rathschlags, wie ein jeder Christen mensch seines Glaubens halben ganzlich vergwißt und gesichert Sein moge: Dermassen, daß er leichtlich nit künde Betrogen noch verfurt werden*, Dillingen: Sebald Mayer.

Eder, Georg (1573), *Orationes II. Gratulatoriae, Ad Rudolphum Sereniss: Ac Potentiss: Regem Hungariae, & Archiducem Austriae, & c. D. Imperat: Max:II. Filium. Una, Inclyti Regni Hungariae Nomine, Habita Posonii Sub Ipsa Inauguratione Per Reuerendiß: Principem ac D.D. Antonium Verantium Archiep: Strigon: eiusdem Regni Primate, Legatum natu, & c. Altera Nomine Celeberrimi Archigymnasii Viennensis, Recitata Post reditum Viennae à Clarißimo Viro D. Georgio Edero I.C.S. Caes: Maiest: Consiliario Aulico Imperiali*, Vienna: Stephan Creutzer.

Eder, Georg (1574), *Evangelische Inquisition Wahrer und falscher Religion Wider Das gemain unchristliche Claggeschray …* , new edition, place of printing and name of printer unknown.

Eder, Georg (1579; 1580 reprint), *Das guldene Flüß Christlicher Gemain Und Gesellschaft, das ist, ain allgemaine richtige Form der ersten, uralten, Prophetischen und Apostolischen Kirchen gleich als ain Kurtze Historia Von der hailigen Statt Gottes, wie es umb dieselbe vor dieser Spaltung ain Gestalt gehabt, und wie sich das ießig Religionwesen darmit vergleiche, Für den anderen Thail Euangelischer Inquisition, mit angehäffter Erinnerung, Was ain Zeit hero zu gütiger Hinlegung und Vergleichung gegenwirtiges Religionstreits für Weg und Mittel gesucht und gebraucht worden, Woran auch dieselben bis daher entstanden, Und welches entgegen die rechten Mittel senen. Durch H. Georgen Eder D.*, Ingolstadt: David Sartorius.

Eder, Georg (1579), *Methodus Catechisimi Catholici Antea docte ex Decreto. S. Concilii Tridentini S.D.N. Pii V. Pont. Max. Iussu scripti, Ad Parochos Nunc vero pio Ecclesiae iuuandae studio Hoc ordine ita accommodati, ut ne Dum Parochis utilis: at publice etiam Pueris in scolis proponi queat. D. Geor. Ederi. S.C.M. Consiliarii cura ac labore*, Lyon: Joannes Parant

Eder, Georg (1580), *Ein Christliche Gutherzige und Notwendige Warnungschrifft An Den Vierten Stand der löblichen Statt und Märckt, ainer Ersamen Landschafft in Oesterreich under und ob der Enns: Daß man Gott in Religion und Glaubenssachen mehr gehorsamen solle, als den Menschen Und Was Innhalt diß Spruchs von dem Gehorsam der Augspurgerischen Confession zuhalten sene. Durch H. Georgen Eder D*, Ingolstadt: David Sartorius.

Eder, Georg (1580), *Evangelische Inquisition Wahrer und falscher Religion Wider Das gemain unchristliche Claggeschray* ... new edition, Ingolstadt, David Sartorius.

Eder, Georg (1580), *Malleus Haereticorum, De Variis Falsorum Dogmatum Notis Atque Censuris Libri Duo. In quibus uniuersa penè hereses & cognoscendi & fugiendi ratio continetur Sive Methodus Contra Sectas Ad Arguendos Et Convincendos haereticos, hoc tempore omninò necessarai. Ex paucorum quidem, sed probatißimorum Patrum praefscriptionibus in unum velut Corpus congesta*, Ingolstadt: David Sartorius.

Eder, Georg (1581), *Confessio Catholica S.S. Concilii Tridentini Paulo III Iulio III Pio IIII & V Pont. Opt. Max De praecipuis Christianae Religionis Articulis, hoc potissimum seculo controuersis. D. Georg Edero I.C. Necnon. S. Caes. M. Consiliario Collectore*, Lyon: Joannes Parant.

Eder, Georg (1581), *Malleus Haereticorum ... Editio Secunda Cui nunc acessit Demonstratio, penes quos hodie vera, aut falsa sit Ecclesia Per D. Georgium Ederum*, Ingolstadt: David Sartorius.

Eder, Georg (1581), *Mataeologia Haereticorum Sive Summa Haereticarum Fabularum. In Qua Brevi Quodam veluti Compendio continentur nongentifere vanißimi errores, de ducentis propè religionis Catholicae capitibus. Quibus homines quidam reprobi, purum Dei verbum plerunq corrumpere, Ecclesiae verò unitatem proscindere, ac fidei Christiane integritatem violare ausi sunt. Unde apparet etiam illa admodum horrenda. Babylonia Sive Confusio Haeresum quae à Christo nato in huncusq; diem exortae: nunc verò in Locos communes, per quasdam veluti Classes sic digestae, ac distributae sunt, ut primo statim intuitu constet, quae, a quibus, & quo tempore, de quouis Articulo controuerso, uel assertae fuerint, uel damnate. Per D. Georgium Ederum*, Ingolstadt: David Sartorius.

Eder, Georg (1581), *Quaerela Iustitiae, Lites nunc fieri omnio fere Immortales. In Coronatione Magnifici Nobilis & Clarissimi Viri, Domini Alexii Strauss, V.I. Doctoris Academiae Viennensis pro tempore Rectoris. Per D. Georg Ederum*, Vienna: Stephan Creuzer.

Eder, Georg (1585), *Symbolum der Evangelischen Predicanten Darauss klärlich erscheinet, dass sie nit einen einigen Articul unsers heiligen, alleinseligmachenden, den sie nichte eintweders verspottet, oder verfalschet, oder gar verworssen hetten. Menigklich zur Warnung Auss Evangelischer Inquisition D Georgii Ederi. Cum Consensu Reuerendissi DD Martini Archiepiscopi Pragensis*, Prague: printer unknown.

Fabricius, Heinrich (1570), *Kurtzer Catholischer Catechismus Wie sich desselben die Heilig Ro. und Apostolisch Kyrch, von anfang biß dahero jeder zeit recht gebraucht. Auß dem grossen Catechismo so hie beuor vermug des Algemeynen Tridentischen Concilii Beschluß außgage, Der Catholische Juge[n]d zu gute– newlich mit fleiß gezogen, und jetzo in hoch teutsch ubergesetzt*, Cologne: Gervinus Calenius and Johanne Quentel.

Fellner, Thomas and Kretschmayr, Heinrich, eds (1907), *Die Österreichische Zentralverwaltung I Abteilung Von Maximilian I. bis zur vereinigung der Österreichischen und Böhmischen Hofkanzlei (1749)*, vol. 2, *Aktenstücke 1491–1681*, Vienna: Veröffentlichungen der Kommission für neuere Geschichte Österreichs.

Fernandez de Navarrete, Martin, ed. (1842), *Por el Marquís de la Fuensanta del Valle (Colección de documentos inéditos para la historia de Espanya)*, vols 101, 103, 110, 111, Madrid: Impenta de la Viuda de Calero.

Freninger, Franz Xaver, ed. (1872), *Das Matrikelbuch der Universität Ingolstadt–Landshut–München*, Friedberg: Eichleiter.

Gall, Franz and Szaivert, Willy, eds (1971), *Quellen zur Geschichte der Universität Wien. I Abteilung. Die Matrikel der Universität Wien*, vol. 3, 1518/II–1579/I and vol. 4 1579/II–1658/59, Vienna, Cologne, Graz: Publikationen des Instituts für Österreichische Geschichtsforschung.

Goetz, Walter, ed. (1898), *Briefe und Akten zur Geschichte des sechzehnten Jahrhunderts mit besonderer Rücksicht auf Baierns Fürstenhaus*, vol. 5, *Beiträge zur Geschichte Herzog Albrechts V und des Landsberger Bundes 1556–1598*, Munich.

Hansen, Joseph, ed. (1892), *Nuntiaturberichte aus Deutschland 1572–1585*, part 3, vol. 1, Berlin: A. Bath.

Hansen, Joseph, ed. (1894), *Nuntiaturberichte aus Deutschland 1572–1585*, part 3, vol. 2, Berlin: A. Bath.

Hosius, Stanislaus (1584), *Opera Omnia, Tom. II.*, Cologne: M. Cholin.

Keussen, Hermann, ed. (1979), *Die Matrikel der Universität Köln*, vol. 2, Düsseldorf: Droste.

Kramer, Hans, ed. (1952), *Nuntiaturberichte aus Deutschland 1560–1572* part 2, vol. 7, Vienna.

Lazius, Wolfgang (1546), *Vienna Austriae. Rerum Viennensium Commentatii in quatuor libros distincti, in quibus celeberrimae illius Austriae civitatis exordia, vetustas, nobilitas, magistratus, familiaeque ad planum (quod ajunt) explicantur*, Basle.

Litters, Jonas (1645), *Catalogus Rectorum et illustrium virorum archigymnasii Viennensis …1237–1644*, Vienna: Rictius.

McHugh, John A. and Callan, Charles J., trans. (1982), *Catechism of the Council of Trent for Parish Priests. Issued by Order of Pope Pius V*, Rockford, IL: Tan Books.

Melanchthon, Philip and Bucer, Martin (1543) *Von Gottes gnaden unser Hermans Ertzbishoffs zu Coln unnd Churfürsten &c. einfaltigs bedencken, warauff ein Christliche ... Reformation und Lehr brauch der Heyligen Sacramenten und Ceremonien, Seelsorge, und anderem Kirchendienst verbesserung ... auzurichen seye.* Bonn: Laurentius von der Mullen.

Nigrinus, Georg (1581), *Lehr, Glaubens, and Lebens Jesa und der Jesuwider, das ist, Christi un Antichristi. Gegensatz, Antithesis und Vergleichung. Sonderlich wider die Evangelische Inquisitio und das Gulden Fluss ... G. Eders, ... und die Jesuitisch Cölnisch Censur, etc ...*, place of printing and name of printer unknown.

Nigrinus, Georg (1582), *Papistische Inquisition und gulde Fliis der Römischen Kirchen. Das ist Historia und Ankunft der Römischen Kirchen, und sonderlich vom Antichristischen wesen, ... nach anweisung der geheymen ... zahl inn der Offenbarung Johannis, ... sonderlich wider Doctor G. Eders Evangelische Inquisition und gulden Flüss zugericht, etc ...*, place of printing and name of printer unknown.

Nigrinus, Georg (1589), *Papistische Inquisition ... Zum andern Mahl ... gemehrt und biss in diss ... 1589. Jar ... erstreckt ... Darzu auch vieler Bäpst eygentliche ... Anbildnussen ... welche ... O.Panvinius aussgehn lassen, gethan worden,* place of printing and name of printer unknown.

Possevino, Antonio (1570), *Kurtzer Catholischer Catechismus Wie sich desselben die Heilig Ro. und Apostolisch Kyrch, von anfang biß dahero jeder zeit recht gebraucht. Auß dem grossen Catechismo so hie beuor vermug des Algemeynen Tridentischen Concilii Beschluß außgage, Der Catholische Jugend zu guten newlich mit fleiß gezogen, und jetzo in hoch teutsch ubergesetzt,* Cologne: Gervinus Calenius and Johanne Quentel.

Possevino, Antonio (1586), *R. P. Antonii Possevini, ... Theologi Societatis Iesu, de Sectariorum nostri temporis Atheismis liber. Confutatio, item, duorum pestilentißimorum librorum, à Ministris Transsyluanie editorum, ac thesewn Francisci Dauidis aduersus Sanctißimam Trinitatem. Praeterea, Antithesis haereticae perfidiae contra singulos articulos Orthodoxae fidei,* Cologne: Birckmann.

Rainer, Johann, ed. (1967), *Nuntiaturberichte aus Deutschland 1560–1572,* part 2, vol. 8, Graz, Cologne: Niemayer.

Reichenberger, Robert, ed. (1905), *Nuntiaturberichte aus Deutschland 1585 (1584)–1590,* Part 2, *Die Nuntiatur am Kaiserhofe. Erste Hälfte,* Paderborn.

Rescio, Stanislao (1587), *D. Stanislai Hosii S. R. E. Cardinalis Maioris. Poeniten. & Episcopi Varmiensis Vita,* Rome: Zannetti and Ruffinelli.

Schellhass, Karl, ed. (1896), *Nuntiaturberichte aus Deutschland 1572–1585,* part 3, vol. 3, Berlin: A. Bath.

Schellhass, Karl, ed. (1903), *Nuntiaturberichte aus Deutschland 1572–1585*, part 3, vol. 4, Berlin: A. Bath.

Schellhass, Karl, ed. (1909), *Nuntiaturberichte aus Deutschland 1572–1585*, part 3, vol. 5, Berlin: A. Bath.

Schrauf, Karl, ed. (1904), *Acta Facultatis Medicae Universitatis Vindobonensis III 1490–1558*, Vienna: Verlag des Medicinischen Doctorcollegiums.

Schrauf, Karl, ed. (1904), *Der Reichshofrath Dr Georg Eder. Eine Briefsammlung. Als Beitrag zur Geschichte der Gegenreformation in Niederösterreich*, Vienna: Adolf Holzhausen.

Schroeder, Rev. H.J., ed. (1978), *The Canons and Decrees of the Council of Trent*, Rockford, IL: Tan Books.

Schuster, Richard, ed. (1896), 'Regesten aus dem Archive des k.k. Ministeriums des Innern,' in Mayer, Anton (ed.), *Quellen zur Geschichte der Stadt Wien*, part 1 vol. 2, Vienna: Verlag und Eigenthum des Alterthums-Vereines zu Wien, pp. 1–94.

Schwarz, W.E., ed. (1891), *Briefe und Akten zur Geschichte Maximilians II. II Theil: Zehn Gutachten über die Lage der katholischen Kirche in Deutschland (1573/76) nebst dem Protokolle der deutschen Congregation (1573/78)*, Paderborn: Druck und Verlag der Bonifacius Druckerei.

Schwarz, W.E., ed. (1898), *Die Nuntiatur-Korrespondenz Kaspar Groppers (1573–1576)*, Paderborn: Ferdinand Schöningh.

Senfelder, Leopold, ed. (1908), *Acta Facultatis Medicae Universitatis Vindobonensis IV 1558–1604*, Vienna: Verlag des Medicinischen Doctorcollegiums.

Sorbait, Paul de (1669), *Catalogus Rectorum et illustrium virorum archigymnasii Viennensis 1237–1669*, Vienna: Matthaeus Cosmerov.

Sorbait, Paul de (1670), *Catalogus Rectorum et illustrium virorum archigymnasii Viennensis 1237–1670*, Vienna: Matthaeus Cosmerov.

Starzer, Albert, ed. (1895), 'Regesten aus dem k.k. Archive für Niederösterreich (Statthalterei-Archiv)', in Mayer, Anton (ed.), *Quellen zur Geschichte der Stadt Wien*, part I, vol. 1, Vienna: Verlag und Eigenthum des Alterthums-Vereines zu Wien, pp. 210–78.

Starzer, Albert, ed. (1906) 'Fortsetzung' in Starzer, Albert (ed.), *Quellen zur Geschichte der Stadt Wien*, part I, vol. 5, Vienna: Verein für Geschichte der Stadt Wien, pp. 11–397.

Steinherz, S., ed. (1914), *Nuntiaturberichte aus Deutschland 1560–1572*, part 2, vol. 4, Vienna: Alfred Hölder.

Stieve, Felix, ed. (1885), 'Briefe des Reichshofrathes Dr G. Eder zur Geschichte Rudolfs II und der Gegenreformation in Österreich unter der Enns', *MIÖG*, 6, 440–49.

Theiner, Augustin, ed. (1856), *Annales Ecclesiastici*, vol. 1, Rome.

Tomaschek, J.A., ed. (1879), *Geschichts-Quellen der Stadt Wien* part 1, vol. 2, Vienna: Hölder.

Secondary sources

Adamson, John, *The Princely Courts of Europe: Ritual, Politics and Culture under the Ancien Régime 1500–1750*, London: Weidenfeld & Nicolson.

Albrecht, Dieter (1988), 'Das konfessionelle Zeitalter Zweiter Teil: Die Herzöge Wilhelm V. und Maximilian I.','Staat und Gesellschaft Zweiter Teil: 1500–1745', and 'Die Kirchlich-Religiöse Entwicklung Zwiter Teil: 1500–1745', in Kraus, Andreas (ed.), *Handbuch der Bayerischen Geschichte*, vol. 2, Munich: C.H. Beck, pp. 393–417, pp. 625–63 and pp. 702–35.

Albrecht, Dieter (1990), 'Ferdinand II', in Schindling, Anton and Ziegler, Walter (eds), *Die Kaiser der Neuzeit, 1519–1918. Heiliges Römisches Reich, Österreich, Deutschland*, Munich: C.H. Beck, pp. 125–42.

Antonicek, Theophil (1985), 'Musik- und Theaterleben an der Alten Universität', in Hamann, Günther; Mühlberger, Kurt and Skacel, Franz (eds), *Schriftenreihe des Universitätsarchivs*, vol. 2, *Das Alte Universitätsviertel in Wien, 1385–1985*, Vienna: Universitätsverlag für Wissenschaft und Forschung, pp. 161–76.

Aretin, Carl Albert von (1842), *Geschichte des bayerischen Herzogs und Kurfürsten Maximilian des Ersten*, vol. 1, Passau: Carl Pleuger.

Asch, Ronald (1991), 'Court and Household from the Fifteenth to the Seventeenth Centuries', in Asch, R.G. and Birke, Adolf M. (eds), *Princes, Patronage and the Nobility: The Court at the Beginning of the Modern Age c1450–1650*, Oxford: Oxford University Press, pp. 1–38.

Aschbach, Joseph Ritter von (1865), *Geschichte der Wiener Universität im Ersten Jahrhunderte ihres bestehens. Festschrift zu ihrer Fünfhunderjährigen Gründungsfeier*, Vienna: Adolph Holzhausen.

Aschbach, Joseph Ritter von (1877), *Geschichte der Wiener Universität. Die Wiener Universität und ihre Humanisten im Zeitalter Kaiser Maximilians I*, Vienna: Adolph Holzhausen.

Aschbach, Joseph Ritter von (1888), *Geschichte der Wiener Universität. Die Wiener Universität und Ihre Gelehrten, 1520 bis 1565*, Vienna: Adolph Holzhausen.

Aulinger, Rosemarie (1980), *Das Bild des Reichstages im 16. Jahrhundert*, Göttingen: Vandenhoeck & Ruprecht.

Babel, Rainer (1999), 'The Duchy of Bavaria. The Courts of the Wittelsbachs c. 1500–1750', in Adamson, John (ed.), *The Princely Courts of Europe: Ritual, Politics and Culture under the Ancien Régime 1500–1750*, London: Weidenfeld & Nicolson, pp. 189–210.

Bagchi, David V.N. (1991), *Luther's Earliest Opponents*, Minneapolis, MN: Fortress Press.

Bahlmann, Paul (1894), *Deutschlands Katholische Katechismen bis zum Ende des sechzehnten Jahrhunderts*, Münster: Regensbergsche Buchhandlung.

Barea, Ilsa (1966), *Vienna. Legend and Reality*, London: Secker & Warburg.

Barton, Peter Friedrich (1977), 'Gegenreformation und Protestantismus in der Einflußsphäre Habsburgs, vor allem im 17. Jahrhundert', in Barton, Peter F. and Makkai, L. (eds), *Rebellion oder Religion? Die Vorträge des internationalen Kirchenhistorischen Kolloquiums Debrecen 12/2/1976*, Budapest: Református Zsinati Iroda Sajtóosztálya, pp. 23–36.

Bast, Robert James (1997), *Honor Your Fathers. Catechisms and the Emergence of a Patriarchal Ideology in Germany 1400–1600*, Leiden: Brill.

Bauer, Johann Jacob (1774), *Bibliothecae Librorum Rariorum Universalis Supplementorum oder des vollständigen Verzeichnißes rarer Büccher*, vol. I, Nuremberg: Martin Jacob Bauer.

Bauerreiss, Romuald (1965), *Kirchengeschichte Bayerns*, vol. 6, Augsburg: St. Ottilien, EOS Verlag.

Baumgarten, Hermann (ed.) (1888), *Sleidans Briefwechsel*, Strasbourg.

Becker, Moritz-Alois (1877), *Die letzten Tage und der Tod Maximilians II*, Vienna: Carl Finsterbeck.

Becker, Winifred (1988), 'Faktoren der Bayerischen Politik im konfessionellen Zeitalter (1522–1648)', *Ostbairische Grenzmarken Passauer Jahrbuch für Geschichte Kunst und Volkskunde*, 30, 47–57.

Behringer, Wolfgang (1994), 'Bausteine zu einer Geschichte der Kommunikation', *Zeitschrift für Historische Forschung*, 21, 92–112.

Bellinger, Gerhard J. (1983), *Bibliographie des Catechismus Romanus Ex Decreto Concilii Tridentini ad Parochos 1566–1978*, Baden-Baden.

Benda, Kálmán (1991), 'Habsburg Absolutism and the Resistance of the Hungarian Estates in the Sixteenth and Seventeenth Centuries', in Evans, R.J.W. and Thomas, T.V. (eds), *Crown, Church and Estates: Central European Politics in the sixteenth and seventeenth centuries*, London: Macmillan in association with the School of Slavonic and Eastern European Studies, University of London, pp. 123–8.

Bérenger, Jean (1994), *A History of the Habsburg Empire, 1273–1700*, London: Longman.

Bergin, Joseph (1992), 'Between Estate and Profession: the Catholic Parish Clergy of Early Modern Western Europe', in Bush, M.L. (ed.), *Social Orders and Social Classes in Europe since 1500. Studies in Social Stratification*, London: Longman, pp. 66–85.

Bibl, Victor (1898), 'Nidbruck und Tanner. Ein Beitrag zur Entstehungsgeschichte der Magdeburger Centurien und zur Charakteristik König Maximilians II', *AÖG*, 58, 381–430.

Bibl, Victor (1900), *Die Einführung der katholischen Gegenreformation in Niederösterreich durch Kaiser Rudolf II*, Innsbruck: Wagner.

Bibl, Victor (1901), 'Erzherzog Ernst und die Gegenreformation in Niederösterreich (1576–1590)', *MIÖG*, 6, 575–96.

Bibl, Victor (1917), 'Zur Frage der religiösen Haltung K. Maximilians II', *Sonderabdruck aus dem Archiv für österreichische Geschichte*.

Bibl, Victor (1929), *Maximilian II. Der rätselhafte Kaiser. Ein Zeitbild*, Hellerau.

Bireley, Robert (1981), *Religion and Politics in the Age of the Counterreformation. Emperor Ferdinand II, William Lamormaini, S.J., and the Formation of Imperial Policy*, Chapel Hill, NC: North Carolina University Press.

Bireley, Robert (1990), *The Counter-Reformation Prince. Anti-Machiavellianism or Catholic Statecraft in Early Modern Europe*, Chapel Hill, NC: North Carolina University Press.

Bireley, Robert (1991), 'Ferdinand II: Founder of the Habsburg Monarchy', in Evans, R.J.W. and Thomas, T.V. (eds), *Crown, Church and Estates. Central European Politics in the Sixteenth and Seventeenth Centuries*, London: Macmillan in association with the School of Slavonic and Eastern European Studies, University of London, pp. 226–44.

Bireley, Robert (1994), 'Confessional Absolutism in the Habsburg lands in the Seventeenth Century', in Ingrao, Charles W. (ed.), *State and Society in Early Modern Austria*, West Lafayette, IN: Purdue University Press, pp. 36–53.

Bireley, Robert (1999), *The Refashioning of Catholicism, 1450–1700. A Reassessment of the Counter Reformation*, Basingstoke: Macmillan.

Bitskey, István (1991), 'The Collegium Germanicum Hungaricum in Rome and the Beginning of Counter-Reformation in Hungary', in Evans, R.J.W. and Thomas, T.V. (eds), *Crown, Church and Estates. Central European Politics in the Sixteenth and Seventeenth Centuries*, London: Macmillan in association with the School of Slavonic and Eastern European Studies, University of London, pp. 110–22.

Bittner, Ludwig (1936), *Inventare des Wiener Haus-, Hof- und Staatsarchivs*, vol. 5, *Gesamtinventar des Wiener Haus-, Hof- und Staatsarchivs*, vol. 4, Vienna: Verlag A. Holzhausens Nachfolger.

Bittner, Ludwig (1938), *Inventare des Wiener Haus-, Hof- und Staatsarchivs*, vol. 6, *Gesamtinventar des Wiener Haus-, Hof- und Staatsarchivs*, vol. 3, Vienna: Verlag A. Holzhausens Nachfolger.

Blum, Paul Richard (1985), 'Apostolato dei Collegi: on the Integration of Humanism in the Educational Programme of the Jesuits', *History of Universities*, 5, 101–15.

Boehm, Laetitia and Müller, Rainer A. (eds) (1983), *Universitäten und Hochschulen in Deutschland, Österreich und der Schweiz: eine Universitätsgeschichte in Einzeldarstellungen*, Dusseldorf: Econ.

Boehm, Laetitia; Müller, Winfried; Smolka, Wolfgang J. and Zedelmaier, Helmut (eds) (1998), *Biographisches Lexikon der Ludwig-Maximilians-Universität München*, vol. 1, *Ingolstadt-Landshut 1472–1826*, Berlin: Duncker & Humblot.

Borromeo, Agostino (1990), 'Tridentine Discipline: the Church of Rome Between Catholic Refrom and Counter-Reformation', in Grane, Leif and Horby, Kai (eds), *The Danish Reformation Against Its International Background*, Göttingen: Vandenhoeck & Ruprecht, pp. 241–63.

Bosbach, Franz (1989), 'Die katholische Reform in der Stadt Köln', *RQ*, 84, 120–59.

Bösel, Richard (1985), 'Von der Plannung der Jesuitischen Gesamtanlage zum Kirchenumbau Andrea Pozzos', in Hamann, Günther; Mühlberger, Kurt and Skacel, Franz (eds), *Schriftenreihe des Universitätsarchivs*, vol. 2, *Das Alte Universitätsviertel in Wien, 1385–1985*, Vienna: Universitätsverlag für Wissenschaft und Forschung, pp. 103–10.

Bossy, John (1985), *Christianity in the West 1400–1700*, Oxford: Oxford University Press.

Bouza, Fernando (1999), 'Docto y devoto. La biblioteca del Marqués de Almazán y Conde de Monteagudo (Madrid, 1591)', in Edelmayer, Friedrich (ed.), *Hispania-Austria II: Die Epoche Philipps II (1556–1598)*, Vienna: Verlag für Geschichte und Politik, pp. 247–310.

Brady, Thomas A. (1995), *Protestant Politics: Jacob Sturm (1489–1553) and the German Reformation*, Atlantic Highlands, NJ: Humanities Press.

Brandmüller, Walter (ed.) (1993) *Handbuch der Bayerischen Kirchengeschichte*, vol. 2, St Ottilien: EOS Verlag Erzabtei.

Brauneder, Wilhelm (1986), 'Die staatsrechtliche Bedeutung österreichischer Juristenschriften des 16. Jahrhunderts', in Schnur, Roman (ed.), *Die Rolle der Juristen bei der Entstehung des modernen Staates*, Berlin: Duncker & Humblot, pp. 629–47.

Brodrick, James (1935), *Saint Peter Canisius, S.J. 1521–1597*, London: Sheed & Ward.

Bucher, Otto (1956), 'Sebald Mayer' in Pölnitz, Götz Freiherrn von, *Lebensbilder aus dem Bayerischen Schwaben*, Munich: Hueber, pp. 165–79.

Bucher, Otto (1960), *Bibliographie der Deutschen Drucke des XVI Jahrhunderts*, vol. 1, *Dillingen*, Bad Bocklet: Krieg.

Bues, Almut (ed.) (1990), *Nuntiaturberichte aus Deutschland 1572–1585*, part 3 vol. 7, Tübingen: Niemayer.

Burkert, Gunther (1991), 'Protestantism and Defence of Liberties in the Austrian Lands Under Ferdinand I', in Evans, R.J.W. and Thomas, T.V. (eds), *Crown, Church and Estates. Central European Politics in the Sixteenth and Seventeenth Centuries*, London: Macmillan in association with the School of Slavonic and Eastern European Studies, University of London, pp. 58–69.

Buxbaum, Englebert Maximilian (1973), *Petrus Canisius und die Kirchliche Erneuerung des Herzogtums bayern 1549–1556*, Rome: Institutum Historicum S.J.

Carsten, Francis Ludwig (1959), *Princes and Parliaments in Germany. From the Fifteenth to the Eighteenth Century*, Oxford: Clarendon Press.

Cesareo, Francesco C. (1993), 'Quest for Identity: The Ideals of Jesuit Education in the Sixteenth Century', in Chapple, Christopher (ed.), *The Jesuit Tradition in Education and Missions: a 450-year perspective*, London: Associated University Presses, pp. 17–33.

Cesareo, Francesco C. (1993), 'The Collegium Germanicum and the Ignatian Vision of Education', *SCJ*, 24 (4), 829–42.

Châtellier, Louis (1989), *The Europe of the Devout: The Catholic Reformation and the Formation of a New Society*, Cambridge: Cambridge University Press.

Chesler, Robert Douglas (1979), 'Crown, Lords and God: The Establishment of Secular Authority and the Pacification of Lower Austria, 1618–1648', unpublished Ph.D. thesis, Princeton University.

Chipps Smith, Jeffrey (1999), 'The Art of Salvation in Bavaria', in O'Malley, John W., et al. (eds), *The Jesuits. Culture, Sciences, and the Arts 1540–1773*, Toronto: University of Toronto Press, pp. 568–99.

Chudoba, Bohdan (1952), *Spain and the Empire 1519–1643*, Chicago, IL: University of Chicago Press.

Coreth, Anna (2004, new edn [1959]), *Pietas Austriaca. Austrian Religious Practices in the Baroque Era*, trans. W. Bowman, and A.-M. Leitgeb, West Lafayette, IN: Purdue University Press.

Cornejova, Ivana (1997), 'The Religious Situation in Rudolfine Prague', and 'Education in Rudolfine Prague', in Fučíková, E., et al. (eds), *Rudolf II and Prague: the Court and the City*, London: Thames & Hudson, pp. 310–22 and pp. 323–31.

Crofts, Richard A. (1985), 'Printing, Reform, and the Catholic Reformation in Germany (1521–1545)', *SCJ*, 16 (3), 369–81.

Csendes, Peter (1981), *Geschichte Wiens*, Munich: Oldenbourg.

Czeike, Felix (1975), *Wiener Bürgermeister. Eine Geschichte der Stadt Wien*, Vienna: Jugend und Volk.

Czeike, Felix (1981), *Geschichte der Stadt Wien*, Vienna: Moldwen.

D'Amico, John (1983), *Renaissance Humanism in Papal Rome*, Baltimore, MD: The Johns Hopkins University Press.

Daniel, David P. (1980), 'Ecumenicity or Orthodoxy: The Dilemma of the Protestants in the Lands of the Austrian Habsburgs', *CH*, 49, pp. 387–400.

Daniel, David P. (1992), 'Hungary', in Pettegree, Andrew, *The Early Reformation in Europe*, Cambridge: Cambridge University Press, pp. 49–70.

Daniel, David P. (1993), 'No Mere Reflection: Features of the Reformation in the Lands of the Austrian Habsburgs', *Archiv für Reformationsgeschichte Sonderband. Die Reformation in Deutschland und Europa: Interpretationen und Debatten*, pp. 81–96.

Delumeau, Jean (1977), *Catholicism between Luther and Voltaire: A New View of the Counter-Reformation*, London: Burns and Oates.

Denis, Michael (1782 and 1793), *Wiens Buchdruckergeschicht bis M.D.L.X.*, 2 vols, Vienna: Wappler.

Denk, Ulrike (2003), 'Schulwesen und Universität', in Vocelka, K. and Traninger, A. (eds), *Wien. Geschichte einer Stadt, vol. 2, Die frühneuzeitliche Residenz (16. bis 18. Jahrhundert)*, Vienna, Cologne, Weimar: Böhlau, pp. 365–422.

Deutscher, Thomas (1981), 'Seminaries and the Education of Novarese Parish Priests, 1593–1627', *JEH*, 32 (3), 303–19.

Diamant, Paul J. (1933), 'Paulus Weidner von Billerburg (1525–1585). Kaiserlicher Leibarzt und Rektor der Wiener Universität', *Mitteilungen des Vereines für Geschichte der Stadt Wien*, 13/14, 57–64.

Ditchfield, Simon (1995), *Liturgy, Sanctity and History in Tridentine Italy*, Cambridge: Cambridge University Press.

Dollenz, R. P. Carolus (1742), *Scriptores antiquissimae, ac celeberrimae Universitatis Viennensis ordine chronologico propositi pars III saeculum tertium ab. anno MDLXV usque ad annum MDLXXXVII.*, Vienna: Kaliwoda.

Donnelly, John Patrick (1981), 'Peter Canisius', in Raitt, Jill (ed.), *Shapers of Religious Traditions in Germany, Switzerland and Poland, 1560–1600*, New Haven, CT: Yale University Press, pp. 141–56.

Donnelly, John Patrick (1994), 'Some Jesuit Counter-Reformation Strategies in East-Central Europe, 1550–1585', in Thorp, M.R. and Slavin, A.J. (eds), *Politics, Religion and Diplomacy in Early Modern Europe: essays in honor of De Lamar Jensen*, Kirksville, MO: Sixteenth Century Journal Publishers Incorporated, pp. 83–94.

Donnelly, John Patrick (ed.), (1999), *Confraternities and Catholic Reform*, Kirksville, MO: Truman State University Press.

Du Boulay, F.R.H. (1983), *Germany in the later Middle Ages*, London: Athlone.

Duggan, Lawrence G. (1978), 'The Unresponsiveness of the Late Medieval Church: A Reconsideration', *SCJ*, 9 (1), 3–26.

Duhr, Bernhard (1901), 'Die Jesuiten an den deutschen Fürstenhöfen des 16. Jahrhunderts' in Pastor, Ludwig (ed.), *Erläuterungen und Ergänzungen zu Janssens Geschichte des deutschen Volkes*, vol. 2, Freiburg im Breisgau: Herder.

Duhr, Bernhard (1907), *Geschichte der Jesuiten in den Ländern deutscher Zunge*, vol. 1, *Geschichte der Jesuiten in den Ländern deutscher Zunge im XVI. Jahrhundert*, Freiburg im Briesgau: Herder.

Duindam, Jeroen (1999), 'The Archduchy of Austria and the Kingdoms of Bohemia and Hungary. The Courts of the Austrian Habsburgs, c. 1500–1750', in Adamson, John (ed.), *The Princely Courts of Europe: Ritual, Politics and Culture under the Ancien Régime 1500–1750*, London: Weidenfeld & Nicolson, pp. 165–88.

Eberhard, Winfried (1992), 'Bohemia, Moravia and Austria', in Pettegree, Andrew (ed.), *The Early Reformation in Europe*, Cambridge: Cambridge University Press, pp. 23–48.

Edelmayer, Friedrich (1989), 'Habsburgische Gesandte in Wien und Madrid in der Zeit Maximilians II', in Krömer, Wolfram (ed.), *Spanien und Österreich in der Renaissance*, Innsbruck: Universität Innsbruck, pp. 57–70.

Edelmayer, Friedrich (1992), 'Ehre, Geld, Karriere. Adam von Dietrichstein im Dienst Kaiser Maximilians II.', in Edelmayer, Friedrich and Kohler, Alfred (eds), *Kaiser Maximilian II. Kultur und Politik im 16. Jahrhundert*, Wiener Beiträge zur Geschichte der Neuzeit, vol. 17, Vienna: Verlag für Geschichte und Politik, pp. 109–42.

Edelmayer, Friedrich (1994), 'Einheit der Casa de Austria? Philipp II. und Karl von Innerösterreich' in Dolinar, France M.; Liebmann, Maximilian; Rumpler, Helmut and Tavano, Luigi (eds), *Katholische Reform und Gegenreformation in Innerösterreich 1564–1628*, Styria: Hermagoras, pp. 373–86.

Edelmayer, Friedrich (1994), '"Manus manum lavat". Freiherr Wolf Rumpf zum Wielroß und Spanien', in Eltz, Erwein H. and Strohmeyer, Arno (eds), *Die Fürstenberger. 800 Jahre Herrschaft unf Kultur in Mitteleuropa*, Korneuburg: Katalog des Niederösterreichischen Landesmuseums, Neue Folge, 342, pp. 235–52.

Eder, Karl (1957), 'Eder, Georg', *Neue Deutsche Biographie*, vol. 4, Berlin: Duncker & Humblot, pp. 311–12.

Ehalt, Hubert C.H. (1980), *Ausdrucksformen Absolutischer Herrschaft. Der Wiener Hof im 17. und 18. Jahrhundert*, Munich: Oldenbourg.

Ehrenpreis, Stefan and Ruthmann, Bernhard (1997), 'Jus Reformandi-Jus Emigrandi. Reichsrecht, Konfession und Ehre in Religionsstreitigkeiten des späten 16. Jahrhunderts', in Weinzierl, Michael (ed.), *Individualisierung, Rationalisierung, Säkularisierung. Neue Wege der Religionsgeschichte*, Wiener Beiträge zur Geschichte der Neuzeit, vol. 22, Vienna: Verlag für Geschichte und Politik, pp. 67–95.

Eilenstein, Arno (1938), 'Die Beziehungen der Abtei Lambach O.S.B. in Oberösterreich zu Wien und Niederösterreich', *Unsere Heimat*, Neue Folge, 11, 113–25.

Elliott, John H. (1987), 'The court of the Spanish Habsburgs: a peculiar institution?' in Mack, Phyllis and Jacob, Margaret C. (eds), *Politics and Culture in Early Modern Europe*, Cambridge: Cambridge University Press, pp. 5–24.

Evans, Robert J.W. (1970), 'Bohemia, the Emperor and the Porte, 1550–1600', *Oxford Slavonic Papers*, New Series, 3, 85–106.

Evans, Robert J.W. (1973), *Rudolf II and his World: A Study in Intellectual History 1576–1612*, Oxford: Oxford University Press.

Evans, Robert J.W. (1975), 'The Wechel Presses: Humanism and Calvinism in Central Europe 1572–1627', *P&P*, Supplement, 2, 1–74.

Evans, Robert J.W. (1977), 'The Austrian Habsburgs: the dynasty as a political institution', in Dickens, A.G. (ed.), *The Courts of Europe: Politics, Patronage and Royalty, 1400–1800*, London: Thames and Hudson, pp. 121–45.

Evans, Robert J.W. (1979), *The Making of the Habsburg Monarchy 1550–1700*, Oxford: Clarendon Press.

Evans, Robert J.W. (1985), 'Culture and Anarchy in the Empire, 1540–1680', *CEH*, 18, 14–30.

Evans, Robert J.W. (1991), 'The Court: A Protean Institution and an Elusive Subject', in Asch, R.G. and Birke, A.M. (eds), *Princes, Patronage and the Nobility*, Oxford: Oxford University Press, pp. 481–92.

Evans, Robert J.W. (1991), 'The Habsburg Monarchy and Bohemia, 1526–1848', in Greengrass, Mark (ed.), *Conquest and Coalescence: The Shaping of the State in Early Modern Europe*, London: Edward Arnold, pp. 134–54.

Evans, Robert J.W. (1994), 'Introduction', in Ingrao, Charles (ed.), *State and Society in Early Modern Austria*, West Lafayette, IN: Purdue University Press, pp. 1–23.

Findlen, Paula (1997), 'Cabinets, Collecting and Natural Philosophy', in Fučíková, E., et al. (eds), *Rudolf II and Prague: the Court and the City*, London: Thames & Hudson, pp. 209–19.

Finkel, Caroline (1988), *The Administration of Warfare: the Ottoman Military Campaigns in Hungary, 1593–1601*, Vienna: VWGO.

Fischer-Galati, Stephen A. (1956), 'Ottoman Imperialism and the Religious Peace of Nürnberg (1532)', *ARG*, 47, 160–79.

Fischer-Galati, Stephen A. (1959), *Ottoman Imperialism and German Protestantism 1521–1555*, Cambridge, MA: Harvard University Press.

Fletcher, John M. (1981), 'Change and Resistance to change: a consideration of the development of English and German Universities during the sixteenth century', *History of Universities*, 1, 1–36.

Forster, Marc R. (1992), *The Counter-Reformation in the Villages. Religion and Reform in the Bishopric of Speyer, 1560–1720*, Ithaca, NY: Cornell University Press.

Forster, Marc R. (1993), 'The Elite and Popular Foundations of German Catholicism in the Age of Confessionalism: The "Reichskirche"', *CEH*, 25, 311–25.

Forster, Marc R. (1997), 'With and Without Confessionalization. Varieties of Early Modern German Catholicism', *JEMH*, 1, 315–43.

Forster, Marc R. (2001), *Catholic Revival in the Age of the Baroque. Religious Identity in Southwest Germany, 1550–1750*, Cambridge: Cambridge University Press.

Frank, Karl Friedrich von (1967), *Standeserhebungen und Gnadenakte für das Deutsche Reich und die Österreichischen Erblande bis 1806 sowie kaiserlich österreichische bis 1823*, vol. 1, Niederösterreich: Selbstverlag Schloss Senftenegg.

Freedman, Joseph S. (1985), 'Philosophy Instruction within the Institutional Framework of Central European Schools and Universities during the Reformation Era', *History of Universities*, 5, 117–66.

Freninger, Franz Xaver (ed.) (1872), *Das Matrikelbuch der Universität Ingolstadt-Landshut-Munich*, Munich: A. Eichleiter.

Frijhoff, Willem (1996), 'Graduation and Careers' in Ridder-Symoens, Hilde de (ed.), *A History of the University in Europe*, vol. 2, *Universities in Early Modern Europe*, Cambridge: Cambridge University Press, pp. 355–415.

Frijhoff, Willem (1998), 'What is an early modern university? The conflict between Leiden and Amsterdam in 1631', in Robinson-Hammerstein, Helga (ed.), *European Universities in the Age of Reformation and Counter Reformation*, Dublin: Four Courts Press, pp. 149–68.

Fučíková, Eliska (1997), 'Prague Castle Under Rudolf II, His Predecessors and Successors', in Fučíková, E., et al. (eds), *Rudolf II and Prague: the Court and the City*, London: Thames & Hudson, pp. 2–66.

Fučíková, E., et al. (eds) (1997), *Rudolf II and Prague: the Court and the City*, London: Thames & Hudson.

Fulton, Elaine (2005), 'Wolves and Weathervanes': Confessional Moderation at the Habsburg Court of Vienna', in Racaut, Luc and Ryrie,

Alec (eds), *Moderate Voices in the European Reformation*, Aldershot: Ashgate, pp. 145–61.

Gall, Franz (1955), 'Die Archive der deutschen Universitäten in Deutschland, Österreich und der Schweiz', *Archivalische Zeitschrift*, 50/51, 141–51.

Gall, Franz (1965), *Alma Mater Rudolphina 1365–1965*, Vienna, Austria Press.

Gall, Franz (1970), *Die Alte Universität*, Vienna, Hamburg: Paul Zsolnay Verlag.

Ganzer, Klaus (1984), 'Ein Unbequemer Reformer am Rande des Konzils von Trient: Der Franziskaner Franziskus von Córdoba als Berater Kaiser Ferdinands I', *Historisches Jahrbuch*, 104, 309–47.

Gatz, Erwin (ed.) (1996), *Die Bischöfe des Heiligen Römischen Reiches 1448 bis 1648*, Berlin: Duncker & Humblot.

Gentilcore, David (1992), *From Bishop to Witch. The System of the Sacred in Early Modern Terra d'Otranto*, Manchester: Manchester University Press.

Gentilcore, David (1994), 'Adapt Yourselves to the People's Capabilities: Missionary Strategies, Methods and Impact in the kingdom of Naples, 1600–1800', *JEH*, 45, 269–96.

Gerstinger, Hans (1968), *Die Briefe des Johannes Sambucus (Zsamboky) 1554–1584*, Vienna: Österreichische Akademie der Wissenschaften.

Gevay, Anton von (1843), *Itinerar Kaiser Ferdinands I. 1521–1564*, Vienna, Strauß's Witwe.

Geyer, Roderick (1956), 'Dr Johann Caspar Neubeck, Bischof von Wien, 1574–1594', unpublished Doktorarbeit, University of Vienna.

Giard, Luce (1997), 'Remapping knowledge, reshaping institutions', in Pumfrey, S., Rossi, P.L. and Slawinski, M. (eds), *Science, Culture and Popular Belief in Renaissance Europe*, Manchester: Manchester University Press, pp. 19–47.

Goffman, Daniel (2002), *The Ottoman Empire and Early Modern Europe*, Cambridge: Cambridge University Press

Goldmann, Arthur (1905), 'In Memoriam. Dr Karl Schrauf, 1835. I. 11–1904. X. 9', *Sonderabdruck aus den Mitteilungen des österreichische Vereins für Bibliothekswesen*, Vienna: E. Kainz & R. Liebhart.

Gollob, Hedwig (1967), *Friedrich Nausea. Probleme der Gegenreformation*, Nieuwkoop: B. de Graaf.

Grafton, Anthony (1985), 'The World of the Polyhistors: Humanism and Encyclopedism', *CEH*, 18, 31–47.

Greengrass, Mark (1998), *The European Reformation c. 1500–1618*, London: Longman.

Greyerz, Kaspar von (1992), 'Lazarus von Schwendi (1522–1583) and Late Humanism at Basel', in Fleischer, Manfred P. (ed.), *The Harvest of Humanism in Central Europe*, St. Louis, MO: Concordia Publishing House, pp. 179–95.

Grolig, Moritz (1909), 'Die Buchdruckerei des Jesuitenkollegiums in Wien (1559–1565)', *Mitteilungen des Österreichischen Vereins für Bibliothekswesen*, 13, 105–20.

Gross, Lothar (1933), *Inventare des Wiener Haus-, Hof- und Staatsarchivs*, vol. 1, *Der Geschichte der deutschen Reichshofkanzlei von 1559 bis 1806*, Vienna: Haus-, Hof- und Staatsarchiv.

Gross, Lothar (1936), 'Reichshofratsprotokolle als Quellen niederösterreichischer Geschichte', *Jb.f.Lk.v.NÖ*, 26, 119–23.

Grössing, Helmuth (1985), 'Die Wiener Universität im Zeitalter des Humanismus von der Mitte des 15. bis zur Mitte des 16. Jahrhunderts', in Hamann, Günther, Mühlberger, Kurt and Skacel, Franz (eds), *Schriftenreihe des Universitätsarchivs*, vol. 2, *Das Alte Universitätsviertel in Wien, 1385–1985*, Vienna: Universitätsverlag für Wissenschaft und Forschung, pp. 37–45.

Gschließer, Oswald von (1942), *Der Reichshofrat. Bedeutung und Verfassung, Schicksal und Besetzung einer obersten Reichsbehörde von 1559 bis 1806*, Vienna: Veröffentlichungen der Kommission für neuere Geschichte des ehemaligen Österreich.

Guinsberg, Arlene Miller (1992), 'Late German Humanism and Hermeticism. A Reassessment of the Continuity Thesis', in Fleischer, Manfred P. (ed.), *The Harvest of Humanism in Central Europe*, St. Louis, MO: Concordia Publishing House, pp. 197–211.

Gutkas, Karl (1964), 'Landesfürst, Landtag und Städte Niederösterreichs im 16. Jahrhundert', *Jb.f.Lk.v.NÖ*, Neue Folge, 36, 311–19.

Gutkas, Karl (1973), *Geschichte des Landes Niederösterreich*, St. Pölten, Vienna: Verlag Niederösterreichisches Pressehaus.

Habsburg, Maximilian von (2001), 'Thomas a Kempis's "Imitation of Christ": Devotional Literature in an Age of Confessional Polarity', unpublished Ph.D. dissertation, University of St Andrews.

Halsted, David (1991), 'Distance, Dissolution and Neo-Stoic Ideals: History and Self-Definition in Lipsius', *Humanistica Lovaniensia*, 40, 162–74.

Hametner, Angelika (1970), 'Die Niederösterreichischen Landtage von 1530–1564', unpublished dissertation, University of Vienna.

Hammer-Purgstall, Joseph Freiherr von (1847–51), *Khlesl's, des Cardinals, Directors des geheimen Cabinetes Kaisers Mathias Leben*, 4 vols, Vienna, Vienna: Kaulfuß Witwe.

Hammerstein, Notker (1983), 'Die Deutschen Universitäten im Zeitalter der Aufklarung', *Zeitschrift für Historische Forschung*, 10, 73–89.

Hammerstein, Notker (1985), 'Zur Geschichte und Bedeutung der Universitäten im Heiligen Römiscen Reich Deutscher Nation', *HZ*, 241, 287–328.

Hammerstein, Notker (1986), 'Universitäten – Territorialstaaten – Gelehrte Räte' in Schnur, Roman (ed.), *Die Rolle der Juristen bei der Entstehung des modernen Staates*, Berlin: Duncker & Humblot, pp. 687–735.

Harline, Craig and Put, Eddy (2000), *A Bishop's Tale. Mathias Hovius Among His Flock in Seventeenth-Century Flanders*, New Haven, CT: Yale University Press, 2000).

Harrington, Joel F. and Smith, Helmut Walser (1997), 'Confessionalization, Community and State Building in Germany, 1555–1870', *JMH*, 69, 77–101.

Hausberger, Karl and Hubensteiner, Benno (1985), *Bayerische Kirchgeschichte*, Munich: Süddeutscher Verlag.

Hauser, Wilhelm (1982–83), 'Ein protestantes Bücherverzeichnis von 1577 aus niederösterreich', *Jb.f.Lk.v.NÖ*, Neue Folge, 48/49, 115–32.

Headley, John M. (1992), 'Rhetoric and Reality: Messianic, Humanist, and Civilian Themes in the Imperial Ethos of Gattinara', in Reeves, M. (ed.), *Prophetic Rome in the High Renaissance Period*, Oxford: Clarendon Press, pp. 241–69.

Heilingsetzer, Georg (1991), 'The Austrian Nobility, 1600–50: Between Court and Estates', in Evans, R.J.W. and Thomas, T.V. (eds), *Crown, Church and Estates. Central European Politics in the Sixteenth and Seventeenth Centuries*, London: Macmillan in association with the School of Slavonic and Eastern European Studies, University of London, pp. 245–60.

Heimann, Heinz-Dieter (1991), 'Neue Prespektiven für die Geschichte der Post', *HZ*, 253, pp. 661–74.

Heiss, Gernot (1978), 'Konfession, Politik und Erziehung. Die Landschaftsschulen in den nieder – und innerösterreichischen Ländern vor dem Dreißigjährigen Krieg', in Klingenstein, Grete, Lutz, Heinrich and Stourzh, Gerald (eds), *Bildung, Politik und Gesellschaft. Studien zur Geschichte des eruropäischen Bildungswesens vom 16. bis zum 20. Jahrhundert*, Wiener Beiträge zur Geschichte der Neuzeit, vol. 5, Vienna: Verlag für Geschichte und Politik, pp. 13–63.

Heiss, Gernot (1981), 'Bildungsverhalten des Niederösterreichischen Adels im Gescellschaftlichen Wandel: Zum Bildungsgang im 16. und 17. Jahrhundert', in Grete Klingenstein and Heinrich Lutz (eds), *Spezialforschung und 'Gesamtgeschichte'*, Wiener Beiträge zur Geschichte der Neuzeit, vol. 8, Vienna: Verlag für Geschichte und Politik, pp. 139–57.

Heiss, Gernot (1982), 'Reformation und Gegenreformation (1519–1618). Probleme und ihre Quellen' in Zöllner, E. (ed.), *Die Quellen der Geschichte Österreichs*, Vienna: Österreichischer Bundesverlag, pp. 114–32.

Heiss, Gernot (1986), 'Die Jesuiten und die Anfänge der Katholisierung in den Ländern Ferdinands I. Glaube, Mentalität, Politik', 2 vols, unpublished Habilitation, University of Vienna.

Heiss, Gernot (1991), 'Princes, Jesuits and the Origins of Counter–Reform in the Habsburg Lands', in Evans, R.J.W. and Thomas, T.V. (eds), *Crown, Church and Estates. Central European Politics in the Sixteenth and Seventeenth Centuries*, London: Macmillan in association with the School of Slavonic and Eastern European Studies, University of London, pp. 92–109.

Heiss, Gernot (1998), 'Educational politics in the Austrian lands and the foundation of the Jesuit university of Graz, 1585', in Robinson-Hammerstein, Helga (ed.), *European Universities in the Age of Reformation and Counter Reformation*, Dublin: Four Courts Press, pp. 169–86.

Herrnleben, Susanne (1992), 'Zur Korrespondenz Kaiser Maximilians II. mit seinen Gesandten in Spanien (1564–1576)', in Edelmayer, Friedrich and Kohler, Alfred (eds), *Kaiser Maximilian II. Kultur und Politik im 16. Jahrhundert*, Wiener Beiträge zur Geschichte der Neuzeit, vol. 17, Vienna: Verlag für Geschichte und Politik, pp. 95–108.

Hoffmann, Alfred (1964), 'Schwaben und Österreich', *Jb.f.Lk.v.NÖ*, Neue Folge, 36, 445–62.

Horn, Ewald (1893), 'Die Disputationen und Promotionen an den Deutschen Universitäten vornehmlich seit dem 16. Jahrhundert', *Elftes Beiheft zum Centralblatt für Bibliothekswesen*, Leipzig, pp. 1–126.

Hueber, Friedmund (1985), 'Zur Entwicklung der Baugestalt des Alten Universitätsviertels in Wien', in Hamann, Günther, Mühlberger, Kurt and Skacel, Franz (eds), *Schriftenreihe des Universitätsarchivs*, vol. 2, *Das Alte Universitätsviertel in Wien, 1385–1985*, Vienna: Universitätsverlag für Wissenschaft und Forschung, pp. 111–25.

Huntston Williams, George (1981), 'Stanislas Hosius' in Raitt, Jill (ed.), *Shapers of Religious Traditions in Germany, Switzerland and Poland, 1560–1600*, New Haven, CT: Yale University Press, pp. 157–74.

Ingrao, Charles (1994), *The Habsburg Monarchy 1618–1815*, Cambridge: Cambridge University Press.

Jansen, Dirk Jacob (1992), 'The Instruments of Patronage. Jacopo Strada at the Court of Maximilian II: A Case-Study', in Edelmayer, Friedrich and Kohler, Alfred (eds), *Kaiser Maximilian II. Kultur und Politik im 16. Jahrhundert*, Wiener Beiträge zur Geschichte der Neuzeit, vol. 17, Vienna: Verlag für Geschichte und Politik, pp. 82–202.

Janssen, Johannes (1885), *Geschichte des deutschen Volkes seit dem Ausgang des Mittelalters*, vol. 4, Freiburg im Breisgau: Herder.

Janssen, Johannes (1886), *Aus dem deutschen Universitätsleben des sechszehnten Jahrhunderts*, Frankfurt am Main: Foesser Nachfolger.

Jedin, Hubert (1946) *Katholische Reformation oder Gegenreformation? Ein Versuch zur Klärung der Begriffe nebst einer Jubiläumsbetrachtung über das Trienter Konzil*, Lucerne: Josef Stocker.

Jedin, Hubert (1949–75), *Geschichte des Konzils von Trient* (4 vols), Freibourg im Briesgau: Herder.

Johnson, Trevor (1996), 'Holy Fabrications: The Catacomb Saints and the Counter-Reformation in Bavaria', *JEH*, 47, 274–96.

Johnson, Trevor (2006), 'The Catholic Reformation', in Ryrie, Alec (ed.), *The European Reformations*, Basingstoke: Palgrave Macmillan, pp. 190–211.

Johnston, Rona (1993), 'The Implementation of Tridentine reform: the Passau Official and the Parish Clergy in Lower Austria, 1563–1637', in Pettegree, Andrew (ed.), *The Reformation of the Parishes*, Manchester: Manchester University Press, pp. 215–37.

Johnston, Rona Gordon (1996), 'The Bishopric of Passau and the Counter-Reformation in Lower Austria, 1580–1636', unpublished D.Phil. dissertation, University of Oxford.

Johnston, Rona (1997), 'Patronage and parish: the nobility and the recatholicization of Lower Austria', in Maag, Karin (ed.), *The Reformation in Eastern and Central Europe*, Aldershot: Ashgate, pp. 211–27.

Julia, Dominique (1999), 'Reading and the Counter-Reformation', in Cavallo, Guglielmo and Chartier, Roger (eds), *A History of Reading in the West*, Cambridge: Polity Press, pp. 238–68.

Kaltenbaeck, J. (1837), 'Die Universität zu Wien um die Mitte des Sechzehnten Jahrhunderts', *Österreichische Zeitschrift für Geschichts- und Staatskunde*, 3, 1–2, 5–6, 13–15, 17–19, 25–6, 42–4, 50–52, 54–5, 63–4, 66–8.

Kasehs, Ulrike (1991), 'Die ersten Jahre der Reformation in Wien. Ein Beitrag zur Rezeptiongeschichte', unpublished Diplomarbeit, University of Vienna.

Kaufmann, Thomas DaCosta (1978), *Variations On The Imperial Theme in the Age of Maximilian II and Rudolf II*, New York: Garland.

Kaufmann, Thomas DaCosta (1988), *The School of Prague. Painting at the Court of Rudolf II*, Chicago, IL: University of Chicago Press.

Kaufmann, Thomas DaCosta (1995), *Court, Cloister and City: The Art and Culture of Central Europe, 1450–1800*, London: Weidenfeld & Nicolson.

Kittelson, James M. (1990), 'Learning and Education: Phase Two of the Reformation' in Grane, Leif and Horby, Kai (eds), *The Danish*

Reformation Against Its International Background, Göttingen: Vandenhoeck & Ruprecht, pp. 149–63.

Klaiber, Wilbirgis (1978), *Katholische Kontroverstheologen und Reformer des 16. Jahrhunderts*, Münster: Aschendorff.

Klingenstein, Grete (1995), 'Der Wiener Hof in der Frühen Neuzeit. Ein Forschungsdesiderat', *Zeitschrift für Historische Forschung*, 22, 237–45.

Knecht, August (1891), 'Katechismus', *Wetzer und Welte Kirchenlexikon*, second edn, vol. 7, Freiburg im Breisgau: Herder, pp. 288–317.

Knod, G. (1895), 'Hugo Blotius in seinen Beziehungen zu Strassburg', *Centralblatt für Bibliothekswesen*, 12, 266–75.

Kobolt, Anton Maria (1795), *Baierisches Gelehrten Lexikon*, vols 1 and 2, Landshut: Hagen.

Koenigsberger, H.G. (1971), 'The Statecraft of Philip II', *European Studies Review*, 1, 1–21.

Kohler, Alfred (1978), 'Bildung und Konfession. Zum Studium der Studenten aus den habsburgischen Ländern an Hochschulen im Reich (1560–1620)', in Klingenstein, Grete; Lutz, Heinrich and Stourzh, Gerald (eds), *Bildung, Politik und Gesellschaft. Studien zur Geschichte des europäischen Bildungswesens vom 16. bis zum 20. Jahrhundert*, Wiener Beiträge zur Geschichte der Neuzeit, vol. 5, Vienna: Verlag für Geschichte und Politik, pp. 64–123.

Kohler, Alfred (1979), 'Flugblatt und Streitschrift in der österreichischen Reformation und Gegenreformation' in Zöllner, Erich (ed.), *Öffentliche Meinung in der Geschichte Österreichs*, Vienna: Österreichischer Bundesverlag, pp. 27–38.

Kohler, Alfred (1986), 'Zur Bedeutung der Juristen im Regierungssystem der "Monarchia universalis" Kaiser Karls V.' in Schnur, Roman (ed.), *Die Rolle der Juristen bei der Entstehung des modernen Staates*, Berlin: Duncker & Humblot, pp. 649–74.

Kohler, Alfred (1989), 'Die spanisch-österreichische Begegnung in der ersten Hälfte des 16. Jahrhunderts. Ein mentalitätsgeschichtlicher Versuch' in Krömer, Wolfram (ed.), *Spanien und Österreich in der Renaissance*, Innsbruck: Institut für Sprachwissenschaft, pp. 43–55.

Kohler, Alfred (1990), *Das Reich im Kampf um die Hegemonie in Europa 1521–1648*, Munich: Oldenbourg.

Kohler, Alfred (1991), 'Ferdinand I and the Estates: Between Confrontation and Co-Operation, 1521–1564', in Evans, R.J.W. and Thomas, T.V. (eds), *Crown, Church and Estates. Central European Politics in the Sixteenth and Seventeenth Centuries*, London: Macmillan in association with the School of Slavonic and Eastern European Studies, University of London, pp. 48–57.

Kohler, Alfred (1992), 'Vom Habsburgischen Gesamtsystem Karls V. zu den Teilsystemen Philipps II. und Maximilians II', in Edelmayer, Friedrich and Kohler, Alfred (eds), *Kaiser Maximilian II. Kultur und Politik im 16. Jahrhundert*, Wiener Beiträge zur Geschichte der Neuzeit, vol. 17, Vienna: Verlag für Geschichte und Politik, pp. 13–37.

Kopallik, Josef (1890–94), *Regesten zur Geschichte der Erzdiözese Wien*, Vienna.

Kratochwill, Max (1965), 'Wolfgang Lazius', *Wiener Geschichtsblätter*, 20 (3), 449–52.

Kratochwill, Max (1980), 'Wien im 16. Jahrhundert', in Rausch, Wilhelm (ed.), *Die Stadt an der Schwelle Zur Neuzeit*, Linz, Donau: Österreichischer Arbeitskreis für Stadtgeschichtsforschung, pp. 75–92.

Kraus, Andreas (ed.), *Handbuch der Bayerischen Geschichte*, vol. 2, Munich: C.H. Beck.

Kraus, Andreas (1988), 'Bayerische Wissenschaft in der Barockzeit (1579–1750)', in Kraus, Andreas (ed.), *Handbuch der Bayerischen Geschichte*, vol. 2, Munich: C.H. Beck, pp. 877–918.

Krawarik, Hans (1981), 'Causa Hoffmann. Methoden der Gegenreformation um 1580', *Jahrbuch für die Geschichte des Protestantismus in Österreich*, 97, 116–23.

Krexner, Martin and Loidl, Franz (1983), *Wiens Bischöfe und Erzbischöfe*, Vienna.

Kronberger, Katharina (1995), 'Der Reichshofrat Dr Georg Eder und sein Werk Evangelische Inquisition', unpublished Diplomarbeit, University of Vienna.

Krones, Ferdinand (1962), 'Kardinal Melchior Klesl' in Hantsch, Hugo (ed.), *Gestalter der Geschichte Österreichs*, Innsbruck: Studien der Wiener Katholischen Akademie 2, pp. 143–56.

Laferl, Christopher F. (1997), *Die Kultur der Spanier in Österreich unter Ferdinand I. 1522–1564*, Vienna: Böhlau.

Lang, Peter Thaddäus (1984), 'Reform im Wandel. Die katholischen Visitationsinterrogatorien des 16. und 17. Jahrhunderts', in Zeeden, Ernst Walter and Lang, Peter Thaddäus (eds), *Kirche und Visitation. Beiträge zur Erforschung des frühneuzeitlichen Visitationswesen in Europa*, Tübingen Beiträge zur Geschichtsforschung, vol. 14, Stuttgart: Klett-Cotta, pp. 131–90.

Lauchs, Joachim (1978), *Bayern und die deutschen Protestanten 1534–1546. Deutsche Fürstenpolitik zwischen Konfession und Libertät*, Nuremberg: Verein für bayerische Kirchengeschichte.

Lechner, Karl (1969), '500 Jahre Diözese Wien. Vorgeschichte und geschichte des Wiener Bistums', *Unsere Heimat*, 40, 53–70.

Lechner, Karl (1982/3), 'Die Herzoglich-Bairischen Lehen im Lande unter der Enns', *Jb.f.Lk.v.NÖ*, Neue Folge, 48/49, 70–98.

Lecler, Joseph (1960), *Toleration and the Reformation*, New York: Association Press; London: Longmans.

Leist, Friedrich (1889), *Zur Geschichte der auswärtigen Vertretung Bayerns im XVI. Jahrhundert*, Bamberg: Buchner.

Leitner, Gertraud (1971), 'Der Wiener Bibliothekar Hugo Blotius und seine Straßburger Korrespondenz', *Österreich in Geschichte und Literatur*, 15, 204–10.

Léonard, E.G. (1967), *A History of Protestantism*, vol. 2, London: Nelson.

Lhotsky, Alphons (1962), *Österreichische Historiographie*, Vienna: Verlag für Geschichte und Politik.

Lichtenberger, Elisabeth (1977), *Die Wiener Altstadt: von der mittelalterlichen Bürgerstadt zur City*, Vienna: Deuticke.

Liebert, Erwin (1986), 'Zwingli in Wien', in Karner, Peter (ed.), *Die evangelische Gemeinde H.B. in Wien*, Vienna: Deuticke, pp. 6–13.

Locher, D. Joanne Joseph (1773–75), *Speculum Academicum Viennense, sen magistratus antiquissimae et celeberrime Universitatis Viennensis, a primo eiusdem auspicio ad nostra tempora chronologice, historice, et lemmatice, exhibitus a D. Joanne Josepho Locher J.U.D.*, 3 vols, Vienna: Kaliwoda.

Lohn, Magdalena (1949), 'Melchior Khlesl und die Gegenreformation in Niederösterreich', unpublished dissertation, University of Vienna.

Loidl, Franz (1983), *Geschichte des Erzbistums Wien*, Vienna: Herold.

Louthan, Howard (1994), *Johannis Crato and the Austrian Habsburgs. Reforming a Counter-Reform Court*, Studies in Reformed Theology and History, Princeton, NJ: Princeton Theological Seminary.

Louthan, Howard (1997), *The Quest For Compromise: Peacemakers in Counter-Reformation Vienna*, Cambridge: Cambridge University Press.

Louthan, Howard (1999), 'Popular Piety and the Autobiography of Athanasius Kircher, S.J.', in Robertson, Ritchie and Beniston, Judith (eds), *Catholicism and Austrian Culture*, Austrian Studies X, Edinburgh: Edinburgh University Press, pp. 3–15.

Lutz, Heinrich (1976), 'Die Bedeutung der Nuntiaturberichte für die Europäische Geschichtsforschung und Geschichtsschreibung', in Lutz, Heinrich (ed.), *Nuntiaturberichte und Nuntiaturforschung. Kritische Bestandsaufnahme und neue Perspektiven*, Rome: Das Institut, pp. 152–67.

Lutz, Heinrich (1987), *Das Ringen um deutsche Einheit und Kirchliche Erneuerung. Von Maximilian I. bis um Westfälischen Frieden 1490 bis 1648*, Frankfurt am Main: Ullstein.

Lutz, Heinrich and Schmid, A. (1988), 'Von Humanismus zur Gegenreformation', in Kraus, Andreas (ed.), *Handbuch der Bayerischen Geschichte*, vol. 2, Munich: C.H. Beck, pp. 861–75.

Lutz, Heinrich and Ziegler, Walter (1988), 'Das konfessionelle Zeitalter. Wilhelm IV. und Albrecht V', in Kraus, Andreas (ed.), *Handbuch der Bayerischen Geschichte*, vol. 2, Munich: C.H. Beck, pp. 322–92.

Maag, Karin and Pettegree, Andrew (1997), 'The Reformation in Eastern and Central Europe' in Maag, Karin (ed.), *The Reformation in Eastern and Central Europe*, Aldershot: Ashgate, pp. 1–18.

MacHardy, Karin J. (1981), 'Der Einfluss von Status, Konfession und Besitz auf das Politische Verhalten des Niederösterreichischen Ritterstandes 1580–1620', in Klingenstein, Grete and Lutz, Heinrich (eds), *Spezialforschung und 'Gesamtgeschichte'*, Wiener Beiträge zur Geschichte der Neuzeit, vol. 8, Vienna: Verlag für Geschichte und Politik, pp. 56–83.

MacHardy, Karin J. (1999), 'Cultural Capital, Family Strategies and Noble Identity in Early Modern Habsburg Austria, 1579–1620', *P&P*, 163, 36–75.

MacHardy, Karin J. (2003), *War, Religion and Court Patronage in Habsburg Austria. The Social and Cultural Dimensions of Political Interaction, 1521–1622*, Basingstoke: Palgrave Macmillan.

Makkai, László (1991), 'The Crown and the Diets of Hungary and Transylvania in the Sixteenth Century', in Evans, R.J.W. and Thomas, T.V. (eds), *Crown, Church and Estates. Central European Politics in the Sixteenth and Seventeenth Centuries*, London: Macmillan in association with the School of Slavonic and Eastern European Studies, University of London, pp. 80–91.

Martels, Zweder von (1992), 'On His Majesty's Service. Augerius Busbequius, Courtier and Diplomat of Maximilian II', in Friedrich Edelmayer and Alfred Kohler (eds), *Kaiser Maximilian II. Kultur und Politik im 16. Jahrhundert*, Wiener Beiträge zur Geschichte der Neuzeit, vol. 17, Vienna: Verlag für Geschichte und Politik, pp. 169–81.

Martels, Zweder von (1993), 'A Stoic Interpretation of the Past: Augerius Busbequius's description of his Experiences at the Court of Suleiman The Magnificent (1554–1562)', *Journal of the Institute of Romance Studies*, 2, 165–79.

Mattingly, Garrett (1955), *Renaissance Diplomacy*, Oxford: Cape.

Maxcey, Carl E. (1979), 'Double Justice, Diego Laynez, and the Council of Trent', *CH*, 48, 269–78.

Mayer, Anton (1883), *Wiens Buchdrucker-Geschichte*, vol. 1, *1482–1682*, Vienna: Verlag d. Comites z. Feier d. vierhundertj. Einführung d. Buchdruckerkunst in Wien.

Mayr, Josef Karl (1954), 'Wiener Protestantengeschichte im 16. und 17. Jahrhundert', *Jahrbuch der Gesellschaft für die Geschichte des Protestantismus in Österreich*, 70, 41–127.

McGrath, Alister E. (1993), *Reformation Thought: An Introduction*, second edn, Oxford: Blackwell.

Mecenseffy, Grete (1967), *Evangelische Lehrer an der Universität Wien*, Vienna: Böhlau.

Mecenseffy, Grete (1974), 'Wien im Zeitalter der Reformation des 16. Jahrhunderts', *Wiener Geschichtsblätter*, 29 (1), 228–39.

Mecenseffy, Grete (1976), 'Maximilian II. in neuer Sicht', *Jahrbuch der Gesellschaft für die Geschichte des Protestantismus in Österreich*, 92, 42–54.

Mecenseffy, Grete and Rassl, Hermann (1980), *Die Evangelischen Kirchen Wiens*, Vienna: Zsolnay.

Meichelbeck, Carolus (1729), *Historiae Frisingensis*, vol. 2, part 1, Augsburg.

Metzger, Edelgard (1980), *Leonhard von Eck (1480–1550). Wegbereiter und Begründer des frühabsolutistischen Bayern*, Munich: Oldenbourg.

Meyjes, G. Posthumus (1984), 'Protestant Irenicism in the Sixteenth and Seventeenth centuries', in Loades, D. (ed.), *The End of Strife*, Edinburgh: T. & T. Clark, pp. 77–93.

Midelfort, H.C. Erik (1992), 'Curious Georgics: The German Nobility and Their Crisis of Legitimacy in the Late Sixteenth Century', in Fix, Andrew C. and Karant-Nunn, Susan C. (eds), *Germania Illustrata. Essays on Early Modern Germany Presented to Gerald Strauss*, Kirksville, MO: Sixteenth Century Journal Publishers, pp. 217–42.

Midelfort, H.C. Erik (1994), 'A Melancholy Emperor and His Mad Son', in Midelfort, H.C. Erik, *Mad Princes of Renaissance Germany*, Charlottesville, VA: University Press of Virginia, pp. 125–43.

Mitterdorffer, R.P. Sebastiano (1724, 1725), *Conspectus historiae universitatis Viennensis ex actis veteribus que documentis erutae atque a primis illius initiis ad annum usque 1701 deductae. (etc.)*, vols 2 and 3, Vienna: Schwendimann.

Moeller, Bernd (1972), 'Religious Life in Germany on the Eve of the Reformation', in Strauss, G. (ed.), *Pre-Reformation Germany*, New York: Harper and Row, pp. 13–31.

Morford, Mark (1991), *Stoics and Neostoics. Rubens and the Circle 0f Lipsius*, Princeton, NJ: Princeton University Press.

Mühlberger, Kurt (1991), 'Zu den Krisen der Universität Wien im Zeitalter der konfessionellen Auseinandersetzungen', *Bericht über den achtzehnten österreichischen Historikertag in Linz veranstaltet vom Verband Österreichischer Geschichtsvereine in der Zeit vom 24. bis 29. September 1990*, Veröffentlichungen des Verbandes Österreichischer Geschichtsvereine 27, pp. 269–77.

Mühlberger, Kurt (1992), 'Bildung und Wissenschaft. Kaiser Maximilian II. und die Universität Wien', in Edelmayer, Friedrich and Kohler, Alfred (eds), *Kaiser Maximilian II. Kultur und Politik im 16. Jahrhundert*, Wiener Beiträge zur Geschichte der Neuzeit, vol. 17, Vienna: Verlag für Geschichte und Politik, pp. 203–31.

Müller, Rainer A. (1996), 'Student Education, Student Life', in Ridder-Symoens, Hilde de (ed.), *A History of the University in Europe*, vol. 2, *Universities in Early Modern Europe*, Cambridge: Cambridge University Press, pp. 326–54.

Murdock, Graeme (2006), 'Central and Eastern Europe', in Ryrie, Alec (ed.), *The European Reformations*, Basingstoke: Palgrave Macmillan, pp. 36–56.

Myers, W. David (1996), *'Poor, sinning folk:' Confession and Conscience in Counter-Reformation Germany*, Ithaca, NY: Cornell University Press.

Myers, W. David (1996), 'Die Jesuiten, die häufige Beichte, und die katholische Reform in Bayern', *Beiträge zur Altbayerischen Kirchengeschichte*, 42, 45–58.

Neck, Rudolf (1970–71), 'The Haus-, Hof- und Staatsarchiv: Its History, Holdings and Use,' *AHY*, 6/7, 3–16.

Neuhaus, Helmut (1982), *Reichsständische Repräsentationsformen im 16. Jahrhundert*, Berlin: Duncker & Humblot.

Niederkorn, Jan Paul (1993), *Die europäischen Mächte und der 'Lange Türkenkrieg' Kaiser Rudolfs II. (1593–1606)*, Vienna: Verlag der Österreichischen Akademie der Wissenschaften.

Nye, Jason K. (2000), 'Catholic Reform and Society: Rottweil, 1525–1618', unpublished Ph.D. dissertation, University of St Andrews.

Oestreich, Gerhard (1982), *Neostoicism and the Early Modern State*, Cambridge: Cambridge University Press.

Olin, John C. (ed.) (1987), *Christian Humanism and the Reformation. Selected Writings of Erasmus*, New York: Fordham University Press.

O'Malley, John W. (1982), 'Catholic Reform', in Ozment, Steven (ed.), *Reformation Europe: A Guide to Research*, St Louis, MO: Center for Reformation Research, pp. 297–319.

O'Malley, John W. (1993), *The First Jesuits*, Cambridge, MA: Harvard University Press.

O'Malley, John W. (1993), 'Was Ignatius Loyola a Church Reformer? How to look at Early Modern Catholicism', in O'Malley, J. W. (ed.), *Religious Culture in the Sixteenth Century*, Aldershot: Variorum XII, pp. 177–93.

O'Malley, John W. (1994), 'The Society of Jesus' in De Molen, Richard (ed.), *Religious Orders of the Catholic Reformation*, New York: Fordham University Press, pp. 139–64.

O'Malley, John W. (2000), *Trent And All That. Renaming Catholicism in the Early Modern Era*, Cambridge, MA: Harvard University Press.

Oswald, Josef (1975), 'Der päpstliche Nuntius Ninguardia und die tridentinische Reform des Bistums Passau (1578–1583)', *Österreichische Geschichte*, 17, 19–49.

Panek, Jaroslav (1992), 'Maximilian II, als Konig von Böhmen', in Edelmayer, Friedrich and Kohler, Alfred (eds), *Kaiser Maximilian II. Kultur und Politik im 16. Jahrhundert*, Wiener Beiträge zur Geschichte der Neuzeit, vol. 17, Vienna: Verlag für Geschichte und Politik, pp. 55–69.

Parker, Geoffrey (1987), *The Thirty Years War*, London: Routledge & Kegan Paul.

Pastor, Ludwig von (1929, 1930), *The History of the Popes From the Close of the Middle Ages*, vols 17, 19 and 20, ed. Ralph Francis Kerr, London: Kegan Paul, Trench, Trubner & Co.

Patrouch, Joseph F. (1991), 'Methods of Cultural Manipulation: The Counter-Reformation in the Habsburg Province of Upper Austria, 1570–1650', unpublished Ph.D. dissertation, University of California.

Patrouch, Joseph F. (1994), 'The Investiture Controversy Revisited: Religious Reform, Emperor Maximilian II, and the Klosterrat', *AHY*, 25, 59–77.

Patrouch, Joseph F. (1999), 'Ysabell/Elisabth/Alzbeta: Erzherzogin. Königin. Ein Forschungsgegenwurff', *Frühneuzeit-Info*, 10, 257–65.

Patrouch, Joseph F. (2000), 'The Archduchess Elizabeth: Where Spain and Austria Met,' in Kent, Conrad, Wolber, Thomas and Hewitt, Cameron M.K. (eds), *The Lion and the Eagle: Interdisciplinary Essays on German-Spanish Relations over the Centuries*, New York: Berghahn Books, pp. 77–90.

Paulus, N. (1893), 'Dr Konrad Braun. Ein katholischer Rechtsgelehrter des 16. Jahrhunderts', *Historisches Jahrbuch*, 14, 517–51.

Paulus, N. (1895), 'Hofrath Dr Georg Eder. Ein katholischer Rechtsgelehrter des 16. Jahrhunderts', *Historisch-politische Blätter für das katholische Deutschland*, 115, 13–28, 81–94, 240.

Pauser, Josef (2003), 'Verfassung und Verwaltung der Stadt Wien', in Vocelka, K. and Traninger, A. (eds), *Wien. Geschichte einer Stadt*, vol. 2, *Die frühneuzeitliche Residenz (16. bis 18. Jahrhundert)*, Vienna, Cologne, Weimar: Böhlau, pp. 47–90.

Pedersen, Olaf (1996), 'Tradition and Innovation' in Ridder-Symoens, Hilde de (ed.), *A History of the University in Europe*, vol. 2, *Universities in Early Modern Europe*, Cambridge: Cambridge University Press, pp. 452–88.

Pelikan, Jaroslav (1984), *The Christian Tradition. A History of the Development of Doctrine*, vol. 4, Chicago, IL: University of Chicago Press.

Peniston-Bird, Corinna M. (1997), *Vienna*, Oxford: Clio.

Perger, Richard (1985), 'Universitätsgebäude und Bursen vor 1623', in Hamann, Günther, Mühlberger, Kurt and Skacel, Franz (eds), *Schriftenreihe des Universitätsarchivs*, vol. 2, *Das Alte Universitätsviertel in Wien, 1385–1985*, Vienna: Universitätsverlag für Wissenschaft und Forschung, pp. 75–102.

Petritsch, Ernst Dieter (1993), 'Tribut oder Ehrengeschenk? Ein Beitrag zu deh habsburgisch-osmanischen Beziehungen in der zweiten Hälfte des 16. Jahrhunderts', in Springer, Elisabeth and Kammerhofer, Leopold (eds), *Archiv und Forschung. Das Haus-, Hof- und Staatsarchiv in seiner Bedeutung für die Geschichte Österreichs und Europas*, Wiener Beiträge zur Geschichte der Neuzeit, vol. 20, Vienna: Verlag für Geschichte und Politik, pp. 49–58.

Pettegree, Andrew (1993), 'The clergy and the Reformation: from "devilish priesthood" to new professional elite' in Pettegree, Andrew (ed.), *Reformation of the Parishes*, Manchester: Manchester University Press, pp. 1–21.

Pfleger, Luzian (1908), 'Martin Eisengrein (1535–1578). Ein Lebensbild aus der Zeit der katholischen Restauration in Bayern' in Pastor, Ludwig (ed.), *Erläuterungen und Ergänzungen zu Janssens Geschichte des deutschen Volkes*, vol. 6, Freiburg im Breisgau.

Pils, Susanne C., and Weigl, Andreas (2003), 'Die frühneuzeitliche Sozialstruktur', in Vocelka, K. and Traninger, A. (eds), *Wien. Geschichte einer Stadt*, vol. 2, *Die frühneuzeitliche Residenz (16. bis 18. Jahrhundert)*, Vienna, Cologne, Weimar: Böhlau, pp. 241–81.

Pleyer, Karl (1964), 'Eine niederösterreichische Schulstiftung aus dem Jahre 1579', *Jb.f.Lk.v.NÖ*, Neue Folge, 36, 320–27.

Po-Chia Hsia, R. (1984), *Society and Religion in Münster, 1535–1618*, New Haven, CT: Yale University Press.

Po-Chia Hsia, R. (1989), *Social Discipline in the Reformation: Central Europe 1550–1750*, London: Routledge.

Po-Chia Hsia, R. (1998), *The World of Catholic Renewal 1540–1770*, Cambridge: Cambridge University Press.

Polleroß, Friedrich (2003), 'Renaissance und Barock', in Vocelka, K. and Traninger, A. (eds), *Wien. Geschichte einer Stadt*, vol. 2, *Die frühneuzeitliche Residenz (16. bis 18. Jahrhundert)*, Vienna, Cologne, Weimar: Böhlau, pp. 453–500.

Pörtner, Regina (2001), *The Counter-Reformation in Central Europe: Styria 1580–1630*, Oxford: Oxford University Press.

Pougratz, Walter (1985), 'Die Alte Universitätsbibliothek', in Hamann, Günther, Mühlberger, Kurt and Skacel, Franz (eds), *Schriftenreihe des Universitätsarchivs*, vol. 2, *Das Alte Universitätsviertel in Wien, 1385–1985*, Vienna: Universitätsverlag für Wissenschaft und Forschung, pp. 127–51.

Power, David N. (1987), *The Sacrifice We Offer. The Tridentine Dogma and its Reinterpretation*, Edinburgh: T. & T. Clark.

Press, Volker (1981), 'Der Niederösterreichische Adel um 1600 zwischen Landhaus und Hof- eine Fallstudie', in Klingenstein, Grete and Lutz, Heinrich (eds), *Spezialforschung und Gesamtgeschichte. Beispiele und Methodfragen zur Geschichte der frühen Neuzeit*, Wiener Beiträge zur Geschichte der Neuzeit, vol. 8, Vienna: Verlag für Geschichte und Politik, pp. 15–47.

Press, Volker (1986), 'The Habsburg Court as Centre of the Imperial Government', *JMH*, Supplement, 58, 23–45.

Press, Volker (1990), 'Rudolf II' and 'Matthias', in Schindling, A. and Ziegler, W. (eds), *Die Kaiser der Neuzeit, 1519–1918*, Munich: C.H. Beck, pp. 99–125.

Press, Volker (1991), 'The Imperial Court of the Habsburgs: From Maximilian I to Ferdinand III, 1493–1657', in Asch, R.G. and Birke, A.M. (eds), *Princes, Patronage and the Nobility*, Oxford: Oxford University Press, pp. 289–314.

Press, Volker (1991), 'The System of Estates in the Austrian Hereditary Lands and in the Holy Roman Empire: A Comparison', in Evans, R.J.W. and Thomas, T.V. (eds), *Crown, Church and Estates. Central European Politics in the Sixteenth and Seventeenth Centuries*, London: Macmillan in association with the School of Slavonic and Eastern European Studies, University of London, pp. 1–22.

Prosperi, Adriano (1988), 'Clerics and Laymen in the Work of Carlo Borromeo', in Headley, John M. and Tomaro, John B. (eds), *San Carlo Borromeo. Catholic Reform and Ecclesiastical Politics in the Second half of the Sixteenth Century*, London: Associated University Presses, pp. 112–38.

Pumfrey, Stephen (1997), 'The history of science and the science of history', in Pumfrey, S., Rossi, P.L. and Slawinski, M. (eds), *Science, Culture and Popular Belief in Renaissance Europe*, Manchester: Manchester University Press, pp. 48–70.

Raab, Heribert (1989), 'Gegenreformation und katholische Reform in Erzbistum und Erzstift Trier von Jakob von Eltz zu Johann Hugo von Orsbeck (1567–1711)', *RQ*, 84, 160–94.

Rall, Hans and Marga (1986), *Die Wittelsbacher in Lebensbildern*, Regensburg: F. Pustet.

Raupach, Bernard (1736), *Evangelisches Osterreich, das ist, Historische Nachricht von den vornehmsten Schicksalen der Evangelisch Lutherischen Kirchen in dem Ertz-Hertzogthum Oesterreich*, Hamburg: Felginer.

Reingrabner, Gustav (1966), 'Der "Alte" und der "Neue" Glaube', *Unsere Heimat*, 37, 6–21.

Reingrabner, Gustav (1968), 'Von Kirche, Schule und Musik im Evangelischen Horn', *Unsere Heimat*, 39, 133–43.

Reingrabner, Gustav (1975), 'Der evangelische Adel in Niederösterreich-Überzeugung und Handeln', *Jahrbuch der Gesellschaft für die Geschichte des Protestantismus in Österreich*, 90/91, 3–59.

Reingrabner, Gustav (1976), *Adel und Reformation. Beiträge zur Geschichte des Protestantischen Adels im Lande Unter Der Enns Während des 16. und 17. Jahrhunderts*, Vienna: Verein für Landeskunde von Niederösterreich und Wien.

Reingrabner, Gustav (1976), 'Über die Anfänge von reformatorischer Bewegung und evangelischem Kirchenwesen in Niederösterreich', *Unsere Heimat*, 47, 151–63.

Reingrabner, Gustav (1981), *Protestanten in Österreich. Geschichte und Dokumentation*, Vienna: Böhlau.

Reingrabner, Gustav (1981), 'Religiöse Lebensformen des Protestantischen Adels in Niederösterreich', in Klingenstein, Grete and Lutz, Heinrich (eds), *Spezialforschung und 'Gesamtgeschichte'*, Wiener Beiträge zur Geschichte der Neuzeit, vol. 8, Vienna: Verlag für Geschichte und Politik, pp. 126–38.

Reingrabner, Gustav (1990), 'Zur Geschichte der flacianischen Bewegung im Lande unter der Enns', *Jb.f.Lk.v.NÖ*, Neue Folge, 54/55, 265–301.

Reinhard, Wolfgang (1985), 'Reformation, Counter-Reformation and the Early Modern State: A Reassessment', *CHR*, 75, 383–404.

Ridder-Symoens, Hilde de (1996), 'Management and Resources', in Ridder-Symoens, Hilde de, *A History of the University in Europe*, vol. 2, *Universities in Early Modern Europe*, Cambridge: Cambridge University Press, pp. 155–209.

Ritter von Otto, Karl (1889), 'Geschichte der Reformation im Erzherzogthum Österreich unter Kaiser Maximilian II (1564–1576)', *Jahrbuch der Gesellschaft für die Geschichte des Protestantismus in Österreich*, 10, 1–60.

Rodríguez-Salgado, M.J. (1988), *The Changing Face of Empire. Charles V, Philip II, and Habsburg Authority, 1551–1559*, Cambridge: Cambridge University Press.

Röhrig, Floridus (1961), 'Protestantismus und Gegenreformation im Stift Klosterneuburg und seinen Pfarren', *Jahrbuch des Stiftes Klosterneuburg*, Neue Folge, 1, 105–70.

Rößner, Maria Barbara (1991), *Konrad Braun (ca. 1495–1563) – ein katholischer Jurist, Politiker, Kontroverstheologe und Kirchenreformer im konfessionellen Zeitalter*, Münster: Aschendorff.

Rossi, Paolo (1997), 'Society, Culture and the Dissemination of Learning', in Pumfrey, S., Rossi, P.L., and Slawinski, M., (eds), *Science, Culture and Popular Belief in Renaissance Europe*, Manchester: Manchester University Press, pp. 143–75.

Rudersdorf, Manfred (1990), 'Maximilian II', in Schindling, A., and Ziegler, W. (eds), *Die Kaiser Der Neuzeit 1519–1918*, Munich: C.H. Beck, pp. 79–99.

Rüegg, Walter (1996), 'Themes' in Ridder-Symoens, Hilde de (ed.), *A History of the University in Europe*, vol. 2, *Universities in Early Modern Europe*, Cambridge: Cambridge University Press, pp. 3–42.

Rummel, P. (1993), 'Jesuiten', in Brandmüller, Walter, *Handbuch der Bayerischen Kirchengeschichte*, vol. 2, St Ottilien: EOS Verlag Erzabtei, pp. 841–58.

Russell, Joycelyne G. (1986), *Peacemaking in the Renaissance*, London: Duckworth.

Russell, Paul A. (1986), *Lay Theology in the Reformation*, Cambridge: Cambridge University Press.

Sánchez, Magdalena S. (1998), *The Empress, The Queen, and The Nun. Women and Power at the Court of Philip III of Spain*, Baltimore, MD: The Johns Hopkins University Press.

Sánchez, Magdalena S. (2000), 'A Woman's Influence: Archduchess Maria of Bavaria and the Spanish Habsburgs', in Kent, Conrad; Wolber, Thomas and Hewitt, Cameron M.K. (eds), *The Lion and the Eagle: Interdisciplinary Essays on German-Spanish Relations over the Centuries*, New York and Oxford: Berghahn, pp. 91–197.

Sattek, Johann (1949), 'Der niederösterreich Klosterrat', unpublished dissertation, University of Vienna.

Scherer, Georg (1584), *Gründlicher Bericht ob es wahr sei, dass auf eine Zeit ein Pabst zu Rom schwanger gewesen und ein Kind gebohren habe*, Vienna: Nassinger.

Schild, X. (1892), 'Die Dillinger Buchdruckerei und ihre Druckwerke im 16. Jahrhundert', *Jahres-Bericht des Historischen Vereins Dillingen*, 102–34.

Schilling, Heinz (1992), *Religion, Popular Culture and the Emergence of Early Modern Society*, Leiden: Brill.

Schilling, Heinz (2001), 'Confessionalisation and the Rise of Religious and Cultural Frontiers in Early Modern Europe', in Andor, Eszter and Tóth, István György (eds), *Frontiers of Faith. Religious Exchange and the Constitution of Religious Identities 1400–1750*, Budapest: Central European University European Science Foundation, pp. 21–35.

Schoder, Elisabeth (1999), 'Die Reise der Kaiserin Maria nach Spanien (1581/82)', in Edelmayer, Friedrich (ed.), *Hispania-Austria II: Die Epoche Philipps II (1556–1598)*, Vienna: Verlag für Geschichte und Politik, pp. 151–80.

Schönfellner, Franz (1987), 'Kirchlicher Alltag in der Mitte des 16. Jahrhunderts am Beispiel der Stadtpfarre Krems', in Kohler, Alfred and Lutz, Heinrich (eds), *Alltag im 16. Jahrhundert. Studien zu lebensformen in mitteleuropäischen Städten*, Wiener Beiträge zur Geschichte der Neuzeit, vol. 14, Vienna: Verlag für Geschichte und Politik, pp. 117–51.

Schramm, Gottfried (1991), 'Armed Conflict in East-Central Europe: Protestant Noble Opposition and Catholic Royalist factions, 1604–20', in Evans, R.J.W. and Thomas, T.V. (eds), *Crown, Church and Estates. Central European Politics in the Sixteenth and Seventeenth Centuries*, London: Macmillan in association with the School of Slavonic and Eastern European Studies, University of London, pp. 176–95.

Schrauf, Karl (1901), 'Zur Geschichte des Wiener Universitätsarchivs', *MIÖG*, 6 Ergänzungsband, 739–59.

Schulze, Winfried (1991), 'Estates and the problem of Resistance in Theory and Practice in the Sixteenth and Seventeenth Centuries', in Evans, R.J.W. and Thomas, T.V. (eds), *Crown, Church and Estates. Central European Politics in the Sixteenth and Seventeenth Centuries*, London: Macmillan in association with the School of Slavonic and Eastern European Studies, University of London, pp. 158–75.

Schwarz, Henry Frederick (1943), *The Imperial Privy Council in the Seventeenth Century*, Cambridge, MA: Harvard University Press.

Scribner, R. (1976), 'Why was there no Reformation in Cologne?', *Bulletin of the Institute of Historical Research*, 49, 217–41.

Seifert, Arno (ed.) (1973), *Die Universität Ingolstadt im 15. und 16. Jahrhundert*, Berlin: Duncker & Humblot.

Seifert, Arno (1978), *Welticher Staat und Kirchenreform. Die Seminarpolitik Bayerns im 16. Jahrhundert*, Münster: Aschendorff.

Sicken, Bernhard (1990), 'Ferdinand I', in Schindling, A. and Ziegler, W. (eds), *Die Kaiser der Neuzeit 1519–1918*, Munich: C.H. Beck, 55–79.

Simone, Maria Rosa di (1996), 'Admission' in Ridder-Symoens, Hilde de (ed.), *A History of the University in Europe*, vol. 2, *Universities in Early Modern Europe*, Cambridge: Cambridge University Press, pp. 285–325.

Simons, Madelon (1997), 'King Ferdinand I of Bohemia, Archduke Ferdinand II and the Prague Court, 1527–1567', in Fučíková, E., et al. (eds), *Rudolf II and Prague: the Court and the City*, London: Thames & Hudson, pp. 80–89.

Skibniewski, Stephan Leo Ritter Corvin von (1903), *Geschichte des Römischen Katechismus*, Rome: Pustet.

Socher, Antonius, S.J. (1740), *Historia Provinciae Austriae Societatis Jesu Pars Prima*, Vienna: Kurtzböck.

Smolka, Wolfgang J. and Zedelmaier, Helmut (eds) (1998), *Biographisches Lexikon der Ludwig-Maximilians-Universität München*, vol. 1, *Ingolstadt-Landshut 1472–1826*, Berlin: Duncker & Humblot.

Soergel, Philip (1993), *Wondrous In His Saints: Counter-Reformation Propaganda in Bavaria*, Berkeley, CA: University of California Press.

Spielman, John P. (1993), *The City and the Crown. Vienna and the Imperial Court 1600–1740*, West Lafeyette, IN: Purdue University Press.

Spitz, Lewis W. (1956), 'Particularism and Peace. Augsburg – 1555', *CH*, 25, pp. 110–22.

Spitz, Lewis W. (1975), 'Imperialism, Particularism and Toleration in the Holy Roman Empire' in Soman, Alfred (ed.), *The Massacre of St Bartholomew: Reappraisals and Documents*, The Hague: Martinus Nijhoff, pp. 71–95.

Spitz, Lewis W. and Sher Tinsley, Barbara (1995), *Johann Sturm on Education. The Reformation and Humanist Learning*, St. Louis, MO: Concordia Publishing House.

Stalla, Gerhard (1971–77), *Bibliographie der Ingolstädter Drucker des 16 Jahrhunderts*, Baden-Baden: Verlag Valentin Koerner.

Steinherz, S. (1901), 'Zwei Predigten des Bischofs Musso in Wien 1560', *MIÖG* Ergänzungsband, pp. 565–74.

Steinhuber, Andreas (1895), *Geschichte des Collegium Germanicum Hungaricum in Rom*, vol. 1, Freiburg im Breisgau: Herder.

Stetten, Paul von (1743), *Geschichte der Heil. Rom. Reichs Freyen Stadt Augspurg*, Frankfurt: Merz und Mayer.

Stieve, Felix (1878), *Die Politik Baierns 1591–1607*, vol. 1, Munich: M. Rieger.

Stieve, Felix (1883), *Die Politik Baierns 1591–1607*, vol. 2, Munich: M. Rieger.

Strauss, Gerald (1993), 'The Religious Policies of Dukes Wilhelm and Ludwig of Bavaria in the first decade of the Protestant era' in Strauss, G. (ed.), *Enacting the Reformation in Germany*, Aldershot: Ashgate, pp. 350–73.

Strohmeyer, Arno (1999), 'Kommunikation und die Formierung internationaler Beziehungen: Das österreichisch-spanische Nachrichtenwesen im Zeitalter Philipps II', in Edelmayer, Friedrich (ed.), *Hispania-Austria II: Die Epoche Philipps II (1556–1598)*, Vienna: Verlag für Geschichte und Politik, pp. 109–50.

Strömmer, Elisabeth (2003), 'Klima und Naturkatastrophen', in Vocelka, K. and Traninger, A. (eds), *Wien. Geschichte einer Stadt*, vol. 2, *Die frühneuzeitliche Residenz (16. bis 18. Jahrhundert)*, Vienna, Cologne, Weimar: Böhlau, pp. 91–108.

Sutter Fichtner, Paula (1975), 'Of Christian Virtue and a Practicing Prince: Emperor Ferdinand I and his son Maximilian', *CHR*, 61, 409–16.

Sutter Fichtner, Paula (1980), 'The Disobedience of the Obedient: Ferdinand I and the Papacy, 1555–1564', *SCJ*, 11 (2), 25–34.

Sutter Fichtner, Paula (1982), *Ferdinand of Austria: The Politics of Dynasticism in the Age of the Reformation*, New York: Columbia University Press.

Sutter Fichtner, Paula (1994), 'Introduction', in Ingrao, C. (ed.), *State and Society in Early Modern Austria*, West Lafayette, IN: Purdue University Press, pp. 27–35.

Sutter Fichtner, Paula (1995), 'Habsburg Household or Habsburg Government? A Sixteenth Century Administrative Dilemma', *AHY*, 26, 545–60.

Sutter Fichtner, Paula (2001), *Emperor Maximilian II*, New Haven, CT: Yale University Press.

Szonyi, Gyorgy E. (1997), 'Science and Magic, Humanism at the Court of Rudolf II', in Fučíková, E., et al. (eds), *Rudolf II and Prague: the Court and the City*, London: Thames & Hudson, pp. 222–31.

Tanner, M. (1992), *The Last Descendant of Aeneas: The Habsburg and the Mythic Image of the Emperor*, New Haven, CT: Yale University Press.

Tentler, Thomas N. (1977), *Sin and Confession on the Eve of the Reformation*, Princeton, NJ: Princeton University Press.

Terpstra, Nicholas (1995), *Lay Confraternities and Civic Religion in Renaissance Bologna*, Cambridge: Cambridge University Press.

Tomek, Ernst (1935–59), *Kirchengeschichte Österreichs*, vol. 2, *Humanismus, Reformation und Gegenreformation*, Innsbruck, Munich, Vienna: Tyrolia.

Trenkler, Ernst (1978), 'Wolfgang Lazius, Humanist und Büchersammler', *Biblos. Österreichische Zeitschrift für Buch- und Bibliothekswesen, Dokumentation, Bibliographie und Bibliophilie*, 27, 186–203.

Trevor-Roper, Hugh (1976), *Princes and Artists: Patronage and Ideology at Four Habsburg Courts, 1517–1633*, London: Thames and Hudson.

Tschernuth, Uta (1985), 'Studentisches Leben in den Bursen', in Hamann, Günther, Mühlberger, Kurt and Skacel, Franz (eds), *Schriftenreihe des Universitätsarchivs*, vol. 2, *Das Alte Universitätsviertel in Wien, 1385–1985*, Vienna: Universitätsverlag für Wissenschaft und Forschung, pp. 153–9.

Uiblein, Paul (1985), 'Die Universität Wien im 14. und 15. Jahrhundert', in Hamann, Günther, Mühlberger, Kurt and Skacel, Franz (eds), *Schriftenreihe des Universitätsarchiv*, vol. 2, *Das Alte Universitätsviertel in Wien, 1385–1985*, Vienna: Universitätsverlag für Wissenschaft und Forschung, pp. 17–36.

Vandermeersch, Peter A. (1996), 'Teachers' in Ridder-Symoens, Hilde de (ed.), *A History of the University in Europe*, vol. 2, *Universities in Early Modern Europe*, Cambridge: Cambridge University Press, pp. 210–55.

Vilfan, Sergij (1991), 'Crown, Estates and the Financing of Defence in Inner Austria, 1500–1630', in Evans, R.J.W. and Thomas, T.V. (eds), *Crown, Church and Estates. Central European Politics in the Sixteenth and Seventeenth Centuries*, London: Macmillan in association with the School of Slavonic and Eastern European Studies, University of London, pp. 70–79.

Vocelka, Karl (2003), 'Die Stadt und die Herrscher', in Vocelka, K. and Traninger, A. (eds), *Wien. Geschichte einer Stadt*, vol. 2, *Die frühneuzeitliche Residenz (16. bis 18. Jahrhundert)*, Vienna, Cologne, Weimar: Böhlau, pp. 13–46.

Vocelka, Karl (2003), 'Kirchengeschichte', in Vocelka, K. and Traninger, A. (eds), *Wien. Geschichte einer Stadt*, vol. 2, *Die frühneuzeitliche Residenz (16. bis 18. Jahrhundert)*, Vienna, Cologne, Weimar: Böhlau, pp. 311–64.

Vocelka, K. and Traninger, A. (eds) (2003), *Wien. Geschichte einer Stadt*, vol. 2, *Die frühneuzeitliche Residenz (16. bis 18. Jahrhundert)*, Vienna, Cologne, Weimar: Böhlau.

Vogt, Johannes (1747), *Catalogus historico-criticus librorum rariorum, iam curis tertiis recognitas et copiosa accessione ex symbolis et collatione bibliophilorum per germaniam doctissimorum adauctus*, Hamburg: Heroldus.

Wappler, Anton (1884), *Geschichte der Theologischen-Facultät der K.K. Universität zu Wien*, Vienna: Braumüller.

Weigl, Andreas (2003), 'Frühneuzeitliches Bevölkerungswachstum', in Vocelka, K. and Traninger, A. (eds), *Wien. Geschichte einer Stadt*, vol. 2, *Die frühneuzeitliche Residenz (16. bis 18. Jahrhundert)*, Vienna, Cologne, Weimar: Böhlau, pp. 109–32.

Wheatcroft, A. (1995), *The Habsburgs: Embodying Empire*, London: Penguin.

Wiedemann, Theodor (1873), 'Die kirchliche Bücher-Censur in der Erzdiöcese Wien. Nach den Acten des Fürsterzbischöflichen Consistorial-Archives in Wien', *AÖG*, 1, 215–520.

Wiedemann, Theodor (1879–86), *Geschichte der Reformation und Gegenreformation im Lande unter der Enns*, 5 vols, Prague: Tempsky.

Wilson, Peter H. (1999), *The Holy Roman Empire 1495–1806*, Basingstoke: Macmillan Press Limited.

Winkelbauer, Thomas (1992), 'Krise der Aristokatie? Zum Strukturwandel des Adels in den böhmischen und niederösterreichischen Ländern im 16. und 17. Jahrhundert', *MIÖG*, 100, 328–53.

Winkelbauer, Thomas (1999), *Fürst und Fürstendiener. Gundaker von Liechtenstein, ein österreichischer Aristokrat des konfessionellen Zeitalters, MIÖG* Ergänzungsband.

Wrba, P. Johann (1985), 'Der Orden der Gesellschaft Jesu im Alten Universitätsviertel von Wien', and 'Hundertfünfzig Jahre von den Jesuiten Geprägte Universität', in Hamann, Günther, Mühlberger, Kurt and Skacel, Franz (eds), *Schriftenreihe des Universitätsarchivs*, vol. 2, *Das Alte Universitätsviertel in Wien, 1385–1985*, Vienna: Universitätsverlag für Wissenschaft und Forschung, pp. 47–52 and pp. 52–74.

Wright, A.D. (1982), *The Counter-Reformation. Catholic Europe and the Non-Christian World*, London: Weidenfeld and Nicolson.

Yates, Frances A. (1975), *Astraea. The Imperial Theme in the Sixteenth Century*, London & Boston: Routledge & Kegan Paul.

Zeeden, Ernst Walter (1967), *Das Zeitalter der Gegenreformation von 1555 bis 1648*, Freiburg im Briesgau: Herder.

Ziegler, Walter (1989), 'Bayern', and 'Nieder-und Oberösterreich', in Schindling, A., and Ziegler, W. (eds), *Die Territorien des Reichs im Zeitalter der Reformation und Konfessionalisierung. Land und Konfession 1500–1650*, vol. 1, *Der Südosten*, Münster: Vereinsschriften der Gesellschaft zur Herausgabe des Corpus Catholicorum, pp. 56–72 and pp. 118–34.

Zika, Charles (1988), 'Hosts, Processions and Pilgrimages: Controlling the Sacred in Fifteenth Century Germany', *P&P*, 118, 25–64.

Zimmermann, Wolfgang (1994), *Rekatholisierung, Konfessionalisierung und Ratsregiment: Der Prozeß des politischen und religiösen Wandels in der österreichischen Stadt Konstanz, 1548–1637*, Sigmaringen: Thorbecke

Zoepfl, Friedrich (1955), 'Kardinal Otto Truchsess von Waldburg', in Pölnitz, Götz Freiherrn von (ed.), *Lebensbilder aus dem Bayerischen Schwaben*, Munich, pp. 204–48.

Index

St Andrews Studies in Reformation History

*The Shaping of a Community: The Rise and Reformation
of the English Parish c. 1400–1560*
Beat Kümin

*Seminary or University? The Genevan Academy and
Reformed Higher Education, 1560–1620*
Karin Maag

Marian Protestantism: Six Studies
Andrew Pettegree

Protestant History and Identity in Sixteenth-Century Europe
(2 volumes) edited by Bruce Gordon

*Antifraternalism and Anticlericalism in the German Reformation:
Johann Eberlin von Günzburg and the Campaign against the Friars*
Geoffrey Dipple

*Reformations Old and New: Essays on the Socio-Economic
Impact of Religious Change c. 1470–1630*
edited by Beat Kümin

Piety and the People: Religious Printing in French, 1511–1551
Francis M. Higman

The Reformation in Eastern and Central Europe
edited by Karin Maag

John Foxe and the English Reformation
edited by David Loades

The Reformation and the Book
Jean-François Gilmont, edited and translated by Karin Maag

The Magnificent Ride: The First Reformation in Hussite Bohemia
Thomas A. Fudge

Hatred in Print: Catholic Propaganda and Protestant Identity
during the French Wars of Religion
Luc Racaut

Penitence, Preaching and the Coming of the Reformation
Anne T. Thayer

Huguenot Heartland:
Montauban and Southern French Calvinism
during the French Wars of Religion
Philip Conner

Charity and Lay Piety in Reformation London, 1500–1620
Claire S. Schen

The British Union: A Critical Edition and Translation of
David Hume of Godscroft's De Unione Insulae Britannicae
edited by Paul J. McGinnis and Arthur H. Williamson

Reforming the Scottish Church:
John Winram (c. 1492–1582) and the Example of Fife
Linda J. Dunbar

Cultures of Communication from Reformation to Enlightenment:
Constructing Publics in the Early Modern German Lands
James Van Horn Melton

Sebastian Castellio, 1515-1563:
Humanist and Defender of Religious Toleration in a Confessional Age
Hans R. Guggisberg translated and edited by Bruce Gordon

The Front-Runner of the Catholic Reformation:
The Life and Works of Johann von Staupitz
Franz Posset

The Correspondence of Reginald Pole:
Volume 2. A Calendar, 1547–1554: A Power in Rome
Thomas F. Mayer

William of Orange and the Revolt of the Netherlands, 1572–1584
K.W. Swart, translated J.C. Grayson

The Italian Reformers and the Zurich Church, c.1540–1620
Mark Taplin